The Last Mile to Huesca

An Australian Nurse in the Spanish Civil War

Judith Keene

The Clapton Press

First edition published in Australia 1988 by:
New South Wales University Press, Kensington, NSW

This new fully revised edition published 2023 by:
The Clapton Press Ltd, 38 Thistlewaite Road, London E5

Cover by Gruffydd Design

Keene, Judith
The Last Mile to Huesca: An Australian Nurse in the Spanish
Civil War.
Bibliography.
Includes Index.
ISBN 978-1-913963-28-2

1.   Hodgson, Agnes—Diaries.
2.   Nurses—Australia—Diaries.
3.   Spain—History—Civil War, 1936-1939—Personal narratives,
     Australian.

Contents

The Last Mile to Huesca
Part One

An Australian Nurse
in the Spanish Civil War

Studio portrait taken in Sydney before departure, Oct 1936.
Back row: Agnes Hodgson, May MacFarlane;
Centre: Una Wilson; Front: Mary Lowson

Chapter One

Introduction

Agnes Hodgson kept a diary during the year of the Spanish civil war in which she served as a volunteer nurse with a medical unit caring for wounded Republican soldiers on the Aragón front. She was an accomplished writer with a sensitivity to her surroundings and a sharp eye for the engaging detail to clinch a story. Several of her written pieces from Spain appeared in Australian newspapers under her own by-line.1 Similarly, she was conscientious in her efforts to include colourful detail about the state of the war in Spain when reporting back to the Sydney Spanish Relief Committee, always avid for usable copy for propaganda and fund raising.

The entries in her diary, however, were never intended for publication. They functioned as a personal *aide-mémoire* in which she jotted down notable events and the striking individuals she came across as well as recording her own unvarnished assessment of nursing conditions and the work of the surgical teams, as viewed by a nurse, proud of her own training and experience. The diary writing also provided a parallel subtext for Agnes's private and often critical reflection on her own behaviour and her sense of self as she attempted to undertake, in her words, 'credible work', while negotiating a place in a world that was differently framed by ideology and expectation from anything within her previous experience.

In facing her own individual challenges, Agnes, like most foreign nurses in Spain, was buoyed by a sense of confidence in her own knowledge and skill that had been acquired in hospital training elsewhere.2 In wartime Spain, however, patient care was

---

1 Listed in the Bibliography.

2 It is worth noting that recent historians of Spanish nursing have demonstrated the inaccuracies in the commonly-held belief among

delivered in mobile and makeshift hospitals often with scarce resources and in the chaotic conditions of managing the injured brought directly from the battlefield. In many cases, medical staff described the situations they were confronting in terms that evoked the First World War, though of course few nurses in the Spanish civil war were of the generation to have experienced the Great War.3 Volunteer nurses in Spain faced an added strain of keeping up professional and personal relationships while living and working in close quarters with a 'very mixed bunch of individuals from widely different social and professional backgrounds' in what often were remote locations that offered little respite. This, in turn, aggravated whatever were the internal differences among foreign medical staff.4 Cross cultural contact

---

foreign nurses and foreign medics (and many of the historians who have written about them) that in pre-civil war Spain, nursing was monopolized by unskilled nuns, while professional nursing training was non-existent. For the scholarly re-examination that has challenged what previously was the standard story, see Siobhan Nelson, Paola Galbany-Estragués and Gloria Gallego-Caminero, 'The Nurses No-One Remembers: Looking for Spanish Nurses in Accounts of the Spanish Civil War (1936-1939)', *Nursing History Review*, 28 (2020): 63-92; a scholarly comparison of training levels in Spanish nursing on both sides in the civil war found that they were closely comparable, in María López, Rubén Mirón-González, María-José-Castro and José-María-Jiménez 'Training of Volunteer Nurses during the Spanish Civil War (1936-1939): A Historical Study', *Plos ONE*, 16 (31 Dec 2021): 1-12; and more broadly with similar conclusions, see Dolores Martin Moruno and Javier Ordez Rodríguez, 'The Nursing Vocation as Political Participation for Women during the Spanish Civil War', *Journal of War and Culture Studies*, 2, 3 (2009): 305-319. See also Bibliography section.

3 According to Kenneth Sinclair-Loutit, Ada Hodson, one of the few in the British Medical Unit who nursed in the Great War remained unfazed in Spain even in the most trying circumstances. KL letter to JK. Rabat 4 Jun 1991. JK private papers.

4 Linda Palfreeman, *Salud! British Volunteers in the Republican Medical Service during the Spanish Civil War, 1936-1939*, (Brighton: Sussex Academic Press & Cañada Blanch Centre for Contemporary Spanish Studies, 2012), p 28.

with the local community as well could be awkward. The behaviour of independent women travelling about unchaperoned, wearing pants, smoking cigarettes, drinking in rowdy bars and mixing freely with the opposite sex, was antithetical to local customs in much of rural Spain.

In light of the singularity of their placement, it is not an exaggeration to suggest that these foreign nurses, whatever the circumstance that prompted their enlistment—political, humanitarian or a sense of adventure—put their bodies on the line in answering the call in August 1936 from the Republican government for urgent assistance. Subsequently, many suffered physical and mental ailments that today would be identified as Post Traumatic Stress Disorder. Yet, almost without exception, these volunteers, looking back over their lives, considered their involvement in Spain as their proudest endeavour, the memory of which sustained them for the rest of their lives.

Agnes penned her first diary entry on 24 October 1936 in the evening of the day on which she and her three *compañeras*, sailed out of Sydney harbour, bound for their Spanish adventure. She noted that at the first possible opportunity, she had approached the Purser to request an on board upgrade in the location of the nurses' shared cabin. It was politely refused but the incident underlined the fact that Agnes was a seasoned traveller. The last entry in the diary, on 21 October 1937, was made in Paris where she passed a couple of free days waiting for a plane to London on the first leg of the return journey home. Leaving war-torn Barcelona with only the clothes that she stood up in, she treated herself to a bottle of 'cheap scent' but thought better of her original plan to take in an opera when she became aware that her bedraggled appearance stood out among the crowd of well-dressed Parisians. She took the opportunity, however, to visit the Paris International Exhibition on the Seine, where the displays of embroidered dresses and flamenco dancers in the Spanish Pavilion caught her attention but, curiously, Picasso's *Guernica*, occupying the pride of place, elicited no comment.

Between the first and the last diary entries, the detail and their length fluctuated with the rhythms of wartime engagement, the overriding demands of the wounded and according to her own state of mind. It varied from exhilaration at the sense of her own part in a drama of world-wide significance while at other times she was cast down by misery at the futility of the war, the wastage of the lives of young soldiers and the limits of her own physical and psychological endurance in face of the challenges that supporting the Republican cause entailed.

I met Agnes Hodgson several months before her death in June 1984. I had returned home from an immersion in post graduate studies in contemporary Spanish history in California where teachers Gabriel Jackson and David Ringrose communicated their own passionate involvement with contemporary Spain. As well, there was the inimitable Herbert Southworth, the visiting Regents' scholar, whose fabulous library was in the Special Collections at UCSD and who knew everything there was to know about Spain and the civil war, including the Australian war correspondents at Guernica and the participation of Australians in the International Brigades.

I had heard about the Australian Aid movement and the medical aid unit sent to Spain, probably from Herbert Southworth. Also, around this time I met Amirah Inglis. As a child in a communist family in Melbourne she had donated her pocket money to the Aid Spain committee and became both a wonderful friend and the author of a fine book on Australians and the Spanish civil war.5

I arrived at Agnes Hodgson's door in suburban Melbourne bearing card indexes and notebook. She was welcoming but reticent about her own part in the Spanish war. By contrast she spoke freely about her life-long love affair with Italy and the rich contribution of Italian immigration to Australian homegrown culture. After an hour or so she mentioned diffidently that she had kept a diary in Spain but feared it was rather inconsequential and did not show herself in a good light. There was an album of

---

5 Amirah Inglis, *Australians in the Spanish Civil War*, (Sydney: Allen & Unwin, 1987); and Keene, 'Amirah Inglis; Activist, Historian and Friend' in Peter Browne & Seumas Spark (eds.), *I Wonder: The Life and Work of Ken Inglis*, (Melbourne: Monash University Publishing, 2020): 240-59.

snapshots, as well, that I might see if I was interested. I sat at her dining-room table reading the diary and following the pictures. Both were riveting.

These were not the self-serving recollections framed in the stultifying mode so often adopted in first person accounts of participants in just causes. The diary chronicled the daily experiences of a lively young woman dropped into the centre of a civil war about which, initially, she knew very little. It described the frivolity of ship board life on the journey to Europe, an experience shared by many an Australian debutante off on the Grand Tour, and the unsettling experience of arriving in Barcelona, to a city caught up in the fraught times in which the vicissitudes of war were overlaid by turmoil between political groups within those fighting against Franco. Indeed, Agnes herself became caught up in a potentially very dangerous incident in the febrile environment in Barcelona that bred internecine fear of fascist spies and Trotskyist traitors. In the main, however, the diary catalogues the dreary slog of a field hospital at the front whereby the rhythm of work see-sawed between inundations of the wounded in periods of intense engagement and the boredom of slack periods in which the isolation of life in a small Aragonese village without amenities or distractions engendered arguments and petty irritations within the medical group. Overall, Agnes's narrow focus on her own individual experience provides a microscopic bead on the large and turbulent landscape of Spain in wartime.

Agnes's husband, Ralph Tonkin, was keen for his wife's work to see the light of day. With his encouragement and my editing, the diary was published in 1988 by the University of New South Wales Press. It included a number of the photographs from Agnes's original album, some of which were taken by herself and by others with whom she worked. Most were of the military hospital units in Aragón as the warfront moved across the region.6

---

6 See the discussion of women photographers in Aragón in, Carmen Agustin-Lacruz and Luis-Blanco Domingo, 'La Memoria en Encuadres. Fotógrafas Extranjeras en Aragón durante la Guerra Civil Española (1936-1939)', *Documentación de las Ciencias de la*

The distinguished American Hispanist, Gabriel Jackson, in his introduction, placed Agnes's experiences against a larger Spanish context, in order to point out the rarity of such an eyewitness account by a young woman whose testimony was untethered from ideology or party politics and notably free of an overburdening self-regard.7 When the diary first appeared, it was at a time when literature about the medical services in Spain was sparse as were first person accounts of nurses, volunteers and otherwise.

In 2005, under the imprint of the University of Zaragoza Press, the Rolde de Estudios Aragones, overseen by Carlos Serrano, arranged the publication of Agnes's diary in Spanish.8 The translation was made by Isabel Pahissa and the journalist Victor Pardo Lancina added a section on the civil war in Los Monegros. The Comarca de los Monegros, Diputación de Huesca and the Gobierno de Aragón, backed the project and these same institutions distributed the book to their own constituents. The Australian Embassy was also supportive and the Ambassador in Madrid, Ms Sue Tanner, participated in several of the

---

Información, 44, 1 (2021): 61-72. The analysis includes Agnes's photography but passes over the fact that, though she prided herself on her use of the camera, her lens was 'as a tourist' and at the front she often traded cigarettes from those wanting to use her camera. Her 'snaps' were retained by the family with the original album. See also, Jane Hanley, 'The Tourist Gaze in the Spanish Civil War: Agnes Hodgson Between Surgery and Spectacle', *College Literature*, 43, 1 (Winter 2016): 196-219. Margaret Michaelis's images of Aragón that are used in this book are held in the Margaret Michaelis-Sachs Archive at the National Gallery of Australia and analysed by Helen Ennis, *Margaret Michaelis: Love, Loss and Photography*, (Canberra: National Gallery of Australia, 2005) and Almudena Rubio Pérez, 'Las Cajas de Amsterdam: Margaret Michaelis y los anarquistas de la CNT-FAI en la Guerra Civil', *Historia Social*, 104 (2022): 71-90. See also the references to photography in Aragón in the Bibliography.

7 *The Last Mile to Huesca* (1988), pp xiii-xvi.

8 *A una milla de Huesca. Diario de una enfermera australiana en la Guerra Civil española* (2005).

discussions of the book that took place at launches in various towns and villages. As with the original version, the Spanish Rolde de Estudios's version with a small distribution has been out of print for at least a decade.

The diary in both forms continued to attract considerable attention. Since its original appearance, there have been a number of developments to enrich an understanding of Agnes's role in the civil war. The Noel Butlin Labour Archives at the Australian National University has acquired more primary material on Spanish civil war matters in Australia, including the papers of Spanish Relief Committee and of Phil Thorne, the leading light on Aid Spain in Australia, as well as Amirah Inglis's papers. Equally importantly, the field of history about medical services in the civil war has richly expanded as have analyses of women, Spanish and others.9 New images unearthed since then and associated with the new materials have been integrated into this edition in order to broaden the understanding of Agnes's narrative. In relation to first person accounts of the civil war in Spain, Clapton Press has made an outstanding contribution in the discovery and recovery of historical writing with its series '1930s and Memories of Spain' in which I am honoured to be represented.

---

9 See the references listed in the Bibliography.

Chapter Two

Agnes Hodgson and the Spanish Civil War

On 24 October 1936, a warm Spring day in Sydney, several hundred people gathered on the Woolloomooloo wharf to give a 'rousing Red Flag farewell' to four nurses setting off to the Spanish civil war. As the ocean liner, SS *Oronsay*, pulled away into Sydney Harbour the cheerful crowd sang the *Internationale* and threw streamers to the beaming women waving from the rails above. Mary Lowson, May MacFarlane, Una Wilson and Agnes Hodgson had answered a call sent out by the Australian Spanish Relief Committee (ASRC) for nurses willing to join a British medical unit to care for the wounded from Spanish battlefields in a conflict in which the legally-elected, democratic government in Spain was confronting a military insurgence led by the Spanish general, Francisco Franco. The ASRC was composed of trade unionists, Labor party members and communist activists as well as various groupings that constituted the Movement against War and Fascism. In a very short time the nurses' fares had been raised with an extra £100 with which in France to purchase a shopping list of medical supplies and equipment to take with them into Spain.

There had been some hostile questions in the Parliament about their departure and whether the government could prevent the nurses leaving Australia. The Attorney-General's opinion, however, was that as long as they had a guaranteed return passage and they remained non-combatants there was no legal ground for withholding their passports.[10] Nor did the Parliament attempt to prevent funds being sent from Australian supporters to the Spanish Republican government or by Australian Catholic organizations to Franco's Nationalists.

---

10 *Sydney Morning Herald* 24 Oct 1936.

It had been decided that the group would be called the Australian-Spanish Nursing Unit. Their uniforms were to be as worn in Australian hospitals, including the starched veil, but with a distinctive oval aluminium badge bearing a Red Cross within an etched outline of Australia encircled by the unit's name. The same insignia was stitched on their arm bands. The additional kit included heavy boots and jodhpurs that suggested a more realistic preparation for the 'rugged outside service' of wartime nursing.11

Badge of the Australian Spanish Nursing Unit, Oct 1936.

The group attracted a good deal of press coverage. It could hardly have been otherwise. Four highly photogenic young women, articulate and seemingly unfazed by the prospect of risking their own lives to care for wounded soldiers in a country about which they knew very little.12

---

11 *West Australian* 3 Nov 1936.

12 *Workers Weekly* front page coverage, 23 Oct 1936.

Newspaper reporters were fascinated by the motivation that had prompted such an undertaking.13 These 'Australian girls', to use the common press denominator, were described in terms of their glamour and that they embodied the finest humanitarian values of the nursing profession. May MacFarlane, 'definitely a brunette' commented that 'despite the dangers it will be a marvellous education for all of us and any risk involved is worthwhile in defence of democratic freedom'.14 Una Wilson, 'platinum blonde', told the *Workers Weekly* that 'if we get captured or shot that's that. It's only a few years off your life and it's better than spending all your days nursing in a private hospital. Danger is the spice of life, that and the feeling that we'll be doing something with real meaning'. Mary Lowson, 'well under five feet in height and possessing great spirit and determination' explained that 'No sacrifice is too great to assist people who are fighting in defence of freedom'.15 Agnes, about whom it was invariably noted 'already had travelled outside

Leaving Sydney SS Oronsay, 24 Oct 1936: Agnes Hodgson, Mary Lowson, May MacFarlane and Una Wilson.

13 *Workers Weekly,* 23 Oct 1936.

14 *West Australian,* 3 Nov 1936.

15 *Workers Weekly,* 31 Oct 1936; Workers Star, 6 Nov 1936.

[Australia]' and was in possession of a 'smattering' of Italian and French, indicated that she 'strongly disagreed' with the 'Rebels using the Moors against the Spanish people'.16 At each port of call before the ship left Australian shores on the five week journey to Europe, the nurses were lavished with praise for their beauty, valour and virtue, garnering donations for the cause from generous admirers.17

Agnes Hodgson had been the last to join the group. Indeed she had only met her three *compañeras* and the members of the Spanish Relief Committee a few days before the departure. Visiting her sister in Sydney, she heard on the radio that a local group was raising money to send nurses to Spain in response to an appeal for assistance from the Spanish government to democratic nations everywhere. On the spur of the moment she had decided to volunteer; and at the very last minute there was a vacant bunk on board ship when the father of one of the earlier aspiring recruits refused his daughter permission to travel. Lloyd Ross, a well-known figure in adult education and the trade union movement had known Agnes's sister at Melbourne University, and vouchsafed Agnes's nursing qualifications, good character and that she would be ready to leave within a couple of days.18

Agnes, thirty years of age and a trained nurse, had spent a number of years abroad. Her family ties were few but close. Her father, William Frederick Hodgson, a commercial traveller, had been killed at Gallipoli in World War One. Her widowed mother, Agnes Rachel, had died when Agnes was 14 years old. By then she had begun secondary schooling in Melbourne at a private girls' school but, with the mother's death, she was sent for a year to live with relatives in Scotland, after which she returned to Melbourne to complete her schooling as a boarder at Presbyterian Ladies' College. At the insistence of her guardian,

---

16 *Workers Weekly*, 23 Oct 1936.

17 *Adelaide Advertiser*, 29 Oct 1936.

18 Michael Easson, 'Lloyd Ross, 1901-1987', *Australian Dictionary of Biography*, Vol 18 (2012).

Members of the Victorian Spanish Relief Committee welcome the four nurses in Melbourne. Back row: Len Fox, Helen Baillie, Dorothy Gibson, Joyce Metcalf and Nettie Palmer. Front row Australian nurses. 25 Oct 1936.

after secondary school she studied domestic science for two years until she was of an age to begin training as a nurse in the Alfred Hospital from which she graduated as a Registered Nurse in 1928, with a speciality in theatre and in paediatrics. Education behind her, Agnes set off to Budapest to visit her older sister Isabel and then remained in Europe to work and travel for several years. She nursed in Rome at the Anglo-American Clinic for a couple of years, and in the summer of 1932 made a long trip through Spain and North Africa.[19] In mid-1933, when Agnes returned to Australia she was an experienced and independent woman, cultivated, speaking fluent Italian, with a yen for meaningful work and a passion for travel. She had contemplated volunteering to nurse in Abyssinia during the Italian invasion but that had come to nothing. After a stint on her brother's farm, she

[19] Agnes Hodgson in conversation with JK, Camberwell, Melbourne 26 Feb 1984; A M Hodgson, 'A Memory of Rabat. An Australian's Experience in Morocco', *Australian Women's Mirror*, 15 Sep 1936.

began nursing privately in Melbourne. Perhaps it is not surprising, facing what was an unpromising future, that the opportunity to return to Europe and ply her professional skills in a worthwhile cause would appeal.20 In her sister Isobel's assessment, the Spanish civil war was an event that 'naturally drew the enthusiasm of the young' and the motive for Agnes's choice to join them was more than anything else a 'function of her being at a loose end'.21 Agnes had no contact with the Australian political left though, when later reflecting on the decision to volunteer in Spain, she noted that from a young age she had been interested in international affairs and in the 'workings of things like the League of Nations'.22

Mary Lowson was the designated leader of the unit. Small in stature, energetic and forthright, at 41 years of age she was the oldest of the group. She brought to her responsibilities the lessons of work, independence and determination that had been hard-won during a tough childhood in Tasmania. After both parents had died, Mary was raised by relatives to work on a farm in southern Tasmania. In her own description, her schooling was spasmodic and incomplete, as she proudly later proclaimed, all her education had been self-acquired.23 She planned to become a teacher, but trained as a nurse at the Hobart General Hospital and then began working as a private nurse in Sydney. When nursing jobs dried up in the early 1930s, much as had been Agnes's experience in Melbourne, Mary moved to a nursing position at Lidcombe Hospital in Sydney. It was state-run, underfunded and little more than a 'dumping place' for ill and destitute elderly men. Medical care was scarce and professional nursing not part of the remit. The nursing staff was demoralized by low pay and bad working conditions. It was during this stark

---

20 AH with JK Camberwell, 26 Feb 1984.

21 Isabel Shutt to Margaret Delmer, 10 Aug 1986. Private collection JK.

22 AH to JK, Camberwell, 1984.

23 *News* (Adelaide) 29 Oct 1936.

time that Mary joined the Communist Party of Australia (CPA). Here she found an active community of people with a coherent purpose, based on a sustaining conviction that the hardship and misery confronting the poor and the working people around her could only be fixed by revolutionary political and economic change. As a member of the Communist Party, Mary availed herself of all the opportunities for self-improvement in the study circles and lectures devoted to Marxist economics, Soviet history and the radical analysis of Australian labour politics. She also became an enthusiastic member of the group around the New Theatre in inner-city Newtown where productions favoured a Brechtian mode focusing on contemporary realities and the moral problems confronting the poor and the marginalized. Increasingly immersed in the party's culture of talks, meetings and actions of solidarity, Mary experienced the unfolding of a new way of viewing the world and of understanding her own place in it. It was at a Party meeting that Mary had first heard about the Spanish generals' *pronunciamiento* to overthrow the new democratic Republic and that these anti-democratic forces were being backed by the ebullient fascist movements emerging in Italy and Germany. She was a participant at the very early meetings in which the decision was taken to form a Spanish Relief Committee among whom a number of central figures, such as Phil Thorne in Sydney and Helen Baillie in Melbourne, were CPA members. As well there were other committed supporters like Nettie Palmer, indefatigable in the movement for Spanish Aid. Nettie had been living with her family on the coast of Catalonia when the uprising took place and her daughter Aileen, in London, had joined the British Medical Aid Unit (BMAU) that was already on its way to Spain. As a trained nursing sister and an activist in the Communist Party in Sydney it was not surprising that it was to Mary Lowson that the ASRC committee looked to lead the nursing volunteers and to function as the *enlace* maintaining communications between the nurses in the field in Spain with their supporters in the Aid Spain movement in

Australia.24

The other two nursing volunteers, May MacFarlane and Una Wilson, both of whom had worked with Mary at Lidcombe Hospital, followed Mary's example in volunteering for Spain in what for them was a new and worthwhile challenge. May, at 27 years of age and the 'baby of the group', was a qualified triple-certificated nurse.25 A West Australian who had nursed in Brisbane and in far northern New South Wales, May completed her midwifery at Crown Street Women's Hospital in Sydney. 'Mac', as she was called by her colleagues, recalled the hard graft of delivering babies in the inner-city slums of Sydney and the desperate poverty of the mothers in families where the bread winner was unemployed during the drawn-out Depression in Australia.

May had grown up in a politically aware family in Western Australia. But, as she herself recalled, it had been the Egon Kisch affair that clinched her radicalization with the series of ploys that the Australian government used in late 1934 in the failed attempt to stop the Czech communist journalist attending a peace rally in Melbourne.26 For May, the Spanish civil war crystallized all these strands in her political development and, indeed, in Spain she joined the Communist Party while meeting the challenge of wartime nursing attached to the dedicated *équipe* of communist surgeons who had volunteered from a spread of European countries to offer their surgical skills in frontline medical units

---

24 'Australian nurses for Spain. Leader Interviewed', *West Australian*, 3 Nov 1936.

25 There are several usages of May's last name; here I use MacFarlane the most common form but without changing Agnes's usages in the diary. 'Pennefather' is May's married name.

26 Egon Kisch, a Czech investigative journalist and part of the Comintern whose 'reportage' revealed the under belly of world affairs. Invited to a peace conference in Melbourne in 1934, he was refused permission to land whereupon jumped from the ship, was arrested and released and eventually toured Australia speaking to large audiences about the threat of international war and the necessity to counter it with world peace.

behind the lines of the Spanish government fighting Franco's army.27

The fourth member of the unit, Una Wilson from New Zealand, was a highly qualified specialist in surgical theatre nursing. Like Mary and May, she had employment at Lidcombe Hospital with little likelihood of progressing in what she had hoped would have been a promising career in surgical nursing. At 29 years of age, Una also was very stylish. A statuesque blonde, she garnered much attention from all whom she met. Her skill and dedication in the work of frontline surgery made her a key figure in the battlefield surgical units in which she served. Her contribution in the theatre was notable as the lynchpin of a surgical *équipe*, led by the Belgian surgeon Dr René Dumont with whom she developed an intimate relationship in the unpromising conditions of demanding surgical work in the most unpropitious conditions.28

On board ship on their way to Europe the nurses, as had many young Australians before them, made half-hearted attempts to study Spanish from the language books presented to them in Melbourne by Nettie Palmer for the ASRC. They threw themselves into the festivities of ship board life: dressing for dinner, playing deck games, sitting about on deck chairs and drinking cocktails as the sun went down over the ocean. At ports of call, the nurses toured the sights, shopped for souvenirs, and took snapshots of each other to send home. As Europe drew closer, Agnes's spirits grew higher.

---

27 ABC Tape, 'May McFarlane [Pennefather] lent to JK by May McFarlane; conversations with JK Sydney, 3 Nov 1996; *The Red Matildas* [documentary] directed by Trevor Graham, Laurie McInnes; and Sharon Connolly et al., with May Pennefather, Audrey Blake and Joan Goodwin, Ronin Films, Melbourne, (1985): 50 minutes.

28 'From Sister Una Wilson to P Thorne, Jul 1937', in *From the Battlefields of Spain: Vivid Pen Pictures from Australian Nurses.* Published by the Spanish Relief Committee Sydney: Forward Press (40-hour week) [1937]: 3-13; Nettie Palmer and Len Fox with the help of Jim McNeill and Ron Hurd, *Australians in Spain*, (Sydney: Current Book Distributors, May 1948), "Una Wilson", in 'Women Who Served", pp 28-30.

The pleasure of the trip was only marred by a growing antagonism between Agnes and Mary Lowson. Agnes was an old hand at overseas travel. She could reminisce and make comparisons with her previous ocean-going voyages. She also knew friends who were friends of one of the officers in the crew and socialized with their circle on board. She announced as well that an old friend of hers in Rome would meet the ship in Naples and they would catch up together with some sight-seeing.

Una Wilson and Agnes Hodgson enjoy life on board, Nov 1936.

It is clear that in Mary Lowson's view Agnes, with her frivolous pursuits and bourgeois friends on board, was not the companion that she would have chosen to be with in heading off to fight an all-encompassing war against fascism. Agnes's politics, if unexamined, were liberal and chary of communism but certainly anti-fascist. This indeterminate state of political awareness undoubtedly irked Mary. Although Agnes had little time for Mussolini and recalled that when in Italy she had heard through friends about the 'club and castor oil' tactics of Italian fascism. But overall, while living in Italy she had been seduced by Italian culture, the warmth of Italian people, and the joys of an

Italian lifestyle. Mary, on the other hand, was a dedicated communist committed to the long haul to the proletarian revolution. From her involvement in the Australian anti-fascist movement, Mary knew that Italy was a fascist state with a bully-boy leader. In her eyes it was inconceivable that anyone could extol the virtues of Italian opera and the wonders of Italian food when these were no more than the superficial facade of a brutal regime. As Mary wrote to Phil Thorne, Agnes was the 'only person among us who had ever lived in a fascist country' and Mary had 'only realized this when they got to Italy'.29 Agnes also insisted on attending shipboard church services and frequently took Una along with her. A more serious cause of antagonism from Mary's point of view, however, was probably the fact that Agnes had lined up contacts with the Australian press to submit articles on her experiences as a woman in a war situation. Mary was perturbed that Agnes would send her own unsupervised opinions to the Australian press.30 In reality, members of the ASRC were delighted with any first hand pro-Republican material that appeared in the Australian press, or was included in the nurses' letters, as it was all grist for the mill of Australian fund raising and pamphlet production.

Once the ship had left the last Australian port of call, the differences between Mary and Agnes fuelled a full-scale confrontation when Agnes announced that in Naples she intended to spend the day visiting an Italian friend.31 Mary insisted that the women should remain on board because four nurses on their way to Republican Spain would attract hostile Italian demonstrations. And, she suspected that Agnes's friend would be a fascist. Agnes considered it risible that Mussolini would have even heard about four Australian nurses and if it

---

29 Mary Lowson to Phil Thorne, 20 May 1937. Phil Thorne Files, P 15/6/52, NBAANU.

30 Agnes's arrangements were with the *Sydney Morning Herald* and the weekly 'Women's Column' in the *West Australian*.

31 May MacFarlane to Phil Thorne, 11 Mar 1938; Phil Thorne Files, P 15/6/52, NBAANU.

were the case he could not have cared less. She was furious, however, that Mary could suggest that she would have a fascist friend. When some of Agnes's friends on board got wind of the story, they teased Mary about Mussolini which further aggravated the situation.32 In any event, in Naples, Agnes's friend did not materialize. She lunched in a local restaurant with one of the ship's officers and spent the rest of the day alone taking in the pleasures of using her Italian and being an invisible part of the cheerful crowd out and about in the bustling city. Certainly, there were no demonstrations even though Mussolini was reported to have visited Naples on that very day. The incident however, continued to rankle and May and Una became more and more troubled by Mary's overbearing manner.

The *Oronsay* berthed at Toulon at the end of November and the Australians disembarked. They had hoped to be met by John Fisher, an Australian Spanish Relief Committee contact and the son of an Australian Prime Minister, at that time travelling in Europe, or even Egon Kisch, who it was said had been contacted by Spanish Aid in Australia about their arrival. No one on the quay had heard of either man. From Aden, Mary had cabled the time of their arrival via the Australian Committee to Spain's Ambassador in Paris who in turn had alerted the office of Toulon Spanish Aid. Four comrades from the Toulon Movement Against War and Fascism eventually came down to the dock, but as they spoke no English and the Australians no French, there was initial confusion about who the Australian women were and where exactly they were headed. Once it was settled, the four were taken in hand by local Spanish Republican support groups and were feted around the town. The Mayor of Toulon presented them with his box at the opera and the Australians were lunched and dined and greeted by a great array of left-wing groups. A public meeting had been scheduled to farewell some French volunteers for Spain and the nurses as distinguished participants were taken along. As the four women were announced and walked towards the stage the crowd in the

---

32 May MacFarlane to Amirah Inglis, 25 May 1984, N171/Box 1/Folder 5, NBAANU.

hall stood, clenched fists upraised, and sang the *Internationale*. In Marseille, a couple of days later, the round of welcomes was repeated.

L'AUSTRALIE

au Secours de l'Espagne!...

Le Comité d'aide à l'Espagne en Australie, avec l'aide du Comité contre la guerre et le fascisme, envoie une ambulance à l'Espagne.

La délégation qui l'accompagne a été solennellement désigné dans des meetings et conférences.

Le fait est vraiment extraordinaire étant donné qu'on met plus de 30 jours pour aller de Sydney en Europe. La mission comprendra quatre sœurs ; Mary LOWSON, May MACFARLANE, Una WILSON et Agnès HODGSON.

VENEZ EN MASSE
saluer la mission australienne
qui sera reçue solennellement
AU CINÉMA SAINT-LAZARE
Samedi **28** *à 18 h. 30*

Le Mouvement des B.-du-Rh
de PAIX et LIBERTÉ
23, Boulevard de la Paix
MARSEILLE

Flyer for Saint Lazare welcome rally, 28 Nov 1936.

A mass rally was arranged for the Australian nurses in the Cinema Saint-Lazare, at which Mary Lowson read the resolution of Australian solidarity with Spanish workers that had been taken at trade union Transport House in Sydney before they left. As Mary rose to speak the crowd cheered and sang the *Internationale*. At a Movement Against War and Fascism dance she was presented with a glorious bouquet of red roses and carnations. These were heady and moving experiences. It is little wonder that Mary found exhilarating the spirit of revolutionary internationalism. Four unknown Australians had arrived unannounced from half way across the world to be embraced by French comrades because they shared a commitment to the Spanish Republic.

Agnes was less impressed. She felt uneasy surrounded by so many communists and was unwilling to give the clenched fist salute. As she explained primly to one of their hosts, she had 'no precise politics' except that she supported the Spanish Republic. The nurses bought medicine in Marseille with the money that had been raised in Australia and, well-equipped and warmly farewelled, they set off by rail to Spain.

Arrival in Barcelona

After the excitement and attention in France, their arrival in Spain was a shock. At the border, their luggage was thoroughly searched by unsmiling officials. When they finally arrived in Barcelona, on 1 December, it was to a war-torn city. Walls were pock-marked with bullet holes and there were sandbags around the entrances to public buildings. People and traffic raced through the streets with furious purpose while overhead loudspeakers blared revolutionary music and the latest news from the front. Every public surface was hung with a welter of flags and pennants in the colours of political groups; vehicles and buildings were painted with a confusion of acronyms and slogans proclaiming different political affiliations. In Barcelona the realization was brought home to them abruptly that they were in a country at war and one in which the existence of four Australians, even if well-meaning nurses, was of small significance.

With some difficulty they managed to make their way to the Plaza de Cataluña where the fine old Hotel Colón had been taken over and transformed into the headquarters of the PSUC, the Unified Communist Party of Catalonia (*Partit Socialista Unificat de Catalunya*). It also housed the Foreigners' Department (*Servicio Extranjero*) that controlled the issue of the necessary visas and permits for foreigners entering Barcelona, and the *vales* (coupons) needed for food and accommodation. As well, the department maintained a register of each foreigner's anti-fascist credentials.33 Eventually, the Australians were directed from there to the flat of the British Medical Aid Unit on calle de Muntaner where they left the luggage they had brought and went to the room assigned to them in the Hotel Lloret where extra members of the British Medical Aid Unit could be accommodated.

Very soon after their arrival, according to Agnes, and as reported later in May's letters to Phil Thorne in Sydney, Mary had alerted Hugh O'Donnell, a member of the British Communist Party and the administrator overseeing British Medical Aid in Barcelona, that she suspected Agnes was a fascist spy.34 Several days later, Agnes was called in for questioning at the Foreigners' Department. In the interview, by 'Fedeli' that took place in Italian, she was asked about her views on fascism, was pressed on the question of how previously she had obtained the funds to travel from Australia to Italy; and what specifically had she been engaged in while there.35 Three weeks went by while Agnes, May

---

33 Kate Mangan, an English woman in Barcelona with a partner in the International Brigades, has left a graphic description of the chaos of the Servicio Extranjero where queues of anxious foreigners waited for hours and days to file and refile lost forms, in order to receive the necessary passes; or to be interviewed before their residence in Barcelona could be approved. She lists some of the questions on the foreigner's application for proof of good character: how many times in prison, when where and for how long; ditto for concentration camp; list all the anti-fascist organizations you have belonged to, in her *Never More Alive: Inside the Spanish Republic*, with a Preface by Paul Preston, (London: Clapton Press, 2020): pp 63-65.

34 May MacFarlane to Phil Thorne, 11 Mar 1938, 6 pps; 17 Feb 1938, NBAANU. The Quaker photographer, Alec Wainman in his diary, included in *Live Souls: Citizens and Volunteers of Civil War Spain*, edited by Serge Alternes (Vancouver: Ronsdale Press, 2015), p 22 describes the main detail of Agnes's experience with the PSUC interrogation but incorrectly attributes it to the New Zealand nurse, Millicent Sharples.

35 Wainman identified the 'Italian high ranking foreign communist' who interrogated foreigners for the PSUC, using the by pseudonym 'Fideli'. In *Live Souls*, p 22.

and Una became acquainted, as tourists, with Barcelona while
they suspected that Mary was 'making trouble in unofficial circles
about Hodgson'. The three of them visited monuments walked
the city, up and down and end to end, spending time sitting in
the Ramblas café that was frequented by English-speaking
volunteers with the International Brigades and foreign visitors
like themselves.

*Plaza de Cataluña, Barcelona, in front of the Hotel Colón.
Mary Lowson, May MacFarlane, journalist John Fisher,
International Brigader Jack 'Blue' Barry, Aileen Palmer,
Agnes Hodgson and Una Wilson. 8 Dec 1936.*

During this time, Mary went off each day ostensibly to deal with the business of where they were to join a medical unit. May and Una, 'increasingly alarmed by Mary's unguarded hatred of Agnes' both agreed that if anything happened to Agnes 'they would leave together'.36 At one stage May confronted Mary about where she went during the day and since they were a 'group of four, not a single person' in charge of arrangements, they would like to accompany her to wherever it was that necessitated her attendance. Mary became very angry and shouted at May in the foyer of a hotel which May found very embarrassing. Writing about the incident several months later to Phil Thorne, May confessed that they had found 'conditions in Barcelona very difficult'; again, in her words, 'everybody seemed to be regarding us with suspicion' in a surrounding ambience that they found very frightening and feared a possibility that 'they would be bumped off'.37

At last word came through that the Australians were to move out. There were four English trucks travelling south to Albacete where the headquarters of the International Brigades was being set up. From there, a destination for them in a battlefront medical unit would be determined. With the gear loaded and at the very point of departure, Mary announced that only three official passes—for Una, May and herself—had been issued from the Foreigners' Department and O'Donnell, who had come to see them off, explained that Agnes was to stay behind. Because of her fluency in Italian she had been chosen to work in an International Brigade hospital that was to be set up in Barcelona.38 May and Una were dismayed at the turn of events

36 May MacFarlane to Phil Thorne, 20 Feb 1938, p 6, pp 2-4 of 6ps Phil Thorne Collection, 171/Box 1/ Folder 6 NBAANU.

37 May MacFarlane to Phil Thorne, Barcelona, 30 Dec 1936, 171/Box 1/ Folder 6 NBAANU.

38 AH to PT, Barcelona 30 Dec 1936; in a warm letter exchange between AH and PT, 14/8/1983, AH asked PT if he had read Orwell's letters and essays, commenting that she 'found them extremely interesting' because he gives 'a good description of the Barcelona as we knew it on arrival'. NBAANU P15/4/Folder 14.

but felt unable to do anything about it by themselves at that minute.39 The convoy drove off, leaving Agnes alone in Barcelona.

The official caution about Agnes's politics, and even her exclusion from the International Brigades, may have been understandable. In reality, however, it was an undeniable stretch based on a misapprehension and the personal animosity between the two women in which the aggravating factors were their differences in class, style, and personality. Undoubtedly, foreign agents and *franquista* sympathisers were at work in Barcelona and the authorities needed to be careful. The larger background to the incident, however, was the increasing distrust leading to an outright struggle between political groups within Republican Spain over the government's determination to dismantle the militias in order to build a new unified Republican Army which increasingly came under the control of the Comintern via the Spanish Communist Party (PCE). In this case, it is worth remembering as well that the support from western democracies, that the legally-elected, democratic Republican government had assumed would be its due, was simply not forthcoming. The Soviet Union provided the only overt aid to the government's struggle to defeat Franco and the insurgent generals, though, as history records, Soviet aid was never untethered from Stalinist foreign policy.40 And the Stalinist obsession with purging Trotskyism in the Soviet Union carried over into the groupings in Spain and within the international volunteers and the International Brigades.41 These political differences and the

---

39 May always regretted not having stood up for Agnes at that moment and years later apologized to her, MacFarlane to Phil Thorne, 3 Jan 1938, N171 P15/6/54; and MMcF to Amirah Inglis, 25 May 1984, N171/Box 1/Folder 5, NBAANU.

40 Soviet aid, military and other kinds, was always tied to Soviet foreign policy.

41 See Len Crome's discussion of denunciations in the medical unit in the International Brigades. 'Document: Walter (1937-1947): A Soldier In Spain', *History Workshop Journal*, 9 (Spring 1980): 120.

tensions growing behind the scenes in Barcelona at the end of 1936, developed into an open struggle in May Days 1937 between the anarchist movement and increasingly communist controlled republican government which for Anglo-Saxon audiences, for good or ill, has been represented in Orwell's *Homage to Catalonia*.42 Allied to this shift in politics was the forced dissolution of the Council of Aragón by the newly centralized military led by General Pozas. And the subsequent savage disbandment and arrest of members of the Trotskyist, or so-claimed, POUMist movement in which Orwell, among others, was a victim. Agnes, however, was apolitical rather than leaning to one group or another. Her unfortunate treatment in the fraught atmosphere of Barcelona, in December 1936 to early February 1937, placed her life in danger. A foreign woman, alone, suspected of harbouring Italian fascist sympathies, with no political faction to call for support and seemingly abandoned by her own *compañeras*, left her in a very vulnerable position. At that time and subsequently, she wrote about her predicament to Phil Thorne in Sydney. Without any doubt, he was a decent man and a Party member who devoted three or more years of his life to the Spanish Aid movement and to fostering an Australian understanding of inter-war European politics and where the Spanish civil war fitted in an ebullient fascist expansion. When Agnes directly appealed to him for affirmation of her mistreatment, he carefully sidestepped the discussion to comment about their shared obsession with the necessity of fund-raising for the vulnerable Republic.43 But, he also was conscientious and tactful in implementing a policy change to ensure that Australian funds were channelled through Paris to the managing organisation for donations outside Spain, *Central Sanitaire Internationale* (CSI); and that if Mary Lowson wished

---

42 Paul Preston, 'George Orwell's Spanish civil war memoir is a classic, but is it bad history?', *Guardian Sunday*, 7 May 2017, [4pp].

43 Phil Thorne to Agnes Hodgson, 23 Feb 1937 p15/Folder 15, Thorne Collection, NBAANU.

to return to Spain after a fund raising tour in Australia, she must accept a nursing position in a Unit as had been the original arrangement. And he alerted the British Medical Aid Committee that the Australian committee would meet any funding needs for Agnes to take some R&R in Britain or at Tossa de Mar on the Catalonian coast.44 From what we now know in a careful perusal of more extensive archives, John Fisher, the journalist son of the former prime minister, was also concerned about Agnes's safety. He wrote to her, but on the condition that she kept the contents of the letter confidential, that he had 'mentioned privately to Thorne that [she] was a trifle worried at not getting down to work straight away' and he spoke for her within the London circles of the British Medical Aid movement to vouch for her genuine antifascism.

The involvement of Hugh O'Donnell, probably, exacerbated the problem. He was an administrator with British Medical Aid in Barcelona, where he had been re-assigned to manage the unit's flat in the city after his 'quixotic character' had found little favour with the other medical volunteers who had set up a military hospital in Aragón. O'Donnell, a member of the Communist Party of Great Britain (CPGB), was criticized on the grounds that he was committed to an agenda that suited party loyalty over medical necessity. The consequences of his erratic stance caused distrust among a number of the English medical staff that, in any event, were divided over political issues between communists versus non-communists. For example, Archie Cochrane, a very capable medical student, a double honours from Cambridge, who had studied in Berlin and Vienna in the early thirties and had volunteered for Spain from University College Hospital in August 1936, found O'Donnell a 'weak leader' whose behaviour was 'stupid, conceited and erratic', certainly not qualities that would be useful in wartime medicine.45 There were

---

44 Nancy Johnstone, *Hotel in Flight*, (London: Faber and Faber, 1939; London: The Clapton Press, 2022).

45 Archie Cochrane noted that in a huge rally for the unit at the Stade Buffalo in Paris calling for planes for Republican Spain, O'Donnell had seized the microphone and made a long-winded and

other incidents with British medical volunteers and equally from British Communist Party members visiting Spain in September 1936.46 Eventually O'Donnell left the English medical unit to work full time in the Foreigners' Department of the PSUC.

For the remainder of the civil war, May MacFarlane and Una Wilson served on the most critical fronts of battle: Madrid, Brunete, Teruel, Ebro and Aragón. May was attached to a medical team with the Austrian surgeon Walter Langer and Una became a core figure in the theatre *équipe* of the Belgian, Dr René Dumont. With these top surgeons, both women nursed the wounded under truly horrendous conditions and were sterling examples of the nursing profession. They remained in Spain for the duration, that is until the International Brigades were withdrawn at the end of 1938. The two returned to Australia together in February 1939, physically and mentally exhausted: heartbroken by the Republican defeat and personally devastated for the loss of their friends, lovers and close medical *compañeros* in those horrendous final months of the civil war.

Mary Lowson, after a few short weeks with May and Una, working in a hospital in Benicàssim on the coast from Albacete,

---

'stupid' speech. Cochrane's assessment was even more scathing later in Spain, in *One Man's Medicine: An Autobiography of Professor Archie Cochrane*, (Cardiff University Press, 2009), pp 20-1, 23.

46 Jim Fyrth noted that before coming to Spain O'Donnell was reputed to have been gaoled for mutiny because of demonstrating against the RAF air show at Hendon, in *The Signal Was Spain*, (London: Lawrence and Wishart, 1986), pp 30, 50-1, 57, 60-1, 77, 189. There were other complaints as well. Sylvia Townsend Warner and Valentine Ackland, English literary figures and influential members of the CPGB, were in Barcelona as ambulance drivers in August 1936 and wrote a damming report to Harry Pollitt about the poor calibre of English party functionaries, in Angela Jackson, *British Women and the Spanish Civil War*, (London: Routledge/Cañada Blanch Studies of Contemporary Spain 2002): pp 134-5. See also Kenneth Sinclair-Loutit's surprise that O'Donnell's appointment was backed by communists within the organizing committee, quoted in Linda Palfreeman, *Salud! Volunteers in the Republican Medical Services During the Spanish Civil War, 1936-1939*, (Brighton: Sussex Academic Press, 2012): p 27.

came back to Barcelona and was attached to the English Section of the Republican Information Service which produced Spanish government propaganda abroad. In this position she met a number of foreign visitors to Spain to report on the war, and regularly sent material to the Spanish Aid Committee to be sent on to Australia. She also used Australian funds, with Hugh O'Donnell's supervision, to make several trips to France to purchase food and medical supplies that she distributed in Spain. She kept contact from a distance with Una Wilson and May MacFarlane but cut all ties with Agnes.

Agnes Alone in Barcelona

Without the protection of the original combined four-person permit for board and lodging in Barcelona, Agnes was forced to re-apply to the Foreigners' Department for a new *vale*.47 This time she was assigned, not to an hotel, but to barracks on the outskirts of Barcelona in an over-crowded ex-convent that housed refugee women and children rescued from Madrid. There, she waited for a hospital appointment that did not eventuate. She was uncertain whether Lowson had made any 'arrangements about the financial side of things' except that she had been told that she should ask O'Donnell if she needed money. Agnes noted to 'Mr Thorne' that she was becoming ravenously hungry and craving sweet things, in the way that MacFarlane had developed a craving for sweet things before she left Barcelona. After several weeks, O'Donnell introduced Agnes to a Hungarian doctor with a small clinic treating local people in an outer suburb of Barcelona. O'Donnell had asked him to take Agnes on as his nurse, indicating to Agnes that the doctor would house and feed her and most probably include some sort of living allowance. Once she began there, however, nothing more was ever said about housing or stipend. Because there were few patients, the pace was leisurely. Surrounded by Spaniards, Agnes's Spanish improved but she felt useless and very isolated:

---

47 For material on Agnes's experiences at this time see AH to PT 30-12-1936, p15/Folder 15, Thorne Collection, NBAANU.

'alone in a strange atmosphere with the mental strain of endeavouring to understand them and do [her] work creditably'. Even more urgently, there was nothing said by Lowson or O'Donnell about how to obtain accommodation and the *vales* needed for every day existence. She felt that she was 'getting a raw deal' and 'her services had been politely shelved'. Having come to Spain 'in all sincerity to nurse the war-wounded' and had not bargained for this mental worry, to be left to cool her heels, alone, in the suburbs. After a couple of weeks at the clinic, and feeling particularly desperate, Agnes confronted O'Donnell, threatening either to leave for London to report her predicament to the BMAC or, on the spot, approach the Catalan authorities herself and volunteer to join the medical corps of the Spanish army. Very hastily, an arrangement was made. Agnes was directed to join a group of Spanish doctors with English nurses who had been part of the first British Medical Aid Unit and had set up a hospital in the village of Grañén on the western Aragón front. In a postscript to Phil Thorne, on 30 December 1936, Agnes added that she was leaving 'imminently' for Grañén, that she had met the Spanish doctor in charge (presumably Gonzalo Aguiló) and he had explained that the hospital was no longer run by British Medical Aid, as it had been before, though there were some English nurses remaining, but that 'I must be very careful what I say and write from there'. Agnes added that she was 'not quite sure what that meant' but it looked as though 'I won't be able to send you (PT) any information useful for propaganda in Australia'. But she added that she was at last 'glad to be going off to work'.48

Grañén

The British Medical Aid unit that had set up the hospital in Grañén, where Agnes was headed early in February 1937, had arrived to a tremendous welcome in Barcelona at the end of

---

48 AH to PT, postscript, dated 10-1-37, to letter dated 30-12-1936 [recd. 16/2/37], Thorne Collection. NBAANU.

August 1936. Cheering crowds lined the street and the unit's leaders were welcomed, personally, by the President of the Catalan *Generalitat*. The British were the first foreign aid unit to have responded to the broadcast request to 'the world democracies' from the Republican government for medical assistance. The swiftness of the BMAC response was read in Republican Spain as a hopeful sign that presaged forthcoming support from other democratic nations. Certainly, the British Medical Aid Unit was an impressive sight as the convoy of Bedford trucks and four English ambulances rolled into Barcelona.

Hospital Staff at the British Medical Unit, Grañén, Dec 1936.

The staff, comprising more than some twenty individuals, were kitted out in military-like uniforms, most bought from Army and Navy Surplus stores in London. There were four doctors (an Indian, an American, an Englishman and a German woman); four medical students; four nurses and two interpreters, Rosita Davson and Aileen Palmer, an Australian

linguist whose mother was active in Spanish Aid in Australia.49
With a view to keeping up publicity for fund raising at home, the
group included a journalist, the Australian, Margot Miller, whose
injury in the early days at the front in itself provided a major
news item;50 and the inspired appointment, in light of the
demands for images to aid in fund-raising, of a cinema
photographer, the Australian-born, William Belcher. Injured in a
road accident on the way from London, he arrived later with the
second British medical group in Barcelona where he promptly
headed off to join up with the militias.

Among the six drivers who managed the fleet of vehicles was
the English Quaker, Alec Wainman, who also proved to be a
skilled photographer.51 There were as well two 'quartermasters',
one of whom was O'Donnell, an ambiguous figure already noted,
who remained in Barcelona, to look after supplies from England
and manage a flat that had been rented to serve as an office and a
place for the medical staff to use on rest and recreation from
frontline service.

First up, for the BMAU, was the question of which political
faction they would be attached to. In Cataluña, the anarchist
movement, comprising the FAI and the CNT, was numerically
and politically most powerful. There was also the POUM, the
Workers Party of Marxist Unity, a dissident Marxist group that
had split from the Communist Party; and by then also on the
horizon was the communist PSUC. Each of the distinct political
groups was backed by their own autonomous militias. The
British Medical Aid Unit chose to align with the PSUC which at

---

49 See Sylvia Martin, *Ink in Her Veins: The Troubled Life of Aileen
Palmer*, (Perth: University of Western Australia publishing, 2016).

50 *Australian Women's Weekly*, 26 Dec 1936; *Sydney Sun*, 30 Nov
1936, 'Sturdy Sydney girl' who had been living in London before
travelling to Spain, addressed a packed Albert Hall in London about
her injuries and her adventures in Aragón.

51 Wainman left a treasure trove of some 1,600 photographs that
after his death were misplaced and decades later unearthed by his
son. See *Live Souls*.

that time included socialists that resonated with the Socialist Medical Group, one of the initial promoters of the BMAU, but was dominated by members of the Communist Party of Great Britain which sat comfortably with the PSUC's affiliation with the Communist International.

The second task was to determine where the British effort of setting up a hospital in Aragón should be focussed. Peter Churchill (Viscount Churchill), who had accompanied the group from London and later was to lead the British Medical Aid in all of Spain, used his First World War skills and a Michelin map, probably acquired on the way in Paris, in order to choose the village of Grañén, some 20 kilometres south east from Huesca and Saragossa, the line between those two towns constituted the frontline in northern Aragón. Both towns, since the *pronunciamiento*, had been held by Franco's insurgents. In terms of geo-military logistics it was an advantageous position: at the railhead for Lérida and Barcelona and at an important road junction with access to the whole Aragón front. Churchill and Kenneth Sinclair-Loutit, the unit administrator, scoped out the area finding an abandoned farmhouse on land that had been seized by the local revolutionary committee in the first weeks after the insurgent generals' uprising. The owner of the farm and the local priest, reportedly, had fled to Saragossa or been executed by local committee members, implementing the new collectivist order across Aragón in the first revolutionary weeks of the war. In relation to the hospital's location, the three main political groupings were strung out across Aragón: the POUM controlled the area on the hospital's left flank; the anarchists were in the centre and the right flank constituted the PSUC's area of influence.

Initially, the English staff on taking over what was to become the hospital building, cleared the rubble from inside and drained the muck from the courtyard in a process that Aileen Palmer described as 'walrus and carpenter' work that is with much activity to little discernible effect.

At first, conditions were primitive and the front was very active which brought high numbers of patients needing emergency care.52 Water, which had to be sterilized, was hauled by mule cart from a nearby stream. But, by the time of Agnes's arrival, in early February 1937, things had improved. Ambulances were unloaded in the court yard at the front; within the building were housed two theatres, two surgical wards, another with 30 beds for locals and the ill in transit; and rough sleeping accommodation for the medical staff on mattresses in the loft above. There were the daily hitches: Loutit had rigged up an improvised washing machine but when it broke down, as was often the case, linen, hospital bedding and clothes were taken to the stream to be washed. There was electricity connected but not with much light and never entirely reliable.

At the end of December 1936, the original medical staff split after increasingly acrimonious differences over whether to remain in Grañén under the London BMAC's oversight as in the original agreement that had brought them to Spain; or whether to leave Grañén and move to Albacete to throw their lot in with the medical services of the International Brigades that were in the process of being formed. Most of the English medical staff chose the latter option on the grounds that the International Brigade fighting was becoming more intense and therefore the English medical staff could be most effective as frontline medical units dispersed to where the need for emergency surgical intervention was greatest.53

---

52 In the first month since the set up in the sector of the Aragón front was very active. Sinclair-Loutit reported 200 wounded treated in 3 days of medical staff in intense working times, in his Oct 1936 Report to SMAC, in Palfreeman, *Salud!*, p 29.

53 Contemporary accounts indicate that there were tensions between communists and non-communist humanitarians, in which personal dislikes were also entangled. Jim Fyrth, without passing over the political tensions lays out the complexity of the disagreements, in *The Signal was Spain*, pp 57-61; and Sylvia Martin, focusing on the contradictory assessment of Aileen Palmer's role also astutely reveals the common tensions and their mixed application and outcome, in her *Ink in her Veins*, pp 135-146.

*Grañén, clearing the 'mud and muck' from the
surroundings of the British Medical Aid Unit hospital,
December 1936.*

The medical team remaining in the hospital in Grañén, ostensibly taken over by the Spanish Army, stayed with the PSUC that provided certain supplies from Barcelona. It comprised three Spanish doctors. The most senior was a Mallorcan, Dr Gonzalo Aguiló Mercader, from the Hospital Clínico in Barcelona, a gifted surgeon, with phenomenal stamina when faced with a surge of incoming wounded.54 As well, he was a highly effective medical administrator, as skilled in overseeing the management of the hospital, whether *in situ* or on the move, as he was in calmly performing major surgery under battlefront conditions.

Admired by all, he was a stout supporter of the Republic, but kept clear of domestic politics. He also spoke fluent English and French and, without a doubt, was the key figure in the whole enterprise. His hospital agenda, even in the most trying conditions at the front, was strictly focussed on providing the best possible surgical outcomes in the operating theatre and in the after care of wounded soldiers.

The staff also included several *practicantes* (wardsmen-cum-medical students), four ambulance drivers, a couple of cooks, and four guards who doubled as stretcher bearers. There was, as well, a designated gravedigger. In addition a number of *chicas*, young women from the village, assisted on the wards and with the cleaning. There were three nurses remaining from the original English detachment, whose number increased with new arrivals, including Agnes, until there were seven trained nurses, all British, again with the exception of Agnes.55

---

54 Ruth Muller, *Margaret Powell: An Extraordinary Life*, (Crickhowell District Archive, 2022), draws on her mother's lively diary of her months after joining the unit in Mar 1937, and served later for the duration of the war, even being held in detention in France with the fleeing Republican exiles.

55 Fyrth, *The Signal Was Spain*, 43-61; Patience Darton nursed in the same hospital in Poleñino with Agnes from March 1937. See Angela Jackson, *For Us It Was Heaven: The Passion, Grief and Fortitude of Patience Darton*, (Sussex Academic Press, with Cañada Blanch Centre for Contemporary Spanish Studies, 2012), pp 38-57; Palfreeman, *Salud!,* Chapter 4.

The rhythm of work was irregular. When there were battles at the front, the staff were run off their feet and the theatres worked full-time as was the case in the first months of the hospital's establishment. When the front was quiet, the hospital would slow to a standstill. In these slack periods staff played shuttlecock, walked in the hills, bathed in the stream or sat in the village bar.

Dr Gonzalo Aguiló Mercader, chief surgeon and administrator of the Grañén and Poleñino hospitals. Poleñino, Jun 1937.

The hospital dealt with the wounded brought in by ambulances from dressing stations at the surrounding fronts. The most urgent cases, usually injuries of the head and the stomach, were operated on in the Grañén theatres and were evacuated as soon as possible by train to base hospitals at Lérida and Barcelona. The less seriously injured, including those with hand injuries, viewed with suspicion by staff and the military as suspected self-inflicted, were usually treated but sent back to the front. Spaniards from the surrounding villages also came to the hospital for surgical and medical care and for the birthing of babies.

There was tension between the Grañén village committee and the medical administrators that dated from the hospital's original establishment and became increasingly acrimonious during Agnes's time in Grañén. In the first few days after the Spanish generals' rebellion the area had been taken by fascist supporters from Huesca. Shortly afterwards it was liberated by the anarchist Ascaso militia column that had been sent from Barcelona. As in many other parts of Aragón, the defeat of the Falangists in Grañén was followed by the seizure of the local estates of the absentee landlords and their reorganization into a collectively-run enterprise. According to contemporary Spanish descriptions, Grañén was managed by a committee, sending representatives to the Huesca regional federation which in turn elected representatives to the Council of Aragón.56 All goods and property were collectivised and distributed among members

---

56 Augustín Souchy Bauer, *Entre los campesinos de Aragón: El comunismo libertario en las comarcas liberadas*, (Barcelona: Tusquets Editor, 1977) [1937]: 70-74; Frank Mintz, *L'autogestion dans l'Espagne révolutionnaire*, (Paris: Bélibaste, 1970): 65-99; Erich-Hans Kaminski, *Los de Barcelona*, (Barcelona: Parsifals, 1976) [1937]. See also the transformation of a nearby anarchist village in the Huesca region in, Susan Friend Harding, *Remaking Ibieca. Rural Life in Aragón under Franco*. (Chapel Hill: University of North Carolina Press, 1984): 59-80; and the definitive scholarly treatment by Julián Casanova, *Anarquismo y revolución en la sociedad rural Aragonesa, 1936-1938*, (Madrid: Siglo Veintiuno de España Editores, 1985).

according to individual needs or were exchanged through the regional federation with other villages. The Council of Aragón and its supporting localities, like Grañén, were extremely wary of the centralizing policies of the non-anarchist Left and solidly defended their own political position, which was that in order to defeat the Franco's Nationalists it was necessary to push on with the social revolution that had begun in areas that had remained loyal to the Republican government.57

The anarchist revolution in Aragón attracted a number of observers from outside Spain: the curious as well as admirers who came with great hopes of seeing the unfolding of the anarchist revolution. Emma Goldman, perhaps the highest profile of these international visitors, made a fact-finding trip across the province in the first of her two Spanish visits during the civil war. She was accompanied by the Dutch anarcho-syndicalist Arthur Lehningin and a translator; the photographic images by the exiled Polish/Austrian anarchist photographer, Margaret Michaelis documented their travels. Michaelis's stunning images of Aragón and the rural life of its inhabitants are included in the diary section of this volume.58

The establishment of an English hospital in Grañén inadvertently plugged into tension that was at the intersection of local and national events.59 The hospital was attached to the

---

57 The English filmmaker, Kenneth Loach's film *Land and Freedom* (1995), beautifully shot in Aragón, and influenced by Orwell's *Homage to Catalonia*, follows a group of foreign volunteers in a POUM unit. The film is highly critical of the role of Communists and the PSUC in the forced demilitarisation of the militias, an interpretation that has raised the ire of veterans of the British and American International Brigades.

58 For the remarkable story of these recovered photographic treasures, see Helen Ennis *Margaret Michaelis: Love, loss and Photography* (Canberra, National Gallery of Australia, 2005); and Almudena Rubio Pérez, 'Las cajas de Ámsterdam: Margaret Michaelis y los anarquistas de la CNT-FAI en la Guerra Civil', *Historia Social*, p 104 (2022).

59 Archie Cochrane was critical of Churchill and Sinclair-Loutit for their choice of this area without considering the local regional

Carlos Marx Battalion of the PSUC, on which it depended for funds and supplies. The hospital, therefore, was perceived by some villagers to be allied to the movement for the centralization of the administration of the war. There was as well an underlying hostility to outsiders discernible in some of the local rejection of hospital policies. For example, when Sinclair-Loutit raised the Red Cross flag above the hospital, to indicate the building's international status as a protected medical site, it caused great agitation among the villagers. They saw the flag as a provocation to outsiders from Catalonia that would ensure attention from Fascist enemy aircraft.60 And, indeed in October 1937, the hospital was destroyed in a bombardment by Franco's allies, the German and Italian air force, despite—or maybe as the villagers claimed—because of the Red Cross that by then had been painted on the roof.

It was also the case that the committee in Grañén had not been consulted about the location of an English hospital in their village. The head of the village committee, with the *nom de guerre* of 'Pancho Villa' had been a leading figure in the first successes of the Ascaso militia in driving off the initial fascist victors.61 He viewed the hospital with increasing distrust.62

---

configuration of political groupings of Anarchist, POUM, and PSUC. Perhaps his displeasure with the two Englishmen was influenced by their having borrowed his first, and much prized Triumph sports car, driven out from London, and 'negligently' allowed it to be 'requisitioned' in Aragón by an anarchist militia. In, *One Man's Medicine*, p 24.

60 Palfreeman, *Salud!*, p 41.

61 Thanks to Almudena Rubio for this information.

62 Loutit in an exaggeratedly amused style, suggests that Pancho Villa's hostility was somewhat assuaged when he suffered a burn in a petrol accident and was treated with fulsome nursing care in the hospital, in 'The Largest Frying Pan in the World' in *The Distant Drum: Reflections on the Spanish Civil War*, edited by Philip Toynbee, (London: Book Club Edition, 1976): pp 105-108. Margot Miller repeats this anecdote, though she refers to 'Pancho Villa' as 'the local dictator whose primitive mind was suspicious of

The original British Medical Unit had had their own stores sent from London and topped up by the PSUC in Barcelona. Once untethered from the British Medical Aid Unit, however, the hospital was dependent much more on the regional committee, especially in the most pressing matter of the need for the increasingly scarce resource of motor fuel. A slow war, a 'sub-conflict within a conflict' simmered between the hospital and members of the village committee.63 The latter were reluctant to provision a hospital in which they had little say and, moreover, that was attached to the Catalan Communist Party with whom the anarchist movement was at logger-heads. Certainly, the hospital and English staff were connected to the international dimension of the Spanish civil war, and the villagers and the concerns of its committee were embedded in the Spanish dimension of the war.

By early March 1937 with local hostility at worrying levels, the hospital staff were forced to move to a new village, Poleñino, several kilometres away, leaving the hospital in Grañén to service the anarchist columns around Grañén. The new site, Poleñino, was sympathetic to the PSUC, to which ostensibly the hospital was aligned and the medical operation was housed in a wing of the *Casa de Pueblo*, the village community centre, which also provided quarters for the Poleñino village committee.

---

foreigners' in her interview in *Australian Women's Weekly*, 26 December 1936. The representation of the mayor and the villagers in the telling of this story is etched with an Orientalist edge that highlights the otherness of the surrounding peasantry in the view of some foreign medical staff. By contrast, Pancho Villa was a notable figure in the region and had played an important role in the Anarchist Ascaso Legion's recapturing Aragón from the Insurgent forces in the early days of the fascist uprising. The exiled German anarchist photographer in Barcelona, Kati Horna, whose images and stunning photomontage were so important in spreading the anarchist message, used her own photograph of Pancho Villa on the front page of *Umbral*, the widely-read anarchist magazine, (no 3, 24 Jul 1937). Agnes Hodgson also refers to another 'Pancho Villa' in Tardiente which suggests perhaps that British medicos used 'Pancho Villa' as a nickname for local anarchist influencers.

63 Sinclair-Loutit, p 106.

"The miliciano, Pancho Villa, leaning on a shotgun, wearing beret, cartridge belt and sash", Banastás, Huesca, March 1937.

As in the case of the differences with the Grañén village, the hospital was affected by political developments taking place in Spain as a whole. The staff listened nightly to news broadcasts from Madrid and Burgos, sceptical of Nationalist exaggerations of Republican losses, but also horrified by news of the Nationalists' victories such as in Málaga in early 1937 and the collapse of Bilbao in June.

The Australian, William Belcher, the ex-driver for the British Medical Aid Unit who became Agnes's friend in Barcelona and was now with an anarchist militia, the Battalion of Death, brought first hand reports of the government's tightening of military discipline over his comrades in arms. A cavalry regiment which had been part of the POUM, now incorporated into the regular Spanish army, came through Poleñino in early July 1937. Rumours were rife that Huesca and Zaragoza, in Nationalist hands since early in the war and the focal points on the Republican line, were about to be retaken by the new centralized military. At each report of an imminent Republican offensive the hospital staff cleaned instruments, made splints and were readied for the surge of wounded into the theatres.

After Agnes had been four months at Poleñino the major Aragón offensive began. The army was reorganized under General Pozas Perea. Agnes observed his much-anticipated visit to survey the new Spain army in Aragón, late in August-September 1937, around which time the hospital became a mobile surgical unit behind the advancing Republican troops and moved up into the sierras of High Aragón above Boltaña, about 40 kilometres from the French border. It was the wet season. The mobile hospital worked under extremely difficult conditions. The theatre was set up in an ex-slaughterhouse on a farmyard and tents and medical staff stood ankle-deep in mud and slush. Bombing was continuous. The wounded were brought down through the steep passes on muleback, arriving soaking wet and caked in mud. Before injuries could be assessed the soldiers' clothes had to be cut off, although the hospital had no pyjamas with which to replace discarded clothes, and was so short of covers and hospital linen that in some cases the wounded were evacuated naked in blankets. There were a great many head and stomach wounds from shrapnel which needed immediate attention, but with no post-operative wards, patients had to be evacuated immediately after surgery. Food, which was hauled up to the front by mules, was in short supply. Many of the wounded arrived not having eaten for several days and the hospital had nothing to give them except 'coffee and milk, and not always milk'. According to Agnes, the conditions at Boltaña were like those which one imagined in the most terrible parts of the Great War.

People's nerves were frazzled and by mid-September Agnes was worn out, ill and at the end of her tether. She dreamed constantly about her family and home and was plagued by a recurring nightmare in which she 'unwound and unwound bandages to find nothing but pieces of skin and the remains of arms and legs'.64 There was a disagreement within the nursing staff about sleeping arrangements and Agnes, impulsively, quit the front and hitch-hiked back to Barcelona. From there it was arranged that she should take a spell away from Spain and the war to enjoy some R & R with her relatives in Scotland in order to recover her health and energy. By the second week of October, however, she was back with her unit that by then was serving as an emergency medical station with an *auto-chir*, a mobile operating theatre set up in a truck, dealing with a number of the fascist wounded as well as their own troops.65 Extreme wet weather turned roads and fields to sticky mud. Aguiló and his team, on the spot, operated on the most urgent, usually abdominal and head wounds. The less urgent others were triaged to be shipped further back from the lines to another farm house converted into a wounded rest station from where they would be loaded on ambulance trains for future transport to a larger hospital at Lérida or even Barcelona. Agnes felt she could take no more.

In Barcelona, when Agnes arrived, there were curfews and blackouts and nightly bombing raids. Peter Spencer, by now the director of all the British Medical Aid services in Spain, and Leah Manning, the British secretary, offered Agnes another posting to the Madrid front, which she considered but then rejected after hearing from someone, who had been posted there, that the staff was riven with disagreements. On 19 October 1937 Agnes left Spain.

---

64 AH to "Darlingest" [hersister] 9 Oct 1937. JK Personal papers.

65 There are references in the first person accounts to this capture of a brace of enemy soldiers, who were in very bad physical condition, under-nourished and fearful of the captors about whom they had heard dreadful reports. Brought into the mobile hospital, by stretcher bearers the enemy prisoners were astonished that Aguiló and the nursing team dealt with them in an unvarying sequence determined by the severity of their injuries and the time in which they had been collected from no-man's land at the front. See for example, Wainman, *Live Souls: Citizens and Volunteers of the Civil War in Spain,* p 35.

Agnes captured by a street photographer, Sydney, mid 1938.

Agnes and the Wound in the Heart

On her arrival back in Australia, Agnes told a reporter: 'Never have I seen such dreadful wounds and suffering as those that result from warfare. What I have seen in Spain has made me a militant pacifist for ever'. In the next few months in Australia, Agnes made a number of public appearances raising money for the Aid Spain movement though she found difficulty in public speaking before large groups. She produced some writing about her Spanish experiences and made a long trip by car into the northern Australian outback gathering material for what she hoped would be a series of newspaper stories about the hardships of life in the outback for indigenous Australians and struggling farmers. However, there was less enthusiasm for her observations on Australian home front affairs than there had been for her writing about her experiences as a young woman in wartime Spain. For a time, she was a relieving housemistress at Sydney Church of England Girls' Grammar School in inner Sydney, Darlinghurst. In December 1938 she was delighted to land a job on the women's pages of the *Daily Mirror*, although it was, as she described it, 'not exactly exciting or original work' and the salary was 'on the breadline'. As she rather drily explained, she was expected to produce 'Sister Sadie's column' in the 'Piccaninnies Page', write captions for fashion photographs, and 'attempt to wean country women from the atrocious brand of cushions that they favour'. The job, however, 'provided experience in the compilation of a paper' and, she hoped, would be a 'toe into the paper world'.66

In the 'placidity of Sydney and its peacetime pursuits', Agnes became depressed suffering what she described as 'periodic attacks of the stupidity of all this tripe when Europe is so full of tension'. Spain's defeat filled her with a 'terrible bitterness', as did the horrendous fate of the Spanish Republican population forced into the *Retirada*, the terrifying retreat before Franco's victorious crusade into Catalonia that drove thousands

---

66 A Hodgson to Margaret Delmer, 24 Apr 1939, JK private papers.

of defeated civilians as well as soldiers to cross the border into an unwelcoming France. And for many, into a life of exile. Held in detention camps and make-shift barracks, defeated Republicans and International Brigaders with home nations that had by now fallen under the aegis of ebullient fascist government, were 'living in France under awful conditions and utterly demoralized', while their western allies 'sold them out'. In face of this Agnes worried that she was 'a curious, perverse creature', as the jingoism of the Australian service groups filled her with dismay, as did equally the enthusiastic activities of local women's war service organizations intimidating their friends into joining up. When the next war came, as it seemed increasingly certain it would, Agnes 'dreaded more than anything being worked up to international hate, and all the dirty work that goes with it'.67

During the Second World War Agnes headed, very capably but without overwhelming enthusiasm, the Tasmanian division of the Australian Women's Land Army, organizing women to take over essential farming tasks to free rural men to enlist. In January 1944, she married Ralph Tonkin, an officer in the Australian Imperial Forces, while he was posted back to Australia from service in New Guinea. They had two children, Rachel and Ian. With her husband, post-war, Agnes travelled in Spain several times and remained a life-long aficionado of Italy and Italian culture. She was a founding member of a number of Italo-Australian cultural groups in Melbourne and returned to her beloved Italy on a number of occasions. Agnes Hodgson died in Melbourne in June 1984.

Recollecting on her time in the Spanish civil war, almost fifty years after it had ended, Agnes declared that it had been the 'experience of her life', but she had always felt guilty that she had not remained in Spain until the bitter end. Having had a lifelong antipathy for people who spoke loudly of convictions but did nothing, she had always feared that in the Spanish civil war she could have done more: been more selfless; endured more stoically. The truth, however, is quite the contrary. Most people's lives follow a narrow furrow defined by the routine and the

---

67 AH to MD, 9 Dec 1939, JK Private Papers.

commonplace, and within which their convictions and their spirit are rarely tested. Individuals like Agnes Hodgson, who are curious and fascinated by the larger world and different cultural ways of being, and respond for larger causes than themselves, step outside the confines of their ordinary existence. These are the truly courageous. They have been willing to risk the vulnerability that is the complement of such engagement and have proved their selflessness by the very act of involvement. Those who volunteered in Spain were courageous in a way that evades the rest of us in our ordinary lives. In the Spanish civil war, as in all wars, nurses like Agnes Hodgson and her comrades were doubly heroic. In their daily work they dealt with the wounded, the most horrible and unglamorous results of war and where death was commonplace and in which they had only their professional training and their common sense on which to rely.

Chapter Three

The Second Republic
and the Spanish Civil War

On 17 July 1936, a group of military officers in Morocco staged a rebellion against the Spanish government in Madrid. On the following morning a manifesto was read over Canary Islands' radio from General Francisco Franco y Bahamonde announcing that the Spanish army, responsible to the nation as a whole, would no longer accept the growing chaos in Spain and the continuous slandering of the army by the 'enemies of order'. The officers therefore had risen in order to 'guarantee Fraternity, Liberty and Equality for all Spaniards'.68 It was a classic military *pronunciamiento* of the sort which had been common in Spain for at least a century. Such rebellions, usually led by liberal army officers, had served as a frequent mechanism for changing the political party in government. In July 1936 neither General Franco nor the politicians in Madrid imagined that this latest *pronunciamiento* would lead to a bloody and prolonged civil war and that at its end, on 1 April 1939, the country would be devastated. Nearly 500,000 Spaniards from both sides were dead, another 300 000 had fled into permanent exile, and for the next 35 years Spain stagnated under the stifling dictatorship of Francisco Franco.69

In the course of the nineteenth century two competing visions of Spain's future had developed. One was liberal and anti-clerical, taking its inspiration from Europe; the other, traditional

---

68 Joaquín Arrarás, *Historia de la Segunda República Española*, 4, (Madrid: Libros de Historia, 1964): p 409.

69 For a compelling overview of the Spanish civil war, see Francisco J. Romero Salvadó, *The Spanish Civil War: Origins, Course and Outcomes,* (London: Palgrave Macmillan, 2005).

and absolutist, was anchored to the examples of Spain's heroic Catholic past. By the end of the century the monarchy and the Spanish Church, the two great institutions which historically had provided the glue of Spanish society, had been challenged by new forces. A succession of inept and disastrous monarchs had discredited the throne. In addition, the supporters of the pretender, Don Carlos and his heirs, had split the monarchist movement and drawn Spain into three civil wars. For a variety of reasons, the Church, too, had lost its position as the source of spiritual and moral unity for all Spaniards. A series of nineteenth century progressive governments, adopting the models of English and French liberalism, had attempted to modernize the Spanish state by economic, educational and secular reform. Church and aristocratic lands were disentailed and much ecclesiastical property was reclaimed by the State and sold at public auction. Separated from an independent source of income, the Church was forced to rely for its support on the wealthy. In addition, an expanding urban working class and a politicized peasantry in the south were alienated from the church and its teachings.

The latter, by the end of the nineteenth century, was seen by the urban poor as a symbol of their economic oppression, and by the liberal sections of the middle classes as the main obstacle to Spain's cultural and social reform. The growth of nationalism in the rest of Europe was reflected in Spain at the end of the nineteenth century by the expansion of regionalism, particularly in the Catalan and Basque provinces. In the former the movement grew out of a Catalan cultural and literary renaissance, and in the latter from indigenous religious and political roots. In both areas there had developed by the early twentieth century strong movements calling for home rule.

Under the Constitution of 1876, Spain was a constitutional monarchy with a bicameral legislature elected by a restricted male suffrage. In practice national politics was dominated by two political parties, the Liberals and the Conservatives, who successively held government and ran electoral affairs from Madrid through a network of *caciques*. These local bosses in the countryside, using a combination of patronage and force, arranged that the vote was achieved as the parties in Madrid required. By the first decade of the twentieth century the hegemony of this Madrid-based system had come under challenge from regional parties and from a politicized working class no longer willing to be passive participants.

Industrialization, the great solvent of traditional society, had been slow and uneven in Spain. Heavy industry was centred around the iron and coal mining areas in the Asturias, in the north, and in the textile and light manufacturing industries of Catalonia. In the early twentieth century, two out of every three Spaniards still earned their living from agriculture Patterns of land ownership and productivity varied widely. Where the soil was fertile with leases and landholdings of a reasonable size, the peasantry was prosperous and usually conservative. In parts of Navarre, the Basque areas, in Catalonia and Valencia, where these conditions existed, much of the peasantry was Catholic and conservative. Where *minifundia* and short leases pre-dominated, many rural families, without the cash or technical skills to lift productivity, eked out a marginal existence. Such was the case in the areas of the Cantabrian Coast and Galicia. Others, for example in parts of Old and New Castile, worked plots that were too small or too tenuously held to overcome the shortcomings of water and soil. The south was the heartland of Spanish *latifundia*. These great estates, owned by absentee landlords and let to large middlemen, were worked by day labourers who lived on starvation wages and uncertain seasonal work and, in the course of the nineteenth century, embraced the revolutionary doctrine of anarchism.

In the 1860s, the ideas of the First International Workingmen's Association had been brought to Spain and the struggle within the parent organization between the anarchist followers of Bakunin and the socialist followers of Marx was replayed on the peninsula. Anarchism found receptive soil in southern Spain, Catalonia and parts of Aragón where an anarchist movement flourished. In 1909, an anarchist syndical organization, the Confederación Nacional de Trabajo (CNT) was formed and by 1931 had approximately a million and a half members.

Peasants in Aragón work the land with a mouldboard plough behind horse and a mule, with a donkey keeping the furrow on line. Oct 1936.

Marx's followers, whose strengths were in Madrid and the Asturias, formed the Partido Socialista Obrero Español (PSOE) in 1881 and seven years later the socialist trade union, the Unión General de Trabajadores (UGT). While the anarchists held a revolutionary position eschewing all institutional political activity, elections, parties and reformist strikes for short term demands, the Spanish Socialist Party followed an orthodox Marxist line. The party laid great store on the role of the industrial working class and on the long preparatory struggle on the shop floor, and in municipal and national politics to build a base in the working class. Although revolutionary change was the socialists' ultimate objective, it was not the immediate goal of day-to-day activities. In 1931, the UGT had approximately a million members including some ten or twenty percent from the Federation of Landowners (FNTT) formed in early 1930 to organize and recruit rural workers and peasants.70

At the beginning of 1931, the moribund Spanish monarchy collapsed, discredited by the King's association with the preceding seven-year dictatorship of General Primo de Rivera. Alfonso XIII packed his bags and, without abdicating, quit Spain. There was widespread agreement throughout the country that the time for change and modernization had arrived.

In the first national elections in June 1931, a coalition of left-centre parties won a majority of seats in the *Cortes*, the Spanish parliament, and socialists, regional republican and left republican parties shared posts in the cabinet. Manuel Azaña, leader of the Left Republicans, became prime minister. The new Cortes, conscious of the historical parallel, held its first session on Bastille Day, 14 July 1931. Like the French Republic before it, members of the government of the Second Spanish Republic saw themselves as the architects of a new era. They held an enthusiastic belief that 'La Niña Bonita'—'the Beautiful Girl', as hopeful Spaniards in the first year called the new Republic—was capable of solving Spain's longstanding social and political problems and leading the nation on the high road to a progressive future. The new Constitution declared that Spain was 'a democratic Republic of workers of all categories organized in a regime of freedom and justice'. A wide-ranging programme of social reform was begun. Aristocratic titles were abolished, the penal code was reformed, and women, after some equivocation, were enfranchised. A great boost was promised for public education. A statute giving autonomy to Catalonia was drawn up, which recognized the separate entity of the Catalan region and its language, and shared its administration between Barcelona and Madrid. The central government retained control of defence, customs and foreign affairs, while local administration, education and the University of Barcelona passed into the jurisdiction of the *Generalitat*, the Catalan regional government. The legislation was passed in September 1932 and won to the Republic its staunchest allies. A similar agreement on a division

---

70 Paul Preston, 'The Great Agrarian War in the South', in his *Revolution and War in Spain, 1931-1939,* (London: Methuen, 1984).

of powers under home rule was planned for the Basque provinces.

Although there was strong opposition to a number of these reforms, it took place within the framework of the parliamentary system. The first serious challenge to the Republic was generated by opposition to the separation of church and state. In May 1931, the provisional government had decreed that Catholicism was no longer the state religion of Spain. The Spanish state henceforth was secular and all forms of religious observance were a matter of private conscience. Divorce, civil marriage and burial were legalized. The last two in fact had been common since the end of the first decade of the twentieth century. The religious articles in the Constitution, particularly Article 26, aroused concerted opposition. The Church was no longer to be tax exempt and within two years the Republic would cease payments for its upkeep, an arrangement which dated from the 1851 Concordat. The Jesuit Order, long viewed as hostile to progressive change and harbouring great wealth, was disbanded and the state reserved the right to sequester its property. It was, however, the disbandment of the Catholic education system which caused most conflict. Catholic schools were closed and church orders disbarred from teaching. The Vatican for many years had been concerned that the control of primary school education should remain in the Church's hands, and in Spain it was the issue which most upset Catholic parents.

Undoubtedly, these laicizing policies antagonized many devout Spanish Catholics. Certainly, much was made by Nationalist supporters during the civil war of the 'Godless Republic' and its anticlerical policies. The latter were presented later as the antecedents of the church burnings which took place in the early days of the war. Viewed with hindsight, the laic policies of the Republican government were perhaps imprudent. The stance towards the Church, however, by liberals like Azaña were predictable. They and the socialists saw themselves in a European anti-clerical tradition of the sort which had produced the secular and educational reforms under the Radicals in the Third Republic in France. Public secular education was the lynchpin of a liberal society in which, at least in theory, entry into

land, overseen by socialist-dominated peasant unions. These differences dragged on as conflicts in the south escalated between increasingly frustrated rural labourers and intransigent landowners. As a consequence of a watered-down agrarian reform and the obstacles to its implementation the socialists, pushed by their rural Federation of Land workers, became disillusioned with the possibility of fundamental reform within the existing system.

An incident in a small village in southern Andalusia brought down Azaña's government. In early 1933, his administration was implicated in particularly savage reprisals at Casas Viejas, where a group of anarchist peasants had proclaimed the village for libertarian communism.72 Their abortive rebellion was put down with unrelenting ferocity by the local Guardia Civil, reinforced by a contingent of Assault Guards. Despite the anarchists having surrendered, the police executed 20 villagers, some of whom quite innocently had been caught up in the siege. When the grisly details came out, Azaña resigned, though it is doubtful that he had any personal knowledge of the affair.

In the national elections which followed in November 1933, there was a swing away from the left-centre. The republicans and the socialists, soured by their experience of shared government, ran on separate tickets and were heavily defeated. The Right and the Catholic parties had gathered strength in the preceding two years and ran as a coalition group, the Confederación de Derechas Autónomas (CEDA). The Confederation of the Autonomous Right consisted of Catholic Action groups, the landowners' Agrarian Party, and the separate Carlist and Alfonsine monarchist parties. This diverse group was held together by a minimal programme of opposition to anti-clerical Republican policies. Its leader José María Gil Robles maintained an 'accidentalist position' towards the Republic, claiming that CEDA was not committed to a particular form of government but would assess each according to its treatment of

---

72 Jerome R Mintz, *The Anarchists of Casa Viejas,* (Chicago: University of Chicago Press, 1982).

the Church. Though CEDA polled the majority of seats it had insufficient numbers to govern alone. The Radical Party, led by Alejandro Lerroux, therefore formed a cabinet with CEDA's backing.

In the next two years this conservative government dismantled or let lapse most of the reforming legislation of the Azaña administration. The state resumed the payment of clerical salaries and confiscated property was returned to the Church. During these years both Left and Right were radicalized.

The Falange, the Spanish Fascist Party, formed in 1933, became an increasingly vocal though small presence on the Right, disrupting rallies of CEDA and the socialists alike. José Antonio Primo de Rivera, the charismatic falangist leader and son of the dictator General Primo de Rivera, called for the establishment of a Spanish fascist state, corporate and organic, on the model of Mussolini's Italy but in which the Spanish Church would hold a central place. CEDA's youth wings became increasingly militant, calling for Gil Robles to take over the Spanish state. On the left, anarchists denounced the shallowness of parliamentary politics and waged a great many strikes. Within the Socialist Party the youth and peasant wings pushed the movement to adopt a revolutionary position.

In mid-1934, a series of political crises exacerbated tensions. There were major strikes in Madrid, Saragossa and the rural south. The cabinet attempted to pass legislation to reintroduce the death penalty. An amnesty was declared for those implicated in the Sanjurjo *pronunciamiento*, and the property of the grandees which had been confiscated as a consequence of their involvement, was returned to them. The central government clashed with the Catalan *Generalitat* over the latter's rural reform legislation which gave land rights to certain categories of long-standing tenant farmers. At the end of September CEDA withdrew its support from Lerroux's government and Gil Robles insisted that CEDA would only re-join a full coalition in which it held three cabinet positions.

The broad Left and the president of the *Cortes* feared that CEDA's real intention was to overthrow the Republic and bring in their much-vaunted corporate Catholic state. Though CEDA had the electoral support to insist on cabinet posts, the Spanish Left was sensitive to the recent defeats of the Left in Austria and Germany. When CEDA entered the cabinet on 4 October a general strike was called. It succeeded only in the Asturias where miners, under socialist leadership, built barricades and set up a revolutionary workers' commune. After three weeks the strikers had occupied the whole area and prepared for a long siege. The government responded by shipping the Spanish Foreign Legion and the Moorish Regulars to the mainland, led by General Franco, where they put down the rising with unremitting violence. Oviedo, the stronghold of the strike, was taken house by house and at its end approximately 1,000 strikers were dead and 3,000 wounded. In a crackdown throughout the country the government arrested approximately 40,000 Spaniards as suspected revolutionaries or for having abetted the strike.73 Among those imprisoned was a most unlikely revolutionary, the ex-prime minister Manuel Azaña, a solid liberal for whom revolution of right or left was totally abhorrent. In the Cortes, CEDA pressed for the execution of the convicted. The capriciousness of many arrests, the reported ill-treatment of prisoners and the sheer volume of people in jail united the Left as it had not been since 1931.

In the last elections of the Spanish Republic in February 1935, Left and Right faced each other in almost evenly-matched groupings.74 The Popular Front, on the Left, ran on a platform of amnesty for all prisoners and a return to the reforming republic of the first years. Composed of socialists, the miniscule Spanish Communist Party, republicans, and the progressive regional parties, the Popular Front was also supported by a considerable number of anarchist voters who normally disdained electoral politicking but throughout 1935 had campaigned for amnesty of the Asturian prisoners. On the Right, CEDA and the monarchist parties ran united lists for the National Front, stressing a minimal platform of support for the Church and traditional Spain against the radical Left. Optimistic observers claimed it

---

73 Malefakis, (1970).

74 Romero Salvadó, pp 53-9.

was the beginning of a genuine two-party system in Spain. The more realistic saw the country polarized into two irreconcilable positions between which any middle ground had disappeared.

The Popular Front won the elections. In many districts the voting was as close as one or two percent. The electoral laws of Spain gave a majority of seats to whichever party or coalition won outright on votes. The procedure had been introduced in 1931, to avoid the situation where a plethora of splinter parties were unable to govern, as had frequently happened in the Italian Assembly and during the Third Republic in France. Later, during the civil war, the Right denied the legality of the Popular Front elections, despite their having being run under the same system that had operated to the Right's advantage in 1933.

The Socialist Party remained outside the cabinet, which was composed of Republican Party members. In the four months of the Popular Front's administration the country was riven with street-fighting, rallies of competing groups, great waves of strikes and almost continuous disorder. Peasants who had waited in vain for land under the Republic seized it under the Popular Front and began their own spontaneous land reform. These land seizures were immediately ratified by the government, and with those allocations made by a reinvigorated Institute of Agrarian Reforms, more than 114,000 peasants were resettled. This number was in strong contrast with the 6,000 to 7,000 settlements made by the Republic until the end of 1933.[75] The most marked feature of the period was the growth on both left and right of the outrigger wings of the Communist Party and the Falange.

The *Partido Comunista Español* (PCE) had come late onto the Spanish scene, where the anarchist and socialist movements had already captured the terrain and left no regional or class position for the PCE to occupy. The party had been further marginalized by its strict adherence to the sectarian position of the Comintern in relations with social democratic groups. Until 1935, liberals and democrats had been vilified as 'social fascists' who differed from true fascists only in that the latter were the

---

75 Malefakis, p 378.

beachhead through Seville and Cordoba to march on Madrid. The first, and perhaps the most decisive international intervention in the Spanish civil war had been the ferrying across to the mainland of the Spanish Foreign Legion and Moorish contingents by Italian and German planes in late July. Probably without this crucial foreign assistance the generals' uprising would have failed, or at least its supporters would have been cooped up in northern Spain.

The Spanish generals had rebelled ostensibly to prevent an imminent social revolution in Spain. Paradoxically, their *pronunciamiento* created the conditions which produced exactly the revolutionary situation they feared. The cabinet in Madrid reacted uncertainly to the news from Morocco but a great popular rising against the generals swept through those areas which remained loyal to the government. In large cities political parties and trade union groups formed volunteer militias to fight the insurgents. Factories and work places were seized by workers' councils and trade union committees. In many rural areas peasants drove off, or executed, landowners and transformed the land into peasant collectives.

Haymaking as an example of collectivised labour
in rural Aragón, 1937.

The most complete revolutionary transformation took place in Catalonia and Aragón, the historic anarcho-syndicalist centres in Spain. Barcelona was gripped by a revolutionary euphoria. The rebellion there had been put down by the Guardia Civil and the Assault Guards, both of which had remained loyal to the government, and by local militias, predominantly anarcho-syndicalist. Enemies of the government had been done away with or gone underground.

Observers newly-arrived in Barcelona were struck by the revolutionary ethos of the city. Everywhere were to be seen people dressed in the uniform of the militias or the blue *mono*, the overall worn by Spanish workmen. Formal address had been abandoned for the informal *tú*, and even among the most servile occupations such as waiters, porters and bootblacks, looked their clients in the eye and called them 'comrade'. Buildings were festooned with the black and red flags of the anarchists and the colours of the other Catalan political groups. Brass plates on buildings were pasted over with signs indicating which political group was now in control. Commandeered taxis and private cars roared through the city with the initials of various political groups hastily painted on their sides, and trucks, bristling with rifles and packed with militiamen, headed off to the Aragón front.

George Orwell, who arrived several months later, found the environment 'startling and overwhelming', a 'town where the working class was in the saddle' and where 'down the Ramblas, the wide central artery of the city crowds of people streamed constantly while loudspeakers bellowed revolutionary songs all day and far into the night.76

All areas of local administration, the police force, the tram and subways, the gas and electrical works, the telephone system, newspapers, hotels and restaurants were seized by workers' management. Collectivization extended even to those tradition-

---

76 George Orwell, 'Homage to Catalonia', in *George Orwell in Spain*, edited by Peter Davison and Christopher Hitchens, (London: Penguin Random House, 2001): p 32.

ally individualized occupations such as boot-black and waiter, in which tipping was abolished and rates determined by union locals. A union notice in Barcelona brothels requested patrons to 'treat the women who work here as comrades'.77

Factories large and small were taken over. In most cases the pattern was the same, with the specifics worked out according to the particular conditions in each place. Where the previous owners had fled, the organization was seized and run directly by workers' committees representing either the CNT or the UGT, depending upon which trade union predominated. If the owners were still on the scene the enterprise was usually run by a combined council with owner and worker representatives.78 Heavy machine shops and car assembly works such as Ford Iberia and Hispano-Suiza were immediately converted to supplying the war effort.

The leader of the Catalan regional government, Luis Companys, gave way before the new numerical superiority of the anarcho-syndicalists. Under their auspices a Central Anti-Fascist Militias Committee was constituted to administer the region and coordinate the revolutionary committees that had sprung up. In a most doctrinally unorthodox step, the anarcho-syndicalists refused to dismantle the existing government and invited the other Catalan political groups to share in administration with them. Anarchist leaders justified the action by claiming that to seize power alone would have constituted a dictatorship by anarchists, which was an anathema to their libertarian principles. In practice, though, the suddenness of the revolution had probably caught the anarchists, like everyone else, unaware and unprepared to administer singlehandedly the Catalan state and economy. Political parties and groups were assigned positions on the Central Catalan Committee according to their

---

77 Mary Low and Juan Breá, *Red Spanish Notebook*, (London: Secker and Warburg, 1973) [1937]: p 198.

78 Frank Mintz, *L'autogestion dans l'Espagne Révolutionnaire*, (Paris: Beltibaste, 1970); Michael Seidmann, 'Work and Revolution: Worker's Control in Barcelona in the Spanish Civil War', *Journal of Contemporary History*, 17 (1982).

local strengths. Anarcho-syndicalists of the CNT-FAI held seven posts. The left republican regional party, the Esquerra, received three portfolios, as did the socialist trade union, the UGT. The POUM, an anti-Stalinist Marxist party, was assigned a single position, as was the PSUC.

Political parties and trade unions raised militias which set off to the Aragón front. Anarchist columns in particular boosted the process of collectivization that had begun in the province since the generals' rebellion. As the militias passed through, resisting landowners were executed and village committees organized. A Council of Aragón was formed to co-ordinate the collectives through provincial and regional assemblies, and to assist in the sale of communal produce and the collective purchase of farm machinery.

It has been estimated that by early 1937, before the Communist Party's efforts to dismantle collectivisation were underway, there were about 450 Aragón collectives comprising approximately 400,000 peasants.79 It is difficult to generalize about their operation. Probably for the short time that it continued unimpededly, individual examples were successful and raised agricultural productivity. Certainly, this was the case where shared technical improvements provided better yields and individual village-cultivators had access to agricultural equipment previously beyond their means. Undoubtedly too, there were instances of unwilling individual collectivists being coerced into communal enterprises by enthusiastic—read vengeful—locals backed by anarchist militias. In any event, the success of individual ventures probably depended on the quality of the land to which they had access, whether the previous landowners were absentee or not, and on their individual

---

79 Hugh Thomas, 'Agrarian Collectives in the Spanish Civil War' in his *The Republic and the Civil War in Spain*, (London, Macmillan, 1971): 242; more recently, and with lower figures in relation to collectivisation, see Julian Casanova's *Anarquismo y Revolución en la Sociedad Rural Aragonesa 1936-1939*, (Madrid: Siglo Veintiuno de España Editores, 1985). Agnes Hodgson's medical unit which was located at Grañén in the anarchist region of Aragón became locally entangled in this internecine conflict.

historical experience in the formation of the collective.

The domestic Spanish conditions that had prompted the military uprising were soon engulfed by the larger configuration of international affairs. Spain, though a minor partner, was locked into what A J P Taylor termed the 'permanent quadrille of the Balance of Powers'. The configuration of the dance settled the outcome of the Spanish civil war and in the process irrevocably transformed internal affairs on both sides. The Nationalists and the Republicans faced each other in July 1936 as coalitions of diverse and often internally opposed political groups. By the end of 1937, both sides had been unified into centralized commands: Nationalists under a military dictatorship by General Franco; and the Republicans under a communist-dominated government in which the historically heterogeneous Spanish Left had been extinguished.

After their initial assistance in bringing the Army of Africa to the mainland, Germany, Italy and Portugal funnelled arms, equipment and boots on the ground to the Nationalists, in the process strengthening the place of the military faction in the Nationalist Junta of Defence and within it, General Franco's hand. Those who had rallied initially to the insurgents were politically a motley group composed of monarchists, with two opposing kings; Catholics of CEDA, many of whom were closet Republicans; disgruntled military officers who were neither clericalists nor for a monarchist restoration; and the Falange which was anti-monarchist and supported a national revolution along fascist lines. Franco's claim to leadership was improved by the fortuitous deaths of his key rivals: Generals Sanjurjo and Mola, killed in air crashes early in the war, and perhaps most significantly, José Antonio Primo de Rivera, a leader with a genuine mass following, was executed by Republicans in Alicante in November 1936. Once in power, Franco moved swiftly to suppress dissident opposition within the Nationalist movement, creating a most curious amalgam, whereby Franco became the chief commander and head of the Nationalist state which adopted the trappings of Catholicism and the rhetoric of fascism, while remaining in substance a military dictatorship.

The chariness of England and France at being drawn into

any incident which might upset the fragile balance of international relations, caught the Spanish Republican government in an invidious situation. Though legally elected and confronted with a military rebellion, the government in Madrid, cut off from normal diplomatic support, had difficulty in purchasing arms for its own defence. In consequence, the Soviet Union, the only major power that entered on the government side, came to carry enormous political clout in Spain. The local prestige of the Soviet Union grew immensely and the Spanish Communist Party was elevated from a minor presence on the Left to a commanding position within the Republican administration. With the carrot of Soviet aid and the stick of its withdrawal, the Spanish communists were able to force government policy to root out relentlessly the anti-communist Left while simultaneously quashing the indigenous social revolution that had begun.

The Popular Front government in France, led by the socialist Leon Blum, had close fraternal relations with the Republican government in Madrid. The latter was the first broad left group to be successfully elected in Europe and was a kind of prototype of Popular Frontism. In addition, Spain and France enjoyed a commercial agreement giving preferential treatment to France in the purchase of Spanish arms. It was to be expected, therefore, that the Spanish government would turn to France in July 1936 for diplomatic support and the purchase of arms and that Blum and the left socialists in his cabinet would favourably respond. As in Spain, however, the Popular Front of Paris uneasily governed a nation polarized between Left and Right. In February 1934 the French parliament had been under physical siege from Action Française and their fascist supporters. According to Blum's own assessment, France was on the brink of a civil war. Radical Socialists and Socialists on the right in Blum's cabinet were opposed to any involvement in Spain which could serve as a trigger to open warfare at home. In addition, and equally importantly, the Conservative government in London, led by Stanley Baldwin, indicated quite unequivocally that it would give no support in any form to French intervention in Spain. With Germany in May 1936 having reoccupied the Rhineland

and France heavily dependent upon Britain within Europe, the French government backed away from its initial commitment to the Spanish Republic.

Britain's objective was to avoid a European war at all costs. In addition, in mid-1936, the British government was angling for an Italian naval agreement which would heal the rift that had widened between the two nations since Mussolini's invasion of Abyssinia. In each of the major diplomatic incidents in the 1930s—the Japanese invasion of Manchuria in 1931, the Abyssinian war in 1935 and Germany's re-occupation of the Rhineland in March 1936—Britain had consistently adopted a policy of appeasing the major powers in order to subvert any possibility of a general European conflict. In the case of Spain, the British government's position reflected a widespread opposition at home to British involvement in all foreign wars. Although the position changed later, in September 1936 the British Trade Union Council opposed intervention in Spain, as did a majority at the Labour Party Conference in October of that same year.

The Conservatives' position was reinforced by British bankers and businessmen with financial interests in Spanish mining, wine and sherry exports. English financiers had been deeply distrustful of the reforming zeal of Spanish Republicans with their intervention in the Spanish economy, their efforts to reform agriculture and industry and their rhetoric about taking back the national estate from international capitalism. A great many English businessmen would have shared the opinion that General Franco was a good Spanish patriot who would pull these Spanish 'reds' back into line. Although Catholic Spain was Protestant England's historic adversary, and the Catholic trappings of Nationalist Spain may have left many British businessmen unimpressed, they had little stomach for the beleaguered Republican government. The collapse into Nationalist hands of the mining and heavy industrial centres of the north in mid-1937, sealed the deal.80

The Non-Intervention Committee was Blum's

---

80 Romero Salvadó, pp 70-71.

compromise. With Britain's backing, its objective was to bind Italy and Germany into a pact that would prevent their supplying the Spanish Insurgents. After a great deal of prevarication, the International Committee for the Appliance of Non-Intervention in Spain met in London on 9 September. It consisted of 25 nations and excluded Spain. Germany, Italy, France, England, and the Soviet Union were the crucial members. Efforts to devise strategies for control of naval and land supplies for the war bogged down in endless committees in which the Italian and German representatives stalled proceedings. Despite massive violations, evident from official documents tabled by the Spanish government and from any cursory reading of the daily papers, the committee did nothing. The policy was never properly implemented and the committee had no powers to punish violations. The absurd situation was reached in mid-1937, when the 'neutral' German and Italian navies patrolled the Republican Mediterranean coast while France and Britain surveyed the Bay of Biscay. Behind the façade of non-intervention, Italy, Germany and Portugal aided Franco and the Soviet Union sent arms to the Republic. Italy, Germany and Portugal supported General Franco from the first days of the war. Of the three, Germany's contribution had the greatest impact on the outcome. In the event of a Franco-German war, and with a government in Madrid sympathetic to Germany, France would be left with three borders to defend while Germany's shared involvement with Italy in Spain would draw the former into Germany's field of influence at a time when the relations between the two countries were made uneasy by their common rivalry in Austria. In the long run Spain was fundamental to the Rome-Berlin Axis. Spain controlled half the world's supply of mercury and pyrites and was a vital source of fine ore from Spanish mines, all essential for German rearmament.

It was the quality as much as the quantity of German aid, and the timing of its arrival, which told in the Nationalist war effort.81 In all, Germany sent about 16,000 men, with probably

---

81 For German and Italian military contribution and its impact see Romero Salvadó, pp 82-91.

no more than 6,000 in Spain at any one time. Vast quantities of heavy equipment were despatched from Germany, of which, in the early days especially, the Nationalists were in great need. In November 1936 the Condor Legion was formed, consisting of some 5,000 crack pilots and 600 planes with ground technical staff to service them. As importantly, Germany provided Franco with a sophisticated communications unit of five companies, which dealt with radio and telephone systems and flight and aircraft security. The military academies that were established in Nationalist territory were heavily staffed by German instructors. All this gave an enormous boost to the Nationalist military effort, and in turn provided the German armaments industry with a ready-made testing range. While it was not Hitler's intention to create a National-Socialist state in Spain, it was in Germany's interest to prolong the conflict. The Spanish civil war distracted international attention from central Europe, bound Italy to Germany's sphere of influence, and tested the limits to which western Europe could be pushed to avoid a general war.

Italy sent approximately 75,000 soldiers with between 40,000 and 50,000 in Spain at any one time. In addition, Italy contributed some 600 planes and pilots to fly them, along with technicians and engineers, tanks, heavy equipment, artillery and machine guns. Mussolini had ideological and strategic reasons for wishing to see a government in Madrid that was sympathetic to Italy. He was pursuing a foreign policy in south eastern and western Europe aimed at restoring the Mediterranean to its former glory as an Italian lake. Spain and the Balearic Islands were of great strategic importance. With the Balearics fallen to the Nationalists, Majorca became the staging post for Italian shipping and planes. From late 1937, daily bombing raids from Majorca pounded Barcelona and Valencia. Italian submarines, part of the largest fleet of its kind in the world, harassed shipping bound with supplies for the Republic. Portugal sent several thousand soldiers to Franco's army. Her most significant contribution was to provide a safe port for the landing of supplies for Nationalist Spain and unhindered access along their shared border.

Like the other major European powers, the Soviet Union's

position was determined by its own foreign policy. Stalin's reading of the international situation dictated an involvement in the Spanish war on the side of the Republican government. His intention was to build diplomatic bridges to France and England for collective security against an ebullient Germany and Britain's palliative attitude towards Germany heightened Soviet fears of being isolated on Germany's eastern flank. The same considerations had dictated the Comintern's change of tack at the Seventh Party Congress in 1935 when a new strategy of broad left popular fronts against fascism was adopted.

For Soviet policy to be successful in Spain it was essential to be seen as defending, not a revolutionary 'red' government, but a bourgeois democratic republic that would be acceptable to liberal opinion in western Europe. The support for bourgeois democracy, perhaps curious to the uninitiated, was not simply a feint behind which revolutionary Russia operated as before. Under Stalin's heavy hand and narrow Russian focus, the Soviet Union had ceased to be the main support of world-wide revolutionary movements and was absorbed in building socialism within the Soviet Union and protecting its place in the rest of the world. Consequently, the Comintern, formed by Lenin to promote world-wide revolution, had been transformed into a vehicle for the promotion of Soviet foreign policy through communist parties outside Russia.

The Soviet Union supplied the Spanish government with about 1,000 aircraft, as well as heavy machinery, artillery and tanks, and food and clothing. In addition, there were Russian military experts and advisors in Spain who assisted in the war effort. Without this material assistance the Republic, most likely, would have collapsed by the end of 1936. Until early 1938 Russian aid arrived steadily. As it became increasingly apparent, however, that England and France were bent on appeasement, Stalin began to disengage from Spain and look elsewhere for Soviet security. The denouement of this new foreign policy was found in the signing of the German-Russian Friendship Pact in August 1939.

The Spanish Communist Party, with the assistance of Comintern advisors, carried out Soviet policy assiduously and was the most unbending opponent of all forms of social revolution in Spain. The PCE rallied against collectivization and the infantilism of 'the uncontrollables' who had brought it about. The party became a shelter for small businessmen and prosperous peasants who opposed collectivization. It is perhaps ironical that while newspaper editorial writers in papers like the *Sydney Morning Herald* and the *Daily Telegraph* were fulminating against the establishment of a revolutionary Bolshevik regime in Spain under Russian auspices, the local communists and Comintern advisors were stamping out all such indigenous endeavours.

In early September 1936, Francisco Largo Caballero became premier of Spain and Minister of War. The leader of the UGT and Minister of Labour under Azaña, Largo Caballero was a towering figure on the Left. He came into office with strong communist support and the promise of replacing, with vigorous and energetic leadership, the uncertain policies of the previous Popular Front cabinet. All Spanish political parties, even the Anarcho-syndicalists after November, were represented in his cabinet. Largo and the Communist Party were in agreement that the only way to win the war was to reconstitute and strengthen the central government. The parallel revolutionary structure which had been thrown up in July would be dismantled and the independent militias brought under a single military command. When Largo took office, he was hailed as the Spanish Lenin, however relations between Largo and the communists steadily soured. He resented the intrusions of the Soviet Ambassador, Marcel Rosenberg, in Spanish affairs and opposed the efforts of the Party to dominate war policy. The showdown, which had been brewing for months, came after May Day in Barcelona in 1937 and was precipitated by Largo's refusal to ban the POUM, an anti-Stalinist Marxist party in Catalonia.

The PSUC, the Communist Party of Catalonia, had grown massively in the last three months of 1936. Its anti-revolutionary and anti-collectivist stance had attracted a great many petty bourgeois urban Catalans and prosperous peasants who opposed the revolutionary excesses of the anarcho-syndicalists. The PSUC supported the disbandment of the political militias and through its members in the Catalan government, backed the central government's policy of starving collectivized industries of credit in order to force their compliance in centralization.

The POUM were the objects of particularly vitriolic communist attacks. A numerically small Trotskyist party that had broken with Trotsky and whose main strength was restricted to Catalonia, the POUM consisted of anti-Stalinist Marxist-Leninists, whose theoretical writings were an important element in left debate. As a result of the paranoia of Stalinism in the 1930s about any form of Trotskyism, the labyrinthine and acrimonious relations between Trotsky and the POUM were disregarded.82 In December 1936, the PSUC forced the POUM's Minister of Justice, Juan García Oliver, out of the Catalan government, and in the first week of May 1937 there was street fighting in Barcelona between anarchists and POUM supporters on one side, and communists and the supporters of government centralization on the other. When the smoke had settled the anti-revolutionary forces had carried the day. Spanish communists demanded that Largo Caballero proscribe the POUM, and when he would not, he was out-manoeuvred and forced to resign. Juan Negrín, also a socialist, became prime minister. If not entirely in the communist camp, Negrín was sensible to the need not to jeopardize Soviet supplies by antagonizing the PCE. By the end of 1937 the POUM was illegal and many of its leaders had been arrested or assassinated. The PSUC, with the backing of the Republican army, moved into Aragón and disbanded many of the peasant collectives. In August 1937, the Council of Aragón was dissolved by the Lister Battalion, council members were arrested and their functionaries dispersed.

It has been estimated that at 'full strength' some 42,000 foreign men volunteered and passed through the ranks of the International Brigades in Spain with some 32,500 actually

---

82 Trotsky castigated the party for its lack of revolutionary rigour in entering the Catalan government and referred to POUM leaders as 'ignorant opportunists', quoted in Burnett Bolloten, *The Spanish Civil War: Revolution and Counter Revolution,* (Chapel Hill: North Carolina Press, 1979): p 382.

serving, and about 18,000 serving at any one time. As a comparison, in Franco's army there were some 167,000 foreigners serving, though not as volunteers: Italian division and pilots and German Condor Legion plus approximately 75,000 Moroccan troops brought to the mainland.83 The small contingent of volunteers-proper numbered some 1,000 individuals, from the European extreme right.84

The non-combatants plied their skills as medical personnel, administrators and drivers, or journalists and observers who came to Spain and returned home to tell the story of Spain in fund raising and propaganda for the Republic. The International Brigaders were from 65 'named countries' with Franco-Belgian speakers providing the largest contingent of just under 10,000. German-speakers made up probably over half the numbers compared with the French, and there was a lesser number of east Europeans and Italians. Among English-speakers the American contingent was the largest with 3,000 men and a fully-equipped up to date medical battalion. Approximately 2,000 British and the British medical aid unit served in the International Brigades. From the Commonwealth countries came 1,000 Canadians, 60 Australians, and a handful of New Zealanders and South Africans.

The first foreign battalions were formed among exiles, particularly German-speakers, already living in Spain. They were joined in the first few months by others who had made their way to Spain independently. From September 1936 a great many foreign volunteers came on an underground Comintern conduit which assisted with fares and arrangements in crossing borders. A great many of these international volunteers, but by no means

---

83 Giles Tremlett, *The International Brigades: Fascism, Freedom and the Spanish Civil War*, (London: Bloomsbury, 2020) provides a comprehensive study of the International Brigades. In Tables, pp 673-79 he drills down into the raw numbers to tease out detail in a series of assays of volunteers and their characteristics at the critical junctures of important battles.

84 Keene, Fighting for Franco, International Volunteers in Nationalist Spain during the Spanish Civil War, 1936-39.

all, were communists. All, however, were anti-fascist.85 Many, in particular those from eastern Europe, Germany and Italy, had come to Spain to fight the battle against fascism that had been lost at home. The American and British contingents, as with those from the Commonwealth countries–like the Australian nurses–knew little about Spain but were impelled by an international spirit to strike a blow against fascism in what they saw as the first round in a looming international war. In hindsight, this analysis of the international situation was correct, but domestic Spanish politics were always far more complex than could be embraced by the simple dichotomy of Democracy versus Fascism.

The military contribution of the International Brigades was particularly important in the early stages of the war when almost the entire Spanish officer corps had deserted the Republican army for the Nationalists. In the first battle for Madrid, in November 1936, the role of the Internationals was probably critical. After the Republican army was reorganized in early 1937 the Internationals became part of the regular Spanish army and were integrated into mixed battalions fighting side by side with Spaniards. Later in the war, their contribution to Republican propaganda efforts in their home countries was probably equal if not more effective than it was by then on the battleground. International volunteers were withdrawn in October 1938 in a last-ditch effort by the Spanish Republic to court western European leaders by being seen to have implemented to the letter the Non-Intervention Agreement. Sadly, the Spanish government's efforts made very little difference. After the Munich Pact in September 1938, it was apparent that governments in western Europe were determined to avoid war at all costs, whatever the moral and practical consequences.

The military campaigns of the Spanish civil war fell into four stages. By the end of 1936 Franco held about one third of Spain in the same configuration, but slightly expanded, that he

---

85 Tremlett estimates political affiliations and language groups, pp 676-77.

had held at the end of July. A full-scale Nationalist attack on Madrid in November had been repulsed and Republican and Republican-Nationalists lines on the outskirts of the city became a permanent fixture.

During 1937 the Nationalists sought to cut off Madrid and drive a wedge through government territory by advancing on Valencia through Teruel. In both cases the offensive finally failed. In March 1937, a large Italian contingent was roundly defeated at Guadalajara and Republicans retook Teruel at the end of 1937. In February 1937, however, Italian and Spanish troops had entered Málaga forcing streams of terrified refugees to flee along the coast to Almería while being shelled by battleships offshore.

In the north east, Franco led a major offensive against Republican strongholds. The Spanish government's attempt to draw the Nationalists' fire with a Republican initiative in eastern Aragón failed. Within the province internal fighting between militias and the central Republican army bogged down the war effort. After particularly bitter and bloody combat in the early months of 1936 the Basque provinces fell to Franco. Guernica, the Basque capital, was razed in April 1937 by aerial bombing from the German Condor Legion,86 and in June, after fierce fighting, the Republican port of Bilbao collapsed.

During 1938 the superiority of the Nationalist armament supplies from German and Italy began to tell. Meanwhile, the Republic was faced with shortages of equipment. After punishing battles in sub-zero conditions Franco retook Teruel in February 1938. By August of that year the Nationalists had pushed across Aragón to reach the coast above Valencia, cutting Republican Spain in two. The Catalan front broke by Christmas 1938 and at the end of January 1939 Franco's troops had entered Barcelona prompting the flight of terrified refugees across the Spanish border into France. Madrid surrendered in the last days of March 1939. The citizens of the Spanish capital, the quintessential symbols of Republican resistance, had withstood continuous

86 Herbert Southworth, *Guernica! Guernica! A Study of Journalism, Diplomacy, Propaganda and History*, (Berkeley: California University Press, 1977).

bombardment, food shortages, and tremendous hardships throughout years of siege. With their capitulation the conventional battlefield dimension of the Spanish civil war was over.

Chapter Four

Australia and the Spanish Civil War

There was no single Australian response to the civil war in Spain. The reactions were as diverse as the groups that constituted Australian society in the 1930s. Even for Catholics and the sections of the Left, for whom the war became a pressing issue, Spain was far away, well outside the orbit of England and the British Empire that historically had defined Australia's involvement in foreign affairs. With the exception of the Australian Spanish community, the Australian mainstream with little information about recent Spanish politics integrated the Spanish civil war into a series of existing political and cultural frameworks. Where the Spanish piece was fitted and what it signified was determined by a conjunction of local factors.

After the war broke out there was considerable coverage of Spanish affairs in the Australian papers, however, the image of Spain that emerged was contradictory and often muddled. The *Daily Telegraph* and the *Sydney Morning Herald,* major Australian dailies, were important sources of information on foreign affairs for local readers.87 Both dailies promoted an image of historic Spain, redolent with aristocrats, flamenco dancers and high culture that was coupled with a view of present-day Spain as peopled by volatile individualists, given to violence and largely incomprehensible politics.88 The two

---

87 The *Daily Telegraph,* with a more popular style, appealed to a lower middle- and working-class readership and the *Sydney Morning Herald* was pitched at the middle classes. See R.B. Walker, *Yesterday's News. A History of the Newspaper Press in New South Wales from 1920 to 1945,* (Sydney: Sydney University Press, 1980): pp 56, 85.

88 Aránzazu Usandizaga has argued that the 'Orientalist stance' discernible in foreign women's writing about the civil war in Spain, is underpinned by a pervasive notion of Spain as 'the great

Spains sat together uneasily. Old Spain was portrayed as a country with an enviable heritage of literature, architecture and art, a place that Australian writers and painters visited to sample the cultural delights of great art collections and picturesque Moorish landscapes. In letters to the editor of the *Herald*, amateur antiquarian scholars could argue at length over the date inscribed on the Saragossa bridge and whether it marked El Cid's entrance to the city in the great Reconquest of Spain from the Moors.89 A columnist waxed lyrical in May 1937 about 'The Architectural Wonders of Old Spain', describing the Alhambra and the gardens of the Generalife and the breath-taking proportions of the great cathedral at Seville. The same writer ended on the gloomy observation that 'though these monuments had survived centuries of old Spanish wars, they would probably be destroyed in the present conflict.'90

Reflecting at that time what perhaps was an Australian obsession with royalty, Spanish kings and queens received much coverage. A potted history of the Spanish royal family in the *Sydney Morning Herald*, a couple of months after the civil war had begun, reminded readers that despite what present-day Spaniards might think of him, Alfonso XIII was very popular in

---

unknown' that harks back to 18th century Romanticism, buttressed by the perception of Spain's cultural location at the European periphery, in *Escritoras al frente: Intelectuales extranjeras en la Guerra Civil*, (San Sebastian: Nerea, 2007): 38-41. This thoughtful analysis can usefully be applied to mainstream foreign commentators, male and female. And one might add, is applicable to the mantra of contemporary Spanish tourism that "Spain is Different". See also Tom Buchanan's telling observations on the 'often crude' ideas about Spanish national character in Great Britain at the time of the civil war. In his, 'British Perceptions of Spain, 1931-1939' *Twentieth Century British History*, Vol 4, No 1 (1993): 1-24. Buchanan's observations equally apply to the Australian press, heavily reliant on syndication from the British press.

89 *Sydney Morning Herald*, 2 Jan 1937; 14 Jan 1937; 19 Jan 1937.

90 *Sydney Morning Herald*, 22 May 1937.

other parts of Europe.91 The ex-king, 'slim and irrepressible', was reported to be a frequent visitor to England, where 'his very aristocratic wife was a close relative of the English Royal Family'. Despite the disruptions of exile, Alfonso XIII was 'quite content with his lot', and 'leading a cheerful life travelling from country to country'.92 Readers were also reminded of the generosity and regard for Australians in 1867 when Queen Isabel II, despite her troubles at home, had presented St Mary's Cathedral in Sydney with a magnificent silver chalice and altar ornaments to replace those lost in the cathedral fire. After Isabel was overthrown by a revolution, the following year, the Spanish Consul, an aristocrat no less, in an incomprehensible public display had 'lost his reason and committed suicide by jumping to his death from his apartment in Macquarie Street in Sydney'.93

During the war years a number of artists from the Iberian Peninsula visited Australia, reinforcing this view of Spain as a centre of culture and old-world refinement. 'La Meri', a flamenco dancer, was photographed in October 1936, warming her castanets 'tucked lovingly into her bodice' before going on stage at Sydney's Theatre Royal.94 A famous violinist, Angel Grande, arrived on SS *Orama* in mid-1938 for a series of Australian concerts. The musician sported a diamond tie-pin presented by ex-Queen Ena of Spain and stowed in his bags was another exactly like it, from ex-King Alfonso.95

There was even a 'Spanish Trend' reported in 1936 in Australian suburban bungalow architecture. Featuring an 'unusual layout' which included 'piazza entrance, ample cup-board space, dining alcove and shower recess', wherever 'private

---

91 *Sydney Morning Herald*, 23 Sep 1936.

92 *Daily Telegraph*, 24 Aug 1936.

93 *Sydney Morning Herald*, 23 Sep 1936.

94 *Daily Telegraph*, 16 Oct 1936; *Daily Telegraph*, 4 Aug 1938.

95 *Daily Telegraph*, 28 Jul 1938.

homes predominated', the Spanish bungalow was popular.96 The humourist, Lennie Lower, whose column appeared regularly on the front page of the *Daily Telegraph*, encapsulated exactly this unworldly Australian view of Spain. Just after news had reached Sydney of the generals' rebellion, Lower wrote, 'You are all, naturally, disturbed about the situation in Spain, the shortage of Queen olives, Barcelona nuts, Spanish onions, rhumbas, shawls and matadors'.97

Present-day Spaniards, however, were shown in quite a different light. They had inherited, it seemed, the 'worst characteristics from *Don Quixote*': Extremely sensitive *to* personal slights and fiercely proud, they were obsessed with maintaining their honour. In daily political activity they were volatile, unstable and given to bloodshed. In this vein a number of correspondents and editorial writers recalled Wellington's experiences in Spain.98 Although the great English general had found 'individual Spaniards brave and reliable', in battle they were 'perfidious' and unreliable.99

Australians who had travelled in Spain, ostensibly attempting to explain the national psyche of the Spanish race, employed the same lexicon and examples. Sir Hugh Poynter, a businessman and a relative of Rudyard Kipling, expounded on the psychological makeup of present-day Spaniards to a Legacy Club gathering a few weeks after the generals' rebellion. The Spanish character was composed of two elements: one of 'Moorish Mohammedan influences' and the other from indigenous Spain. From the former came a 'fatal disregard for human life', while the Spanish legacy had left the Inquisition and the bullfight. These traits, which Sir Hugh had observed on several visits to the country, ensured that 'Spanish people are

---

96 *Daily Telegraph*, 12 Oct 1936.

97 *Daily Telegraph*, 28 Jul 1936.

98 Wellington produced a great many references, for a typical example see *Sydney Morning Herald*, 27 Jun 1936.

99 *Sydney Morning Herald*, 12 Sep 1936.

thoroughly inured to the sight of cruelty and of blood'. As a consequence, he predicted that the present war in Spain would be bitter and bloody.100

C E W Bean, the historian of the First World War at Gallipoli, attempted to no avail to dispel the myths current in Australia about Spanish people. Ostensibly written to refute the claim of a Sydney radio announcer that 'most Australians look on the Spanish as an effete un-progressive people almost as backward as the Chinese', Bean's piece reproduced the standard Anglo-Saxon stereotype of the Latin people. Spaniards were like Australians, so Bean argued, as both nations rejected all forms of class distinction. However, the unfortunate influence of the Catholic Church coupled with a lack of education was responsible for the Spanish nation's 'least lovable traits': their 'cruelty to animals, the national enthusiasm for bullfighting and their rapacious attitude to public office'. While 'dilatory and unreliable as tradesmen' they were inherently courteous and proud. A sense of personal honour made them brave but rarely successful fighters whereby when confronting an injustice 'the whole people will rise suddenly and seethe over like boiling milk'. Bean predicted, too, that this war would be fought 'Spanish fashion, with no quarter given and the killing of hostages and similar cruelties'.101

While these national characteristics might explain the Spaniards' propensity to war, it was not clear what the specific domestic issues were that had triggered recently this particular conflict. There were few reports in the daily papers dealing with the Spanish political background that had led to the military rising. Those that were published often contained inaccuracies, or relied heavily on historical analogies from the Russian and French revolutions.

Three days after the *pronunciamiento*, the *Daily Telegraph* announced that 'Toreador Politics' had swept over Spain and the vital and violent Spanish temperament. It was

---

100 *Sydney Morning Herald*, 18 Sep 1936.

101 *Sydney Morning Herald*, 19 Aug 1936.

predicted that a 'new dictatorship was imminent unless the political parties moderated their murderous blood feuds'.102 A week later the same paper pondered whether the Spanish revolution would follow the Russian Revolutionary schedule and if so whether the present situation was the 'Kerensky period' and therefore inevitably would be followed by a communist dictatorship'.103 In the words of the *Telegraph* it was a 'queer happening in Spain, a war in which the obvious things never take place'.104

The *Sydney Morning Herald* unequivocally disapproved of contemporary Spanish politics, whether 'Red or Black'. The paper frequently referred to the government and the Nationalists as 'both factions', with no indication that one was the legitimately-elected government while the other was a group of military rebels. According to the *Herald*, the five years of the Second Spanish Republic had been marked by 'turmoil, bloodshed and pillage' under a government 'modelled on the Russian Soviet system'. During the Popular Front, 'the mob was allowed to vent its passions as it would, with burning, bombing and reckless shooting in the streets which revolted foreign observers'. As in the Popular Front in France, Spanish strikes began over workers' grievances but were 'continued apparently in a sheer love of mischief', and 'each union struck and resorted to pillage independently of any direction'.105

In this analysis, the domestic causes of the war were irrelevant. It was like a 'ship on fire at sea', or 'some great earthquake in this country or that in which it was not the background to the incident that mattered but only the calamity itself'.106 An editorial in the *Sydney Morning Herald*,

---

102 *Daily Telegraph*, 20 Jul 1936.

103 *Daily Telegraph*, 28 Jul 1936.

104 *Daily Telegraph*, 28 Jul 1936.

105 *Sydney Morning Herald*, 24 Jul 1936.

106 *Sydney Morning Herald*, 14 Aug 1936.

immediately after the coup, likened the war to an inscription found on two Spanish tomb-stones: 'these two brave men fought to death over a melon'. In succeeding articles, the *Herald* frequently used the analogy of a war over a melon to underline the folly of Spaniards who willingly waged 'wars of extermination' for useless causes while 'treating each other like wild beasts'.107

Not surprisingly, Spanish anarchists were the most unambiguously portrayed. A political group entirely outside the Australian pale, Sydney newspapers had no time at all for anarchists, who, it was claimed, constituted 'one person in every twenty in Spain'. They were 'prone to hoist the black flag whenever there is trouble' and could not be considered 'good mixers'.108 The best that could be said for them was that they were 'idealists born to destroy' with 'their chill philosophy' that 'one must learn to kill without hate'. A report of May Days in Barcelona in 1937, accompanied by a photo of the anarchist Minister of Justice, García Oliver en-captioned 'Anarchist Chief with gun at hip', described the heaping of bodies shot by anarchists at the Telephone Exchange. Included was a tight-lipped and oblique statement by Sr Luis Companys, the leader of the Catalan government, that about this incident 'he was keeping his comments to himself and urged everyone else to do the same'. Spanish anarchists, the *Telegraph* added primly, operated from the assumption that 'violence from whatever source it comes is every man's opportunity'.109

It was difficult to gain from the newspapers a coherent picture of what was actually taking place in Spain. The presence of Spanish militiawomen among Republican troops aroused considerable interest. Their exploits occupied a disproportionate amount of the news space devoted to Spain in the first days of the war. These 'young Amazons' were shown grimly going about

---

107 *Sydney Morning Herald*, 6 Aug 1936; 4 Sep 1936; 8 Jan 1937.

108 *Daily Telegraph*, 6 May 1937.

109 *Daily Telegraph*, 6 May 1937; 7 May 1937.

their warlike business. They were in the columns which the Socialist government sent to storm mountain passes and 'a mother of four' was with another battalion marching on Saragossa. Front page pictures showed these astonishing creatures being wounded, taking over the Madrid tramways, or, like militiawoman Matilda Ortez 'leader of a communist women's section', at the front after a hard day's fighting and even 'at mealtimes with her rifle at the ready'.110

From the Nationalist side came fewer but equally unworldly reports. The tennis professional, Enrique Maier, sent Christmas greetings to his friends at the tennis tournament at White City (Sydney) at the end of 1936, in which he described how after a 'romantic but horrible escape' from Barcelona he had joined the Nationalists and survived several incidents in which he had thought it was 'match point'. Unlike his Christmas in Australia, there would be for him this year 'no oysters and parties at Rose Bay'.111 An English airman, it was reported, had been in a daring escapade in 1937 while delivering a case of wine to General Franco from an admirer in San Sebastian. Forced to put down behind the government lines, this erstwhile Biggles had only been freed in return for flying out two government generals bound for Gijón.112

Reports from people newly-arrived from the war zone were not clear about from whom they were fleeing. Most of these refugees were comfortable members of the bourgeoisie concerned with the danger the war posed to their property. In the reportage the source of the threat is imprecise, and though readers might agree with a *Telegraph* editorial that 'the Spanish civil war was a conflict of the passionate partisans of two irreconcilable causes', whose causes and which conflict was often

---

110 *Daily Telegraph*, 28 Jul 1936; 11 Aug 1936; 16 Sep 1936; 22 Sep 1936; 22 Oct 1936; *Sydney Morning Herald*, 20 Aug 1936; 4 Sep 1936.

111 *Daily Telegraph*, 2 Jan 1937.

112 *Daily Telegraph*, 9 Dec 1938.

obscure.113

A Czech couple, owners of a 'fashionable hotel' on the Balearic Islands, arrived on the SS *Orford* in early 1937, describing 'the soldiers sacking and looting everything they could lay their hands on'. Mrs A R Hecht, who 'conveyed her horror of the war chiefly by gesticulation', explained that Ibiza had been taken first by the rebels and then bombed by the government. Their hotel, originally 'filled with English tourists', was now 'just walls sheltering scores of Spanish refugees'.114 A German family who arrived on the same liner had a similar tale of woe. They had fled Barcelona only to find that the value of their home in the city had dropped, their car was in danger of being requisitioned and all the decent food was being sent to the front.115

The observations of several Australians in Spain at the time of the generals' coup d'état echoed the 'war for a melon' theme. An English teacher from Melbourne had 'a lucky escape from the Balearics'. She described Palma as having been 'laid waste' and had watched 'a mob of strikers', presumably government supporters, kick the head from a statue of Christ like a football along the main street. Rebel troops in their turn had 'battered communists to death in a house-to-house hunt'.116 The Australian artist Hal Missingham and his wife made 'a nightmare journey' from Barcelona to Málaga to join a British battleship. They had been saved only by flying the Union Jack and by displaying their pet marmoset monkey, whose antics had 'fascinated' both the 'armed communists' and the dark Moorish troops.117

An interview with a returning Spaniard and a government

---

113 *Daily Telegraph*, 12 Nov 1936.

114 *Daily Telegraph*, 9 Apr 1937. *Sydney Morning Herald*, 9 Apr 1937.

115 *Sydney Morning Herald*, 9 Apr 1937.

116 *Sydney Morning Herald*, 5 Aug 1936.

117 *Sydney Morning Herald*, 29 Jul 1936.

supporter contained the same ambiguities about which side could be trusted. Ellis Zamora, a nineteen-year-old 'Australian-born refugee from Spain' was visiting Madrid relatives when the war broke out. His sister and he had wanted to stay and fight with the government troops. Describing the upheaval in the country he explained that horseflesh was the only meat available; boys and girls of twelve were armed to the teeth; and dead fascists lay 'tied together in bundles strewn all over the parks in Madrid'. There was, according to him, something curious about 'this war business in Spain'.118

The example that, perhaps, most egregiously reveals an Orientalist view of events in Spain existing outside the pale of Anglo-Saxon-cum-Australian comprehension, is demonstrated in the first-person account filed by Brian Penton. He was a journalist who later became editor of the *Daily Telegraph*. When the Spanish civil war began, Penton and his wife and children were living in Torremolinos, a small village on the Andalusian coast near the 'red stronghold of Málaga'. The local people whom he described, presumably with whom Penton had at least some acquaintance, are comic characters from a burlesque opera. In the village, where 'death was taken very lightly', fat, jolly and ignorant *señoritos'* drank copious amounts of wine and knew only that Granada and England were equally remote from Torremolinos. After much bungling, the 'starving peasants in the village shot the landlords' and then decided to 'greet the dawn of a new age in Spain by burning the church'. Their 'enthusiastic solidarity' lasted a couple of weeks, during which time great confusion had broken out among the 'three different kinds of communists, four different kinds of socialists, and seven different kinds of anarchists'. At this point the sensible Pentons decided that they had had enough of comic-book Spanish revolutionaries and headed back to a safe harbour in England. There is a heavy smug overlay to Penton's report: the Spaniards are ludicrous, stereotypical Latins, uneducated and lacking any sense of order. His underlying message is that Australian readers

---

118 *Daily Telegraph*, 13 Nov 1936.

are lucky to be separated by half a world from such people. What is most disappointing, perhaps, in Penton's writing about Spain from his stance as a first-person observer and a self-proclaimed qualified journalist—later to become an editor of the *Daily Telegraph*—is that he willingly foreclosed on an opportunity to explain the complexities and the context of the civil war in Spain that had just begun.119

The single exception to these newspaper reports of extravagant Spaniards engaged in incomprehensible conflict were those filed by the Australian writers Nettie and Vance Palmer. At the time of the generals' rebellion they and their daughter Aileen, who subsequently volunteered with a British Medical Unit, had been living in a village on the Catalan coast where they planned to live cheaply in Europe while Vance and Nettie followed their various writing commitments. In Nettie's descriptions of the effect of the generals' uprising in the peaceful village of Montgat, Spaniards are credible, human figures. The militiamen who searched the Palmer's house were courteous, and the villagers and the Palmer's Spanish acquaintances, are portrayed as not at all unlike their neighbours in Melbourne.120

In contrast with a haziness on the domestic causes of the civil war in Spain, Australian newspapers spelt out in great detail the international ramifications and the importance to the Dominions of a policy of strict neutrality. Such a position was consistent with a general fear within the Australian community of another major war.121 Spain, a 'second Balkan cockpit', was a

---

119 *Daily Telegraph*, 21 Jul 1936.

120 Nettie Palmer, *Fourteen Years*, (Melbourne: Meanjin Press, 1948); *Sydney Morning Herald*, 14 Aug 1936; Keene, 'A Spanish Springtime: Aileen Palmer and the Spanish Civil War', *Labour History*, 52, (1987); Sylvia Martin, *Ink in Her Veins: The Troubled Life of Aileen Palmer*, (Perth: UWA Publishing, 2010): 120-129; and Vance Palmer's article, *Sydney Morning Herald*, 3 Aug 1936.

121 The terms in this paragraph were used, over and over, similarly in the following issues: *Sydney Morning Herald*, 14 Aug 1936; 7 Jan 1937; and 8 Jan 1937.

'menace to world peace', 'a danger spot to the rest of Europe', 'an unlucky accident that could bring down the frail structure of European diplomacy'. Like 'medical efforts to segregate an epidemic disease within an affected area', the 'Pyrenees must be sealed off to prevent all of Europe catching the Spanish infection'.

In this picture, Germany was presented as having an economic interest in Spain but it was the Italians and the Russians who were the wild cards in the European pack. 'Signor Mussolini' had his eye on the Mediterranean, and would threaten British and Australian sea lanes in the Straits of Gibraltar while the Russians would inevitably back their own 'Red Spanish government'. Blum's efforts in setting up the Non-Intervention Committee were applauded as were in both major papers, predictably, the ever-sensible policies of the British.122

The *Sydney Morning Herald*, in particular, displayed an almost mystical belief in the power of England and the British navy to straighten out the world's problems. According to the *Herald,* the only redeeming feature of the outbreak of the war in Spain had been 'the unflagging work of the British Navy in restoring calm' and the 'moral effect of the British example upon Spaniards and other nationalities alike'.123 In its analysis of foreign affairs the *Herald* found the League of Nations a spent force but, as in the heyday of the Empire, Britain could still solve all major diplomatic problems alone. A blockade of Spain by Britain should bring an end to the civil war. Better if Britain's allies would join her, but if not, the presence of the British Bulldog and His Majesty's ships would have 'a salutary effect' all over Europe. In an extraordinarily partial and inaccurate survey of recent international events, a *Herald* editorial claimed that the 'peacefulness and highly successful plebiscite in the Saar' had been caused by the moral effect of a British military presence. In Manchuria, too, the British had set the correct tone but had been

---

122 *Daily Telegraph*, 12 Aug 1936.

123 *Sydney Morning Herald*, 19 Jul 1936.

left high and dry by the other Powers.124

Most Australians in the 1930s shared the newspapers' concern to avoid a general European war and any international entanglements in which Australia could be enmeshed. As well, it is worth noting that when Australian Spanish Aid activists, on the Left, created a strong movement demanding the end of arms sanctions against the Spanish Republic, their case was often framed in terms of the need for military support for the Spanish Republic in order to defeat fascism in Europe and thereby prevent the world being drawn into another world war. Within this over-riding orientation, however, there were a number of other factors and sets of priorities, some of which overlapped, and some of which were in conflict with each other. In many cases these sub-sets of factors were not related to the question of war at all, and certainly not to the specifics of a civil war in Spain. It was the conjunction of all these local priorities which conditioned the Australian take on the civil war in Spain. The local response to reports of the presence in Spain of Italian soldiers is a good example of the complex effect which local political and social strands produced. In the 1930s, within certain sections of the Australian community, there was a strong element of anti-Italian sentiment, allied with an antagonism to Mussolini as a Mediterranean bully.125 Evidence, frequently reported in the press, of Mussolini's having sent troops to Franco, produced a corresponding and quite serendipitous sympathy for the Spanish Republic in its misfortune in having been invaded by Italians.

The Spanish civil war similarly tapped long-standing Australian sectarianism. Extravagant protests by Australian Catholics and their clergy at the manhandling of the Spanish brethren by secularists and Spanish anti-clericals drew forth equally exaggerated denials from members of the Protestant

---

124 *Sydney Morning Herald*, 14 Aug 1937.

125 Janis Wilton & Richard Bosworth, *Old Worlds and New Australia: The Post War Migrant Experience*, (Harmondsworth: Penguin, 1984): 1-7.

clergy and parishioners. The reactions from both groups were less a matter of being prompted by new events in Spain than of responses that triggered a manifestation of historic grudges.

The official government policy of non-intervention in Spain, too, was determined by the conservative United Australia Party and the Country Party's historic ties to British foreign policy. The conservative Australian government's indifference to the plight of Spanish war victims was consistent with an historic opposition to non-British migration to Australia. Within the Australian Labor Party (ALP), arguments about non-intervention in Spain plugged into a much deeper and longer discourse about the merits or otherwise of an independent Australian foreign policy, disengaged from Britain's leading strings. Similarly, within other leftist groups, the issue of Spain crossed a number of political strands whose origins had little to do with the civil war. In New South Wales, Spain became a vehicle for the working out of a series of tensions and challenges over the domination of the state party by the radical Jack Lang's faction. Within groups influenced by the Communist Party, the Spanish war coincided with a new Comintern direction to form united fronts with socialists and liberal democrats.

In light of all this, it is superficial to judge the meaning of the Australian response to the Spanish civil war solely on a yardstick of the amounts of money raised, or by comparisons of that amount with other contemporary Australian fundraising efforts. It was to be expected, for example, that the £262,476 of the Sydney Lord Mayor's fund for relief of victims in the Black Friday bushfires in 1938 would far outstrip the £17,115 raised by the Australian Spanish Relief Committees.126 Nor is it surprising that the Australian labour movement would have despatched an amount, twice that sent to Spain, to aid fellow unionists in the London dock strikes in the 1980s.127

---

126 E M Andrews, *Isolation and Appeasement in Australia: Reactions to the European Crises 1935-1939*, (Canberra: National University Press,1970): p 87.

127 See the discussion between Amirah Inglis and Laurie Aarons on the meaning of difference levels in contributions, in Philip Holcroft,

Fundraising for bushfire victims and for fellow strikers in Britain fitted unambiguously into Australian social and political traditions.

The response by Spanish residents in Australia to the war in Spain was probably the single exception to a pattern of reactions refracted and reflected through other networks.128 For them the war was unambiguously Spanish, and their response was direct. Not surprisingly, the Spanish community in Queensland raised proportionately far more for Spanish relief than did any other group in Australia and the community backed a brace of volunteer enlistments who heeded the call to democratic nations to come to the aid of Republican Spain.

The Official Government Response

Framed by economic depression and war, the 1930s was a 'mean decade' in Australia.129 The United Australia Party in alliance with the Country Party led a government in which farmers and country voters were the lead keel which kept the coalition to a narrowly conservative course along which prime minister and cabinet tacked carefully within the bow wave of the British Navy. In the words of the Treasurer, R G Casey, 'in every sense British policy would be regarded as Australia's policy'.130 Perhaps

---

'Crusaders of '36: Australians in the Spanish Civil War', *National Times*, 11-17 Jul 1986, p 15. The contrasting amounts was pointed out by J B Miles, the general secretary of the Australian Communist Party, in *Workers Weekly*, 19 Feb 1937.

128 Judith Keene, 'The Word Makes the Man: A Catalan Anarchist Autodidact in the Australian Bush', *Australian Journal of Politics and History*, 47 No. 3 (2001): pp 311-329. Judith Keene, 'A la recerca de la vida a Acràcia. Un anarquista català a Austràlia', *El Contemporani*, 33-34 (gener-desembre, 2007): pp 85-99.

129 J R Robertson, '1930 to 1939', in Frank Crowley (ed.), *A New History of Australia*, (Melbourne: Heinemann, 1974), p 415.

130 *Sydney Morning Herald*, 31 Jan 1938.

understandably so, as there was not a separate Australian Foreign Ministry until 1935 and no Australian legation abroad until 1940.

Australia's official policy of appeasement during the 1930s fitted both the tradition of adopting England's position on foreign affairs, and a genuine fear within the community of war. The Prime Minister, J A Lyons, returned from the Imperial Conference in 1935 having already committed Australian support to Britain's call for sanctions against Italy over the invasion of Abyssinia. When Britain backed away from this position in late 1936, Australia did too.

During the Munich crisis, the Australian government urged Whitehall to make even more radical concessions to Germany in order to keep the peace. This stance was applauded by many Australians. When the Munich settlement was reached a national day of thanksgiving was held in Australian churches, and on hearing the news a crowd of 33,000 at the football final at the Adelaide Oval stood and sang the national anthem.131 The schizophrenic other face of this determined appeasement was a rush into print by 'amateur defence planners' explaining their crackpot schemes for Australian defence.132

During the Spanish civil war, the Australian government policy was like Britain's one of non-intervention. The Prime Minister urged Australians to stay out of a Spanish war which was none of their business. When Australians volunteered for Spain, government ministers spoke loudly of their folly, but had neither the legal means nor the inclination to do anything about it.133 R G Menzies described the war as a conflict in which 'we have no very great concern whether Communism defeats Fascism or vice versa'. Each system of government while it may

---

131 *Sydney Morning Herald*, 3 Oct 1938.

132 Between 1935 and 1939 more books and pamphlets appeared on this subject than in the whole of the preceding 34 years, Robertson, p 456.

133 *Daily Telegraph*, 14 Oct 1936; 29 Jun 1937; *Sydney Morning Herald*, 12 Sep 1936.

be admirable for Spain is of no possible value in a British community.134 As far as official relations were concerned, perhaps, Menzies' description was not far off the mark. There had been little exposure to Spain except for individual artists and performers arriving on tour. The handful of Spaniards in Australia had come after World War I.

Historically, as we have seen, there had been, off and on, since the 1860s, a Spanish Consul in Sydney. Between 1936 and 1938 the position was filled, successively, by three men who came and went through the revolving door of politics in metropolitan Spain. When the war began, Don Pedro Ygual y Martínez Daban was the Spanish Consul. In March 1937, he declared for Franco and with a certain public flourish went home to join Franco's forces.135 The interim acting consul, Sr Ramón Mas, a well-known Spanish resident and ardent supporter of the Republican government, ran a business in mushroom culture through a shop at Circular Quay.136 He took charge of the consular papers and Spanish government business until the arrival of the new Consul General and his family at the end of September 1937. Don Ricardo Baeza Duran, was a distinguished doctor of law, had taught at Cambridge, was a respected economist and expert on international relations and, at various times, had been the representative in London of *El Sol* a liberal Spanish national newspaper. With the establishment of the Spanish Republic, Baeza had been appointed the Ambassador and Plenipotentiary for Latin America. In his Australian post, he worked tirelessly and tactfully for his government's cause. He consistently pointed out the folly of the major democratic powers, especially Britain, that had let down the ordinary Spanish people by preventing the Republican state from

---

134 *Argus* (Melbourne), 23 Sep 1936.

135 *Sydney Morning Herald*, 6 Jan 1937; *Sydney Morning Herald*, 6 Mar 1937.

136 *Sydney Morning Herald*, 22 Apr 1937; and personal communication Phil Thorne, Nowra, N.S.W. 1985.

purchasing arms with which to defend itself and to prevent an escalation of what was becoming a world war by proxy. At the same time Baeza was subjected to an unrelenting barrage of egregious attacks on the Consul General, himself, and the 'illegal Red mob' masquerading as the legitimate Republican government he represented. The Catholic Archbishops of Sydney, Dr Norman Gilroy and in Brisbane, Bishop James Duhig led the charge in the Catholic press and from the pulpit and were unflagging letter-writers in the mainstream press challenging any positive reporting on the elected Spanish government or its social policies.137

Recalled to Madrid in October 1938, Baeza Duran was farewelled with great regret by Australian Republican supporters. By then the Spanish government, stretched to the limit by the war and with the International Brigades withdrawn, was no longer able to maintain an outpost in far-flung Australia. The Consul General's son, who had turned 18 in Sydney, returned home to enlist in the Republican Army, while his father was transferred to the Spanish Embassy in Paris.138

Trade between Australia and Spain was small, though in some sectors not insignificant. Spanish exports consisted of specialized goods like olive oil, cork, wine and nuts. As one might expect, the civil war had a disastrous effect on these industries. Shipping was disrupted and, in the upheaval of wartime, crops were neglected. Spanish imports into Australia fell from £196,939 in 1935 to £70,715 by the end of the war.139 In the

---

137 In the year of Ricardo Baeza Duran's appointment in Sydney the local press was filled with acrimonious back and forth commentary between the Consul General and the Catholic Church. See for example: *Sydney Morning Herald*, 16 Sep 1937, 8 Nov 1937; *Daily Telegraph*, 23 Sep 1937, 13 Nov 1937; *Maryborough Chronicle*, 27 Sep 1937; *Tweed Daily*, 28 Sep 1937; *Age*, 28 Sep, 1937; *Labour Daily*, 1 Oct 1937, 13 Oct, 1937; *Workers Weekly*, 12 Oct 1937, 15 Dec 1937, 22 Feb 1938; *Sydney Truth*, 20 Feb 1938.

138 *Sydney Morning Herald*, 18 Oct 1938.

139 *Commonwealth of Australia Yearbook*, No. 29, 1936, p 261; No. 33, 1940, p 781.

same period the export of Spanish nuts to Australia fell from the considerable sum of £51,319 to a negligible amount of £3,528. Spanish oil followed the same decline. Before the war the main supply of mercury used in the Australian armaments industry came from the Almadén mines in southern Spain. Their export to Australia provided an average annual return to Spain of approximately £10,000 for 60,000 landed tons.140 It was not a great deal, but the demand was steady. Without accessible local sources Australia relied heavily on Spanish mercury. Apart from being used in making percussion caps, bombs and shells, mercury was an essential ingredient in a number of Australian medicines, in the vapour in street lights and, no less significantly, in the manufacture of fur felt hats. By 1938 the supplies of mercury to Australia had dried up. The sole importers, C W Macleod and Son of Melbourne, reminded the government in 1938 that if Franco continued to cut off Spanish exports of mercury, Australia would be left short. With Germany rearming and now in Franco's camp, the world's entire mercury supplies could be placed in the hands of Germany and Italy.141 None of the arguments had any effect.

Australian exports to Spain consisted of wool, oil cake, hides and skins, and in 1935 totalled £554,564.142 After a year of war, the value of Australian exports to Spain had dropped to £133,448, which represented a single purchase by the Spanish government in early 1937 of 11 million bushels of Australian wheat.143 The war had indirect effects, too, on Australian primary producers. As Spanish markets were closed to many European primary products, European farmers looked elsewhere to sell. Australian egg exporters, for example, were outraged that European producers had flooded the English market. The

---

140 *Daily Telegraph*, 19 Aug 1938.

141 *Daily Telegraph*, 19 Aug 1938.

142 *Commonwealth of Australia Yearbook*, No. 29, 1936, p 261.

143 *Daily Telegraph*, 8 Feb 1937.

Australian High Commissioner warned that in the future Australian farmers could not rely on England to protect their interests. Local egg farmers called loudly and predictably for the immediate establishment of subsidies.

After a series of bumper crops, Australian wheat growers in 1938 lobbied the government to lend all support to an English delegation which was putting out feelers for a trade agreement with Nationalist Spain.144 For the same economic motives, they probably applauded the alacrity with which the Australian government at the end of February 1938 recognized General Franco as the legitimate leader of Spain.145 In light of this it is curious, perhaps, that wheat growers' organizations responded coolly to an approach by the Spanish Relief Committee in mid-1938 to export wheat to the Spanish government on credit provided by the Bank of Spain. Rejected out of hand by the Prime Minister and rebuffed by the farmers, the plan collapsed.146

The ungenerousness of the decade was echoed in the mean-spiritedness of the conservative government's behaviour towards Spanish victims of the war. A tight-fisted £3,000 was the total allocated to the International Red Cross for the care of all Spanish refugees, and by June 1938 only £500 of this amount had been spent.147 The government was equally unbending in its opposition to the settlement of homeless Spaniards in Australia. After the Basque countries fell to the Nationalists, English and French aid groups had stepped in to provide temporary homes for Basque refugee children.

A request by the Friends of Spain in Adelaide that

---

144 *Daily Telegraph*, 7 Mar 1939.

145 *Daily Telegraph*, 1 Mar 1939.

146 *Daily Telegraph*, 29 Dec 1938; interview PT with JK, Nowra, 1984. There is evidence that the ASRC purchased grain for Spain from elsewhere via the CSI, the international medical aid organization in Paris. See image 406, Chapter 4.

147 Robertson, p 453; Commonwealth of Australia, *Parliamentary Debates*, 1938, Vol. 157, p 2057.

Australians be permitted to take some of these children was rejected out of hand. Members of the cabinet considered it 'impracticable' as such children 'would inevitable become a charge on the Australian state'.148 A young 'Spanish stowaway from the war zone', Elias Gurtubay, who arrived in Sydney in April 1939 was quickly bundled back on ship despite protests from the Spanish Relief Committee and promises of employment from Spaniards in Queensland.149 His treatment was in strong contrast to the official support provided for the Church of England Migration Council Scheme whose first non-British migrant arrived in Sydney with much fanfare a fortnight after the Spanish stowaway. A dancer from the Austrian national ballet, she had been forced to leave Austria because of her 'non-Aryan background'. She was reported to be 'glad' that she had been assigned by the Migration Council to domestic service. Her future as a maid in Australia may not have been a bed of roses, but at least she had been offered residency.150

At the end of the civil war the Spanish Relief Committees, the International Peace Committee and the Australian Council for the Relief of Spanish Distress urgently petitioned the government for assistance on behalf of the thousands of Spaniards in desperate circumstances stranded in camps in southern France.151 All appeals fell on deaf ears. It seemed that the nation that prided itself on having given the world 'the little battler' and 'the egalitarian digger' felt no obligation to offer 'a fair go' to destitute Spaniards.

---

148 *Daily Telegraph*, 13 Jul 1937.

149 An appeal for entry on compassionate grounds for Elias Gurtubay was made to Cabinet by the Spanish Relief Committees. *Daily Telegraph*, 15 Apr 1939.

150 *Daily Telegraph*, 6 Apr 1939.

151 *Daily Telegraph*, 6 Apr 1939.

Australian Catholics and the Spanish Civil War

Since end of the nineteenth century the Vatican had perceived itself losing ground before a rising tide of secularism, socialism and left-wing trade unionism. The liberals in a new unified Italy had separated church and state. The national revolution in Mexico in 1910 had done the same. An even more powerful threat for the Church had appeared with the Russian revolution in 1917, whose supporters were seen as bent on exporting their revolutionary and atheistic doctrines. In comparison, Mussolini was decidedly the lesser of two evils. Not only had fascist squads vigorously wiped out communists and socialists but Mussolini himself had restored the temporal power of the Church. The Lateran Accords in 1929 returned control of births, deaths, marriages and education to the Church and declared that Catholicism was again the state religion of Italy. In pastoral letters, at commemorations and stone-laying ceremonies the Australian Catholic hierarchy defended the Vatican's position on all these matters. The *Catholic Freeman's Journal* (CFJ), the *Catholic Advocate* (CA), the *Catholic Press* (CP), the *Catholic Worker* (CW) and the *Australasian Catholic Record* (ACR) thundered against communism and atheism and their sinister threat to the devout. The papers chronicled the dire fate of the clergy in Russia and Mexico, two epicentres of a wave of revolution intended to destroy the Holy Church, and reported sympathetically on events in Italy. Under Mussolini's form of fascism 'religion prospered, Freemasonry had been banned and the Crucifix was restored to its rightful place' in Italian schoolrooms.152

In the Abyssinian crisis in mid-1935, Australian Catholic sympathies with Italy were tested in a number of ways. Catholics, like many Australians, had little interest in the League of Nations or in the workings of the League system. Britain's call for sanctions against Italy for that country's aggression in Abyssinia, however, changed the situation. As a League signatory, Australia

---

152 CFJ, 29 Jan 1931.

was bound to uphold sanctions. However, if the latter were ineffective, a war with Italy was a possibility. Australian Catholics, predominantly of Irish descent, probably cared little for Mussolini or Italians, and were horrified at the news of unarmed Ethiopian tribesmen being mown down by Italian machine guns, but a war with Italy would inevitably embroil the Vatican. Sanctions against Italy, therefore, were unacceptable. The opposition to sanctions by Catholic members of the Australian labour movement was reinforced by the Labor Party, which was opposed to allowing any possibility of Australia's being drawn into war on Britain's coat-tails. Under the general umbrella of Catholic opposition to sanctions, however, there were a variety of responses, many of which evolved as the Abyssinian crisis developed.153

The Australian Catholic response to the Spanish civil war was less complex and changed little over the course of the war. Catholics in Australia had a deep but symbolic attachment to Spain, that most Catholic of countries. However, apart from Don Quixote and Francis Xavier, most Catholics, like Australians in general, would have been hard pressed to name a single Spaniard who was eminent on the pre-war scene. Francisco Franco, who became a household word after July 1936, was unknown before the uprising, as was Dolores Ibárruri, 'la Pasionaria', the leader of the Spanish Communist Party. Certainly, none of the leaders during the Second Republic had cut much lead in the press in Australia. Not even the leader of the Catholic coalition, José María Gil Robles, had figured in the Catholic papers, perhaps because for English readers he was saddled with an unintelligible name and led a faction with an unpronounceable acronym.

In Australia the civil war in Spain was a symbol for the larger Catholic struggle: a station on the long haul to save the Church. From an Australian Catholic stance, the war in Spain was like a mechanical tableau which whirred and clanked through its paces. The figures on stage were placed in their familiar groupings; when they gestured or changed places their

---

153 Pauline Kneipp, 'Australian Catholics and the Abyssinian War', *Journal of Religious History*, X, (Dec 1979).

movements were within familiar fixed arcs. The audience needed very little elaboration on the character of the protagonists or the development in their relationships because, as in an Easter tableau, everyone watching knew who they were and how they would respond even before the performance had begun.

There had been news from Spain in Australian Catholic papers during the time of the Republic which uniformly represented the relationship between the Spanish Church and state as a national version of the international pattern whereby progressive reform was a thin wedge behind which communism would destroy religion.154 The 1931 Constitution separating church and state was 'laical, atheistic and almost pagan in some sections' as it 'permitted divorce, confiscated Church property and accorded illegitimate children equal rights with those born in wedlock'.155 Articles on the expulsion of the Archbishop of Toledo and his stoic opposition to the disestablishment of the Spanish Church were corroborated by the Vatican press.156 Considerable attention was given to the Republic's secular education policy and the dissatisfaction it had aroused among Spanish Catholic parents. The latter would have struck a sympathetic chord with Australian Catholic parents engaged in an embattled defence of government aid to Australian church schools. As Archbishop Duhig of Brisbane explained, it was part of an all-encompassing pattern: 'Yesterday it was Russia and Mexico, today it is Spain, tomorrow it may be Britain and the day after Australia'.157

Against this background the Australian Catholic response to the Spanish Nationalists' uprising against 'the Reds', as government supporters were always called, was consistent and predictable. A pastoral letter by Bishop Kelly read in New South

---

154 See CA, 11 Oct 1934; 27 Dec 1934; 14 Feb 1935; 21 Feb 1935.

155 CFJ, 8 Oct 1931.

156 CFJ, 8 Oct 1931; 8 Feb 1932.

157 *Sydney Morning Herald*, 3 Aug 1936.

Wales churches in the first week of September 1936 defined the terms. The Spanish generals had risen to defeat those who 'persecuted the national religion, demolished churches, schools, monasteries and convents and tortured and murdered priests and nuns'.158 There was little change in the Catholic position over the course of the war. General Franco at its end was exactly as he had been from the beginning. In Cardinal Gilroy's words, he was, 'a man who seemed to be raised up by Almighty God, a military genius, the like of whom has rarely been seen in the history of the world—a mighty organizer, but in addition a God-fearing and God-loving man'.159

Since the settlement of the Australian colonies, Catholics had been predominantly of Irish extraction and Irish priests had ministered to their spiritual welfare. Strong bonds had been forged between hierarchy and laity in a shared opposition to the British Anglican establishment. The violence of Spanish anti-clericalism was inconceivable to Australian Catholics who were appalled at the excesses of the reported mistreatment of the clergy at the hands of Spanish Republicans. The Australian Catholic press was unrestrained in detailing the grisly minutiae of an endless stream of ghoulish incidents. Priests had been decapitated, strung up on gibbets, their heads stuck on church railings, or hung by their feet in mock crucifixions. Nuns were being manhandled, stripped naked and forced to dance in chorus line. Together, priests and nuns had been stripped and tied together while the crowds jeered.160 The pornographic element in many of these descriptions, contrasting with the traditional chasteness of the clergy, underlined the horror of the Spanish war for Australian Catholics.

The wanton extravagance of the destruction of church buildings in Spain probably also struck a raw nerve. Between the wars Australian Catholics were engaged in an ambitious church

---

158 *Daily Telegraph*, 7 Sep 1936.

159 CFJ, 9 Mar 1939.

160 CW, 2 Nov 1936; FJ, 27 Aug 1936; 1 Oct 1936; *Daily Telegraph*, 26 Oct 1936.

and school building scheme, paid for from the hard-pressed parish purse.161 For Australian Catholics there was the grotesque juxtaposition that, as fast as Catholics in Australia were putting up buildings, anti-clericals in Spain were burning them down.

The place of the Spanish Basques in the civil war posed some problem. The most devout and staunch of all Catholics in Spain, the Basques, supported by their priests, had been stout members of the Republic and fought fiercely and bravely against the Nationalists until their defeat in mid-1937. The destruction by incendiary bombing of the Basque capital, Guernica, on 26 April 1937, by German and Italian planes aroused massive and anguished protest from European and English Catholic communities.162 In Australia, the Catholic press explained that Basques were not 'proper Catholics' as they had chosen to meddle in politics 'instead of putting their religion before everything else'. Those that supported the Republic were not Basques at all but 'foreigners and non-Basque communists'. A few of their priests, like technicolour Darth Vaders, had 'turned to the Red side'. The bombing of Guernica, 'the biggest lie of the Spanish war', was 'a yarn' spread to the gullible non-Catholic press in Sydney when 'the Reds themselves had planted the bombs' to discredit General Franco.163 In 1953, Cardinal Gilroy was still maintaining this position and attempted to have an Australian Broadcasting Commission journalist officially reprimanded for having mentioned on air that Guernica had

---

161 CFJ during the 1930s published a regular section 'When Catholics Build and Decorate' which surveyed Church and school building projects.

162 Michael Alpert, 'Humanitarianism and Politics in the British Response to the Spanish Civil War', *European History Quarterly*, 14 (26 Apr 1984): pp 423-40.

163 The discussion of the Basques and Guernica in CP, 25 Feb 1937; 1 Jul 1937; 16 Sep 1937 and CFJ, 21 May 1937.

been destroyed by German planes.164

The Australian clergy railed from the pulpit against Republican excesses, rallied church groups and, wherever possible, attempted to counter the publicity of the Spanish Relief Committee. Except in Victoria, the lead in these activities came from the clergy themselves. The Catholic Evidence Guild provided speakers, the Apostolic Delegate spoke to Catholic Boy Scouts, and there were meetings and evenings in church halls to explain the Catholic interpretation and point out the misguidedness of the Republican position.

Republican supporters, in turn, tried to counter Catholic efforts.165 When the movie 'With Franco in Spain' was shown in St Paul's church hall, Dulwich Hill, it was interrupted by the arrival of two ambulances, three fire engines and a carload of police brought out on a bogus call.166 In Adelaide in the first week of 1937, a Spanish Relief Committee meeting disintegrated into a riot of booing and jostling between Nationalist and Republican supporters when it was attacked by members of the Catholic Guild of Social Studies.167

In Melbourne the impetus and organization came from enthusiastic members of the laity. Young men in the Campion Society like Kevin Kelly, Stan Ingerwersen and B A Santamaría gave energetic service to the Catholic cause. Twenty-five years later Santamaría identified the Spanish civil war as the critical event in his own political development, and the main factor that

---

164 Edmund Campion, *Rockchoppers: Growing up Catholic in Australia*, (Ringwood: Penguin, 1982): pp 40-41.

165 Lloyd Ross edited a collection of statements from European Catholics who supported the Spanish Republic. It was published by the Victorian Movement Against War and Fascism as, *Catholics Speak Out*, Melbourne, 1938.

166 *Daily Telegraph*, 1 Oct 1937.

167 *Workers Weekly*, 11 May 1937; *Sydney Morning Herald*, 6 May 1937.

had set the future course of Australian Catholic Action.168 The differences in the organization between Melbourne and Sydney probably reflected the dissimilarities in the relative positions of the hierarchy and the laity in both places; and the personal and political styles of Archbishops Mannix and Kelly. Whatever the organizational differences, the analysis made in both places was the same.

Debates were favoured in Victoria. In Ballarat at one of a series of debates in country areas between the Campion Society and Spanish Relief organizations, Nationalist supporters occupied the hall early, forcing their opponents to listen and vote from an annexe.169 The most famous debate was the Melbourne University Debating Club meeting in the University Great Hall on 22 March 1937. The motion that 'the Spanish Government is the ruin of Spain' was debated on the government side by Santamaría, Kelly and Ingerwersen, while Nettie Palmer, Dr G P O'Day and Jack Legge opposed it. The speakers could scarcely be heard above the din of stamping and heckling from both sides. At the end, Nationalist supporters as a body stood and chanted the slogan, 'Long Live Christ the King'. The *Catholic Worker* commented in glowing terms that the slogan had 'resounded in the Temple of Australian Secularism' within whose 'halls so much heresy had been preached'.170 Interestingly, a similar debate scheduled a few weeks later at Sydney University had to be cancelled when the four speakers outnumbered the audience.171 Sydney University students, perhaps, were more phlegmatic than their Melbourne peers, but it is more likely that the different sources of the organization in the two cities produced audiences for different activities. In any event, Sydney was the only city which produced a volunteer fighting for

---

168 See his, *Against the Tide*, (Melbourne: Melbourne University Press, 1981): pp 33-38.
169 CW, 19 Jun 1937; CA, 21 Apr 1937.

170 Santamaría, *Against the Tide*, pp 37-38.

171 *Daily Telegraph*, 1 Apr, 1937.

Franco.172

Despite appeals from the pulpit the Australian Catholic community raised little money for Spanish aid. Although Australian and New Zealand bishops launched a Catholic Spanish Relief Fund in November 1936 in the name of 'all those that stand for God against the power of evil and atheism and wish to rebuild the desecrated altars and shrines of Catholic Spain', by the end of 1936 they had collected £650. At the end of March 1937, £6,702 had been contributed by the Australian Catholic dioceses.173 It was not a vast sum. In the 1930s the most pressing financial priority facing Australian Catholics was their support of the local parish and church schools.

In claiming that there was a fairly uniform *response to* the Spanish civil war among Australian Catholics it is not that Catholics throughout the 1930s shared 'a monolithic unity', in which the Church was their only reference point.174 Individual Catholics held a series of allegiances and a hierarchy of beliefs. In a conflict within these in relation to Spain, however, the defence of the Church won out. Catholic trade unionists may have identified with Spanish workers and may have been challenged by fellow workers for their anti-Republican sentiments, but the Australian labour movement as a whole was never united in defence of the Spanish Republic. The Australian Labor Party and a number of right-wing unions remained firmly committed to isolationism and under this umbrella there was a place that Australian Catholics who supported Franco could comfortably occupy. For whatever local or religious reasons, it may have been

---

172 Nugent Bull, educated at St Joseph's College was the son of a prominent Sydney family. Keene, 'An Antipodean Bridegroom of Death: An Australian with Franco's Forces in the Spanish Civil War', *Journal of the Royal Australian Historical Society*, 70 (Apr 1985); and *Fighting for Franco: International Volunteers in Nationalist Spain during the Spanish Civil War, 1936-39*, (London: Continuum, 2007): pp 106- 110.

173 *Argus*, 20 Mar 1937.

174 Ken Inglis, 'Catholic Historiography in Australia', *Historical Studies*, 8 (1958).

adopted, however, a policy of non-intervention in the long run favoured Franco.

The Australian Labour Movement and Spain

Most members of the labour movement in Australia were sympathetic to the plight of Spanish workers who, for non-Catholics at least, were identified with the Republican side. The assessment by individual Australian workers of what they and their labour organizations should do about Spain, however, depended on the part of the labour movement in which they were involved. The national political wing of the movement, the Australian Labor Party, held firmly to non-intervention in Spain and avoided any public commitment to the Spanish Republic. This stance was consistent with the party's long-standing policy of pushing for an Australian foreign policy that was independent of Britain and disengaged from traditional European conflicts. This position had been forged during the anti-conscription struggles in World War One and was tested in the Abyssinian crisis. In contrast, the state Labor parties, with the exception of Jack Lang's group in New South Wales, all came around to overt support for the Spanish Republic in the first quarter of 1937. In New South Wales, Spain was the vehicle through which a series of tensions and challenges for control of the party were worked out between Jack Lang's faction and those groups on the left.

In the industrial wing of the unions, the stance on Spain depended on where the union stood on the political spectrum. Those on the right, with Catholics frequently predominant in the leadership, tended to remain silent on the Spanish war, or to ostentatiously adopt the lead of the federal ALP, which in effect amounted to the same thing. Left-wing unions, with communist leadership, since 1935 had pushed the need for collective security in Europe and Australia in order to defeat fascism. Consistent with this was a strong commitment to the Spanish Republic. As a result of pressure from New South Wales left-wing unions, the Australian Council of Trade Unions, the national body of the union movement, abandoned its traditional isolationism in July 1937 for a platform favouring collective security against fascism, support for the Soviet Union and a commitment to the defence of the Spanish government. A number of state Trades and Labor Councils followed suit.

The Spanish civil war had come hard on the heels of the world economic depression. In 1933, one quarter of the Australian labour force was still unemployed. In 1934 the basic wage, which had been cut by ten per cent in the Commonwealth Court of Conciliation and Arbitration, was restored to its 1931 level. During the Depression employees in industrial sectors and those reliant on public works projects had been hardest hit. In consequence, as the economic recovery began, the efforts of the labour movement were geared to restoring the hard-won gains which had been lost to the working class and their unions during the preceding six or seven years. This was a perfectly legitimate domestic priority. Even when there were differences within the movement over foreign policy, which often involved Spain, there remained a general agreement about the overriding importance of traditional bread and butter struggles for improving wages and conditions for the Australian working class.

The attitude is best summed up in an editorial in July 1938 in the *Labour Daily*, the newspaper of the New South Wales labour movement. The sentiments expressed are particularly significant as the newspaper by this time was controlled by left-wing, anti-Lang unions who strongly rejected the previous isolationism of their opponents. Since the Left's ascendency, the paper had made consistently strong public statements for the Spanish Republic, and had urged its readers to do likewise. On the need for Catholic working-class support in the struggles of the New South Wales miners, however, the *Labour Daily* stated that 'questions of religious belief and free thought need not enter co-operative discussions on economic matters'. Despite the fact that Catholic and non-Catholic members of the union movement may 'not see eye to eye on Spain', and 'some Catholics are unable to believe that the Spanish government is fighting in the widest interests of world democracy' such 'sincere differences of opinion are no reason for men who work side by side not to regard each other with the highest respect and help each other in every way to secure a better life for themselves and their children'.175

The Australian Labor Party in 1936 was carefully rebuilding its electoral base in order to return from the political wilderness into which the party had been cast. In 1931, the ALP members as well as a number of Labor parliamentarians had rejected Arthur Scullin's federal Labor government, which had adopted deflationary policies in order to deal with the Depression. To many party members it appeared that the Labor cabinet had caved in before foreign capitalists and financiers such as Sir Robert Gibson and Sir Otto Niemeyer, the heads of the Commonwealth Bank of Australia and the Bank of England respectively. Both bankers had urged a savage slashing of public works, a reduction of Australian living standards and a balancing of the federal budget in order to meet foreign loan repayments. Jack Lang, the Premier of New South Wales, refused to implement the deflationary policies of the Gibson-Niemeyer plan, and proposed instead his own solution which included, among other things, the repudiation of New South Wales's loan repayments to England. In consequence, in 1932 the State Governor of New South Wales dismissed Lang from office.

In the 1931 elections, the federal Labor Party suffered a resounding defeat to a conservative coalition led by the United Australia Party. Labor retained only 19 out of the total 75 seats in the House of Representatives. In the preceding parliament they had held 46 seats. In the debacle six Labor cabinet ministers were defeated, including the Treasurer and John Curtin, who was to become the party's next leader. Of the seats Labor retained, five were controlled by the Lang group from New South Wales which rejected control by the federal ALP caucus.

For the next decade the federal Labor Party began painstakingly to rebuild the party's electoral base and unify its support within the states. Where possible, divisive issues were eschewed. A defensive isolationism in foreign affairs was both consistent with the ALP's avowed independence from Britain and in the issues of Abyssinia and Spain avoided any overt conflict

---

175 *Labour Daily*, 27 Jul 1938.

with Catholic members of the party. As a policy, isolationism reflected the minimal interest in foreign affairs of most ALP members coupled with an historic opposition to Australian conscription for foreign wars, and the belief that Australia's own interests should take precedence over those of Britain and the Empire. In the Abyssinian crisis the ALP had opposed the application of sanctions against Italy which could draw Australia into a war in Europe, and at home lead to a confrontation with Catholic Labor supporters.

John Curtin, ALP leader after 1935, consistently defended isolationism in the Spanish civil war despite it placing his party out of step with brother labour parties in Britain and New Zealand. Decrying the ACTU's abandonment of isolationism in support of the Spanish Republic, in mid-1937, Curtin argued that Australian unionists could never 'solve the perennial disputes which mark the old world'.176 In October 1938, after the Munich settlement, he stated unequivocally that 'it would be suicidal for the workers of Australia to join in supporting pacts, treaties, understandings or obligations of any sort which would involve them in war against the workers of another nation, or a number of nations, at the dictates of capitalist governments'.177

When Curtin became Australian prime minister during World War II he was an independent figure who defended Australia's interests against the British war cabinet. Under Curtin's hand, Australian foreign policy was reoriented away from Britain and focused in a more realistic way towards the Pacific and the United States. Though the shift has left the ambiguous legacy of Australia as an American client, it is the independence of Curtin's administration which succeeding Australians have most applauded. His stance of non-intervention in the Spanish civil war grew out of a consistent if narrowly nationalistic and domestic logic. The ALP's policy was unfortunate for the Republican Spanish Aid movement in Australia as it hindered fund-raising by the Australian Council of

---

176 *Australian Worker*, 4 Aug 1937.

177 *Australian Worker*, 9 Nov 1938.

Trade Unions, the state Labor Councils, and even within those left-wing unions which from the start had favoured the Spanish government.

The Spanish Aid Movement

A Spanish Relief Committee was formed *in* Sydney at the end of August 1936 in order to 'render moral and material aid to the anti-fascist people of Spain who are waging a heroic struggle against the reactionary forces of that country'.178 The original 26 members of the Spanish Relief Committee were drawn from communist and leftist groups and unions, together with a handful of Protestant clergymen. A stable core of people carried out the legwork of running Spanish Relief in Australia. The central figure was the General Secretary, Phil Thorne, who worked steadfastly and with total dedication to the cause of the Spanish Republic and after defeat for its citizens in exile. With unflagging energy, he wrote letters, organized fund-raisers, made press releases, set up Spanish support groups and tactfully and efficiently held together an effective and broadly based pollical campaign. A member of the Communist Party and a law clerk, Thorne came to the committee from the International Labour Defence organization which provided legal support for 'the victims of capitalist justice'.179

The meetings of the Spanish Relief Committee in Sydney, held at Moony's Club in the Haymarket, were chaired by ex-Labor Senator Arthur Rae. Dr Lloyd Ross was active on the executive. A communist and General Secretary of the Australian Railways Union, Ross was one of the most articulate and informed voices of the Australian Left. J B Miles, the General Secretary of the Communist Party of Australia, was also a regular

---

178 ASRC Circular, 10 Sep 1936. Thorne Collection, Noel Butlin Archives, Australian National University. NBAANU.

179 Phil and Betty Thorne, interviews JK, Sydney and Nowra, 1984, 1985.

presence, as was Mary Lowson, until she left with Agnes Hodgson, May McFarlane and Una Wilson to nurse in wartime Spain. J Harley, of the Hurstville ALP, was active, as at various times were A W Thorpe of the Milk, Ice and Dairy Employees Union, Mr Harrison of the New South Wales Movement Against War and Fascism and Miss Alice Holloway, President of the Ladies' Auxiliary of the Australian Railways Union. She spoke for the movement on conditions in Spain following her visit to the Republican zone in mid-1938.180 Mrs Ada Holman, wife of the ex-Premier of New South Wales, whose daughter Portia was active in the British movement providing medical aid for Spain, also worked solidly for Spanish Relief in New South Wales. The Republican ambassadors in Australia, Ramón Mas, and later Don Ricardo Baeza, attended Spanish Relief meetings and kept in active contact with the activities.

The Sydney group became the headquarters of the Australian Spanish Relief movement. There were branches and groups set up in each of the state capitals and in large and smaller provincial towns like Newcastle, Broken Hill and Ballarat but, as well, in small towns like Innisfail in Northern Queensland and Casino, a rail junction in northern NSW, where the Women's Auxiliary of the Australian Railway Workers Union fostered a refugee child in Spain.181

In northern Queensland 16 branches of Spanish Relief flourished. Before the Sydney committee had been established a group of Italians in the sugar town of Ingham had formed a committee and raised £30, which they sent to the Australian Council of Trade Unions to be forwarded to Spain. The two small towns of Ayr and Innisfail together raised twenty per cent of the total Australian funds in the early months of the war. The depth of the northern Queensland response grew out of the strong anti-fascist movement among southern European immigrants. The Innisfail committee was run by a Spanish-Australian, Trini García, whose husband Joe had returned to Spain early in 1937

180 *Sydney Morning Herald*, 23 Sep 1938.

181 *Northern Star* (Lismore), 11 Mar 1938.

to join the Republican army. Mrs García and her daughters
organized house parties, May Day processions, speakers and
even held a contest for Spanish Relief Queen. Ray Jordana,
whose family was among the first Spanish anarchist migrants to
have settled in Innisfail, were devoted activists and fund raisers
during the Spanish civil war. He volunteered as a CNT
ambulance driver in Aragón.182 During 1939, Spanish sugar
workers in Innisfail adopted a voluntary wage levy for Spanish
relief.183

*Fund-raising stamps issued by the
Australian Spanish Relief Committee.*

The group in Melbourne was drawn from a broad
community base. Len Fox, a communist and a foundation
member of the group, recalled that Victorian Spanish Relief
'seemed at first to be a fragile mixture of a few individuals of
vastly differing religious and political beliefs'.184 The character
of the committee was strongly influenced by its central figures.

---

182 Judith Keene, "Catalan anarchists in Australia in search of
Acracia', Memories of Migration edited by Ignacio García and
Augustín Macarthur, Spanish Heritage Foundation, Ministerio de
Trabajo y Asuntos Sociales de España, 1998, p111-124

183 Diane Menghetti, *The Red North: the Popular Front in North
Queensland*, (Townsville: James Cook University of North
Queensland, 1981): p 73.

184 Len Fox, *Broad Left, Narrow Left*, (published by the author,
Chippendale, 1982), pp 31, 39.

The secretary, Helen Baillie, 'a self-sacrificing Christian and a tireless worker', had previously been active on the Ethiopian Relief Committee.185 Len Fox and Arthur Howells brought their experience from the organization of the Movement Against War and Fascism.

In October 1938, Arthur Howells travelled from Melbourne to Spain with the intention of volunteering as an ambulance driver. By the time he and his wife, Margaret, arrived all international volunteers were being withdrawn and the two spent a couple of weeks in Catalonia. The pamphlet, *We Went to Spain*, describing their impressions of war-torn Barcelona and the Aragón front, was published in Melbourne in 1939 to raise money for the movement.

Ray Jordana driving an ambulance for the CNT in Aragón.

185 Louis L J, 'The Victorian Council against War and Fascism: A Rejoinder', *Labour History*, 44 (1983).

The most prominent member of Spanish Relief in Melbourne and perhaps in all of Australia, was Nettie Palmer who, with her husband Vance, worked solidly throughout the civil war years for the Spanish Republic. Nettie Palmer's commitment was personal as well as political. The Palmers, with their daughter Aileen, had been in Catalonia when the *pronunciamiento* had taken place. Subsequently, Aileen returned to Spain with the first British Medical Aid Unit.

The Sydney group became the headquarters of the Australian Spanish Relief movement. There were branches and groups set up in each of the state capitals and in large and smaller provincial towns like Newcastle, Broken Hill and Ballarat but, as well, in small towns like Innisfail in Northern Queensland and Casino, a rail junction in northern NSW, where the Women's Auxiliary of the Australian Railway Workers Union fostered a refugee child in Spain.186

The Palmers were both informed first hand from their own, if rather brief, experience in Spain, and from Aileen's letters from the war zone. Through their writings, book reviews in Australian papers and their literary talks on national radio, Vance and Nettie were well known and widely respected. They were cultivated, liberal civil-libertarians and internationalists in the best sense of the term. From the time of their arrival back in Australia they lectured on the dangers of fascism in Europe and the importance of defending the Spanish Republic as a bulwark against fascism currently engulfing Europe. Their self-appointed mission of explaining the Republican side of the war task of was not always plain sailing. For example, when Vance gave a series of lectures, billed as 'The war of fascism against democracy' on his return to Melbourne, a member of Catholic clergy in the audience reported that Palmer's 'studied pose was that of the quiet cultured observer' but when he began 'debunking the idea of red atrocities' and that 'he had walked all over Barcelona but seen no evidence of public disorder or of the ill-treatment of priests or nuns' and that at the end of his speech he raised his

---

186 *Northern Star* (Lismore), 11 Mar 1938.

right arm with clenched fist he 'revealed himself as a crafty Soviet propagandist using the ploys of the Red Monster'.187

As President of Spanish Relief in Melbourne, Nettie organized delegations, addressed meetings, wrote publicity material and pamphlets and racked her brains for schemes to raise money. She travelled widely helping Republican support groups and shepherded travelling speakers from venue to venue. Frequently exhausted and occasionally disheartened, Nettie Palmer gave her full energy during the years of the Spanish civil war to work for Australian Spanish relief.

The composition of all these Spanish relief groups was fairly similar. Most of those involved were from communist and left-wing unions, the broad anti-fascist movement, together with a seeding of concerned Christians from the Peace Movement. The Spanish Relief Committees were sensitive to charges by their opponents that they were no more than 'communist fronts'. The president, the secretary, and the treasurer of the Sydney Committee emphatically denied the accusation in a letter to the editor of *Labor Call* on 21 October 1936. Spanish Relief, they claimed, was 'composed of an overwhelming majority of people who don't belong to Communist Party, but have put aside any question of party politics'. It was the case that many communists who were active in the movement, were concerned with the expanding role of fascism in Europe and the threat it posed to the security of the Soviet Union. None of this however detracts from the dedicated work that Australian communists undertook in the cause of Spanish Relief, nor invalidates the energy of the great many non-communists who worked beside Party members.

The Spanish Relief movement aimed to raise awareness of the civil war in the Australian community in order to bring pressure on the Australian government to abandon its policy of non-intervention and of course to raise money for aid to Republican war victims. The Relief organizations spread their message through Spanish Weeks with fiestas and exhibitions, and 'National Solidarity Days' that marked important dates on

---

187 CFJ, 31 Dec 1936.

the Republican calendar. Supporters took to the streets with trays of badges in the yellow, red and violet of the Republican flag, engraved with slogans like 'Defend Spanish Democracy' and 'Food for Spain'. The New Theatre in Melbourne and in Sydney produced Spanish plays. The traditional May Day processions included decorated trucks carrying messages about the war and the plight of refugees.

May Day Parade Sydney SRC Aid Spain float, 1937.

In Cessnock, on the New South Wales coalfields, a competition for schoolchildren offered a prize for the best drawn map of Spain.188 There were typical community fund-raising efforts with cake stalls, raffles and bazaars like the one at Connibere YMCA hall where the Oakleigh ALP Spanish Relief group sold homemade jam and sweets, and the Communist Party grocery table was judged the best-decorated stall.189 As in World

---

188 *Daily Telegraph*, 19 Jul 1938.

189 See news sheets and Minute Books of the ASRC, Thorne Collection, NBAANU.

War I, people donated food, knitted socks and balaclavas, and collected tinned milk and meat which was transported free of charge by P & O with their ship calling at Marseille.190 A number of dramatic strategies were devised to capture public attention. Four women dressed in black with their faces covered by black veils 'paraded up and down' outside the Italian embassy in Bligh Street, Sydney in early December 1937. Their banner carried the message, 'We mourn for the Spanish children killed by Italian Fascist bombs'. The police took their names and moved the women on; the protest caught the eye of a great many Sydney Christmas shoppers, and a photograph with a report appeared prominently in the next morning's papers.191 In the May Day procession in 1938, as part of a strategy of attracting attention to the beneficiaries of the international arms ban by amusing the spectators, a truck blaring Spanish music carried a row of dancing dictators, carefully accompanied on the foot path by fund raisers with donation buckets.

May Day Procession Sydney, 1 May 1938.

---

190 *Spanish Relief Committee News Bulletin*, No 4 (Jan 1939).

191 *Daily Telegraph*, 2 Dec 1937.

They were, left to right, Mussolini, Mosley (in top hat) Hitler with the signature moustache, Daladier in natty three piece suit and a most un-Franco-like figure representing the in-real-life portly General Franco. The banner proclaimed 'Demand the Lifting of the Arms Embargo. Help Suffering Spain'.

The combined Spanish Aid groups sponsored speakers, or shared foreign visitors on national tours. Dr Madeleine Ekenburg, on a world speaking tour from a non-partisan group aiding women and children in Spain, visited Victoria and New South Wales in mid-1937; and Miss Anne Caton from the Duchess of Atholl's National Joint Committee for Spanish Relief made a tour in April 1938.192 The Australian group, the National Joint Committee for Spanish Relief, adopted the British group's title and objective 'to relieve distress and suffering among non-combatants, especially children and irrespective of race, creed or politics'. The non-partisan message attracted a number of distinguished Protestant clergy such as the Anglican Bishop of Bendigo and high profile jurists and business people who responded to the Duchess of Atholl's graphic descriptions of the plight of Spanish refugee children and her urging Australians to commit a few shillings regularly to sponsor a refugee family or a single child.193 This message was underlined several months later by an appeal from Esme Odgers, a Sydney woman who initially had travelled to Spain with her partner Sam Aarons who joined the international Brigade. She volunteered in a children's colony in Catalonia, providing refuge for children of families displaced in wartime. The call for aid to ease the wartime plight of Spanish children evoked responses across the social landscape. In Northern New South Wales, in the small town of Casino, the Women's auxiliary of the Railway Workers Union sponsored a Spanish child from late 1937 and by January 1938 members of the central Victorian committees of Spanish Relief were jointly sponsoring a six-year-old refugee, and in the wealthy

----

192 *Daily Telegraph*, 20 Jul 1937.

193 *Daily Telegraph*, 13 May 1938; 13 Jun 1938.

eastern suburbs in Melbourne a Spanish relief group had accepted responsibility for another child. Most of these children were living in the colony at Puigcerdá where Esme Odgers was stationed.194

In return for their funds, sponsoring foster parents received exquisitely penned letters decorated with beautiful drawings by the children depicting the hardships of their wartime lives.195

The return of Australian volunteers were occasions for public meetings and press publicity. Mary Lowson, the leader of the Australian nurses' group in Spain, carried out a highly effective tour through the Australian states and New Zealand at the end of September 1937 and the three other nurses were warmly welcomed home: Agnes Hodgson returned in February 1938 and May McFarlane and Una Wilson arrived back together in January 1939.196 There were also welcome rallies for returning International Brigaders who returned after the withdrawal of the International Brigade in October 1938. They addressed rallies at each of their Australian ports of call and spoke about their first-hand experiences of the war and its horrors. A number of contemporaries of this time vividly recollected the seaman Dick Whateley speaking at work site rallies. Shell-shocked and frail, Whateley spoke haltingly but with great emotion about Spain and the need for Australian unionists to continue to defend Spanish Republicans forced to flee before Franco's Army but now abandoned in desperate

---

194 Joy Damousi, 'Humanitarianism and Child Refugee Sponsorship: The Spanish Civil War and the Global Campaign of Esme Odgers', *Journal of Women's History*, Vol 32 No 1 (Spring 2020): 111-134.

195 The Saffin Collection, La Trobe Library, Melbourne, contains a number of these decorated children's' letters sent to Australian sponsors.

196 *Daily Telegraph*, 12 Oct 1937.

conditions in refugee camps in Southern France.197

A great many films about the civil war were shown by the Spanish Relief Committees, or lent to community and local groups. Usually, at the conclusion of viewings a collection was taken up for Spanish relief. The dramatic film, *The Defence of Madrid*, drew enormous audiences. The Spanish Aid movement had received serendipitous publicity when the film was banned by the Commonwealth Film Censorship Board. Sections of film dealing with child victims of aerial bombardment had been declared too gory for public screenings in Australia. The censored version was shown to packed houses: in Melbourne people were turned away at the doors and £100 was raised in a single collection.198 During the Czech crisis at the end of 1938 the film *Non-Intervention*, which documented the role of Italians in Franco's army, was withheld initially by the Australian censor on the grounds that an Australian screening could 'complicate international relations'. This banning, too, produced fortunate publicity and lucrative returns at subsequent screenings.

In its informational role the Spanish Relief Committee published news bulletins and information sheets. The pamphlets, *Australians in Spain*, *The Spanish People Present Their Case*, and *Vivid Pen Portraits: Australian Nurses Present Their Case*, which Nettie Palmer produced, were fairly widely distributed. In addition, the Sydney group put out several news-sheets which were based on information supplied from the Overseas Service of the Republican Ministry of Information. On a number of occasions Phil Thorne wrote to Constancia de la Mora, the head of the Overseas Service, about the difficulties of keeping up with the Spanish news at such a distance, begging for more up to date information.

From diverse sources, the Australian Spanish Relief Committees provided information on the war and commented on reports and policy on Spain in the papers. In their literature, the

---

197 A number of interviewees in the research for this book recalled the impact of these returned international volunteers as told in the stories from their parents' generation.

198 *Daily Telegraph*, 12 Jun 1937; 16 Oct 1937.

Spanish Republic was presented as a united and democratic government under siege from Franco and his foreign fascist supporters. The only report of any internal dissension within the Republic was a brief explanation of May Days street fighting in 1937, which was described as the work of 'Spanish Trotskyist agents of Fascism'. According to the report, 'a large conspiracy of espionage' against the Popular Front by the POUM had been unearthed. The latter were in 'contact with foreign elements, some belonging to the Gestapo and others to international Trotskyists'. The POUM newspaper, *Batalla,* was reported to have been published in Burgos. These singular tendentious reports of internal Republican disturbances sank without a ripple in uniformly upbeat reports about Republican health, morale and unified leadership.

In answering Catholic charges of suppression of the Church under the Republic, Spanish Aid in Australia denied that the Republic was anti-religious or anti-Church. Instead, Franco's support from German and Italian fascists was emphasized. This approach evaded the uncomfortable contention that there may have been many Catholics who genuinely supported the Nationalists because they had rejected the Republic in the earlier years. The Australian Republican supporters' analysis was in the same mode as that adopted by their Australian Catholic opponents in which the Republican 'Reds' were entirely at the beck and call of Moscow and the catastrophic bombing of Guernica by German and Italian planes was ignored as was carefully avoided any evidence of the existence of Spanish Catholics and non-communist who favoured the Republican side. Both pro-Republicans and pro-Nationalists in Australia adopted different versions of a 'single struggle thesis'. Though neither was adequate, the perspectives of each fitted the local frameworks which conditioned their separate views of foreign affairs, and the place of the Spanish civil war within the larger picture.

Despite the assiduous efforts of Australians in the Spanish Relief movement throughout the states, the Australian government remained firmly committed to non-intervention. The Prime Minister and the cabinet rejected all delegations that were demanding a lifting of the arms embargo on Spain.

Similarly unsuccessful were requests for condemnation of the bombing of Spanish Republican civilians. All attempts to interest the government and its primary producers in exports of Australian wheat on credit to Spain produced a blank. Despite constant rebuffs, Spanish Relief Committee members wrote to the papers and their local members, keeping up a barrage of correspondence with the Prime Minister and the cabinet. All was to no avail. Conservative Australian governments had always followed Britain's lead in European affairs, and the specific rights and wrongs of a war in Spain were unlikely to alter the pattern.

According to the careful accounts kept by the committees, a total of £17,115 was raised in Australia for Spanish Republican relief, of which £4,000 was officially contributed by unions. The amount was not large. Given the obstacles to fund-raising in Australia for the Spanish civil war, the money represented the effort of a small number of committed and hard-working Australians, and was put to good use. It provided the fares to Spain of Agnes Hodgson and the other Australian nurses, along with seven ambulances and the despatch to Spain of some £10,000 worth of food and medical supplies.

With the capitulation of the Republic in March 1939, the Spanish Relief movement turned its efforts to assist Spanish refugees in the camps in southern France. However, with the conflict in Spain decisively ended and a European war imminent, it was difficult to raise community interest. Calls to sponsor Spanish immigration to Australia went unanswered. The Australian trade union movement, openly in favour of the Republic since 1937, was cool on the matter of refugee migration. The NSW Trade Union Council expressed concern that Spanish refugees would increase competition for jobs among unemployed Australian unionists. Similar doubts were aired during the fourth section of the Australian Council of Trades Unions Congress in June 1939. In any event, the matter never arose as the Australian government remained emphatically opposed to the Australian immigration of Spanish refugees or their children.

The defeat of the Spanish Republic was a heavy blow to those who had worked for Spanish Relief in Australia. In a letter to Constancia de la Mora in mid-1939, Phil Thorne described his shock at the news that Barcelona had fallen, and 50 years later he declared that the Spanish civil war had made him 'sadder and wiser in the ways of the politics of fascism'. Nettie Palmer's assessment of the role of the Spanish Aid movement in Australia is telling. Of it, she said that while those that worked for the Spanish Republic 'were few and not powerful and we seemed often to be shouting against the wind, it was a brave chapter in Australian history and one about which we all should know'.

Nettie's statement graces the memorial to the Australian International Brigaders in Lennox gardens, beside Lake Burley Griffin in the Australian national capital, Canberra. The organizing committee comprised Len Fox, Amirah Inglis, Netta Burns and Judith Keene and the memorial was unveiled in December 1993 by Lloyd Edmonds, the last surviving Australian volunteer in the International Brigades. The Spanish ambassador to Australia, whose father had been a Republican pilot during the civil war, planted a row of olive trees in remembrance of that past time, so long-gone, but never forgotten.

The Last Mile to Huesca

Part Two

The Diary of Agnes Hodgson

Agnes in the operating theatre at Poleñino.

24.10.36—Sydney

Left Sydney per SS *Oronsay*. Weather fine and warm, a light breeze blowing. A large gathering of workers' organizations down on the wharf to see us off, some sang and cheered as the steamer drew away from the wharf. When the ship was well under way, we adjourned to the cabin to arrange our belongings. After lunch we asked the assistant purser to change our cabin. Polite refusal advised to go to the Melbourne office—this we propose doing. All went to bed and slept well.

25.10.36

Up in time for breakfast, weather cold and drizzling. Spent most of the day writing and reading, sitting on deck.

26.10.36—Melbourne

Arrived in Melbourne at 8 a.m. Miss Helen Baillie, Miss Alexander, Mrs Vance Palmer, Mr Howell and others met us and were all very kind.199 Mrs Vance Palmer told us something about the unit already in Spain. Had snapshots taken and were asked what medical supplies we need most. Miss Helen Baillie had telephoned the Alfred Hospital and sent a notice there. I left the ship at 9.20 a.m. thereby missing the reporters. It was not

---

199 Members of the Victorian Spanish Relief Committee. Helen Baillie previously had been secretary to the Abyssinian Relief Committee, in L J Louis, 'The Victorian Council Against War and Fascism: A Rejoinder', Labour History, 44, (1983). Vance and Nettle Palmer had been living in Catalonia at the outbreak of the Spanish Civil War. Their eldest daughter, Aileen, was with the first Medical Aid Unit that went to Spain in August 1936, in Nettie Palmer, Fourteen Years, (Brisbane, University of Queensland Press, 1948), pp 213-227; and Judith Keene, 'A Spanish Springtime: Aileen Palmer and the Spanish Civil War', *Labour History*, 52, (1987). Arthur and Margaret Howells travelled to Spain in October 1938, in A F Howells, *We Went to Spain*, (Melbourne, Spanish Relief Committee, 1938) and *Against the Stream, The Memoirs of a Philosophical Anarchist, 1927-1939*, (Melbourne, Hyland House, 1983).

expected they would come then. I spent a busy day shopping, seeing friends and relatives. I called at the Herald Office and Mr Jenkins, the magazines' editor, invited me to send him contributions of interesting news.

In the afternoon I went to the Alfred Hospital and saw Sister Rowe—the matron being in bed with bronchitis. It had not been made clear to them that I was going with the unit and nothing could be arranged just then. Apart from her interest in our going, had she been well, Miss Wilson could not have taken an active part owing to her position as Matron-in-Chief of the Returned Army Nurses. The notice of our meeting had been put on the board, and several nurses promised to attend the meeting. The chief dispenser whom I had hoped to see there has now left. Through him I hoped to be able to get supplies at wholesale prices.

8 p.m. Attended meeting in the Old Temperance Hall, Russell Street—the hall was three quarters full but our reception was most enthusiastic. The speakers were—the Chairman, the Secretary, Miss Helen Baillie, Dr Cantor, Sisters Lowson and Wilson, Mrs Vance Palmer, Reverend Farnham Maynard,[200] Mr Brian Fitzpatrick,[201] Mr H Payne.[202] An appeal for funds was

---

200 An Anglican Minister at St Peter's, Eastern Hill, Victoria, Farnham Maynard had urged the Church to come to terms with contemporary movements like fascism and communism in, Daily Telegraph, 9 Oct 1936, p 2.

201 An independent left-wing intellectual, Brian Fitzpatrick was a founder of the Australian Council for Civil Liberties in, Don Watson, *Brian Fitzpatrick: A Radical Life*, (Melbourne, Hale & Iremonger, 1979).

202 Herbert Payne, a member of the Victorian Committee Against War and Fascism had vigorously supported League of Nations sanctions against Italy in the Abyssinian crisis. As a result, he was expelled from the Labor Party and dismissed from the executive of the Victorian Trades Hall Council, in line with ALP and ACTU policy in, L.J. Louis, 'The Victorian Council Against War and Fascism: A Rejoinder'.

made by Mrs McIntevy. The chairman introduced us, then Miss Helen Baillie as secretary read the report of the committee's activities: of how the committee had been formed at short notice and the arrangements made for the meeting to welcome us and appeal for funds. Sisters Lowson and Wilson replied on our behalf, speaking well both in subject matter and delivery. Mrs Vance Palmer then spoke on the British Medical Aid Unit—she had been at the farewell given to it in London. She told of the work being done in Spain by the British Medical Aid Unit, talked a little of Barcelona; assured the audience that even if the war was over by the time our ship arrived in Toulon, there would plenty of work for us to do among the refugees in France. People need not worry about that. Mrs McIntevy appealed for funds and £28 was collected. Mr Brian Fitzpatrick spoke on the political situation in Spain, and of the life and customs in Spain, particularly in Catalonia. Dr Cantor spoke of nursing in time of war and appealed for equipment.

27.10.36

More farewells, private, and back to the ship. Weather wet and uncertain. Only a small but enthusiastic gathering to farewell us. Packages of drugs, dressings, and of serum worth £10 were brought on board and handed to Sister Lowson and an inventory made of them. Sailed from Melbourne at 5 p.m.

28.10.36

Raining and very cold, the ship rolling a bit. Began to study Spanish, left the books on a chair during luncheon and can now find no trace of my Spanish grammar book, or a library book. Feeling sick because of it. All the sisters spent much time in our cabin.

29.10.36—Adelaide

Arrived at Adelaide. Met by Mr Cavanagh. We were driven up to Adelaide city. 10.30 a.m. Received by Lord Mayor and Acting Lady Mayoress (Mr Cain welcomed us personally, quite apart from any party politics.) All members of the unit responded.

Sisters Lowson and Wilson spoke very well—other two murmured their thanks and appreciation.

Miss Elizabeth George of the *Adelaide Advertiser* invited me to send her contributions for her column.

12.30 p.m. Meeting at Rechabite Hall. Mr Cavanagh and others on the platform spoke of the difficulties they had met endeavouring to organize an appeal, to get press advertisement for the meeting, and for equipment. They spoke of the aims and objects of the unit as going from the workers of Australia to the Spanish workers. Mention was made that so great was the lack of supplies that the Spanish Loyalists had to shoot some of their severely wounded having no other means of alleviating their sufferings. The four nurses autographed copies of *World Peace* which then sold for double the usual price. Called on Dr Duguid, as suggested by Miss Baillie, taken driving round Lofty Ranges of Unley and Breezy Point. Saw Adelaide through a *camera oscura* and returned to the ship via Bay Road.

People all very kind. One woman told us she did not care if we never put on a bandage and gave the impression that if she found a wounded rebel she would twist the knife. That attitude I will not tolerate. Day windy and cool, the ship sailed later than scheduled at 6 p.m. We all retired early to bed.

30.10.36

Wilson still seedy; I wrote, studied Spanish, played games and danced. The weather is improving.

2.11.36—Fremantle

Arrived at Fremantle and were met by members of the Movement against War and Fascism, and interviewed by reporters. Went up to Perth with Bill and Mione Robertson. 12 noon went to luncheon given us by the Women's Committee against War and Fascism. I sat next to Mrs Susannah Pritchard (Throstle)203 and found her very attractive. Joined in light

---

203 Katherine Susannah Prichard (Throssell), a leading literary figure and founding member of the Communist Party of Australia

conversation. Mrs Throstle said if we encountered Señor Aligos Gomes in Spain to convey her greetings. Mrs Throstle offered us Insectiban for our future comfort in Spain.

1 p.m. Attended a meeting in Theosophists Hall, where members of various organisations were present. The chairwoman introduced us in a moving fashion. Sister Lowson explained how our mission came into being and the purpose for which we were being sent to Spain. An excellent and telling speech. Sister Wilson also spoke a few words. Other speakers painted lurid pictures of atrocities committed in Spain and enumerated the difficulties we would have to face. Mr Greville, a member of the ALP Peace Organisation, spoke of wartime nursing conditions and the horrors of war. Mr Ralph Gibson204 spoke wishing us success in our mission. Other speakers and well-wishers were Mr Roberts, Movement Against War and Fascism; Mrs Robinson, Society of Friends; Mrs Mason, President of the Women's Labour Organisation; Mr J Lindsay, Sec. of the Consultative Council of World Peace; Miss Houten, Sec. of the Parents and Citizens Association; Mrs J Brydon and Miss Anderson, members of the ATNA.205 We were all particularly pleased by the presence of these last two women and also with the flowers received by Sister Macfarlane from the ATNA as it is the only recognition either official or unofficial we have received from nurses, apart from stray members of the profession. At the close of the meeting a collection was taken and we autographed copies of *World Peace* to bring in extra money. We were all given bouquets of flowers and holding same were photographed for one of the daily papers.

(CPA), worked tirelessly for the Spanish Republican cause. See Ric Throssell, *Wild Weeds and Wildflowers. The Life and Letters of Katharine Susannah Prichard,* (Sydney, Angus and Robertson, 1975), pp 81-82.

204 Ralph Gibson had recently returned to Melbourne from the World Peace Congress in Brussels. See his *The People Stand Up,* (Melbourne, Red Rooster Press, 1983), pp 155-169.

205 Australian Trained Nurses' Association.

The kindness shown to us by all those women was very moving. Some of them came down to the ship with us and stayed until we sailed. Received letters and telegrams from family and friends, among whom Mr Thorne and Mr Lloyd Ross.206

3.11.36

All four inoculated with TAB. Reaction immediate *ma non troppo severa*.207 Studied Spanish in the a.m. and slept between lunch and tea. Studied again and danced at a Carnival Dance in the evening. Enjoyed myself immensely. By dancing I was able to make the acquaintance of more passengers.

4.11.36

Feeling rather sick; arm aching and feverish. Sister Lowson is the worst of us. Not sleeping too well.

5.11.36

Feeling better; played in some tournament games; won deck quoits mixed first round and quoit tennis first round; beaten in bucket quoits. Studied Spanish.

6.11.36-10.11.36

Continued to study Spanish in a.m. Played tournament games and attended at various ship functions—dances, cinema, etc. Other three more severely affected by the second inoculation. I had a minor dissension with Lowson re going ashore at Naples. She fears a hostile demonstration there and since I mentioned my friend belongs to some Italian society, which society I believe is purely cultural in purpose, Lowson suspects my friend and is unwilling for me to see her. Knowing my friend I think it is

---

206 Phil Thorne was the Secretary of the New South Wales Spanish Relief Committee; Lloyd Ross who had vouchsafed for Agnes's skills and serious commitment to Republican Spain, was General Secretary of the Australian Railways' Union and active in the Spanish Aid movement in Sydney.

207 'mine not too severe'.

absurd, but expressed my willingness to abide by her decision. If my friend comes to Naples to see me, of which there is only a faint chance, I shall see her even if only onboard ship. The misunderstanding is making Lowson sick. I gave her my promise but I still regard the whole thing as exaggerated and her caution premature.

11.11.36—Colombo

Arrived at Colombo. All four joined a party from the ship touring Colombo by bus. We were driven around the city past native and European quarters, barracks and sports grounds, new Town Hall, and Victoria Park to the Cinnamon gardens. We walked there, lovely and cool under the trees. Banyan trees, cinnamon, bread trees, cocoa and lots of exotic tropical flowers and fruits. Then we were driven to Mount Lavinia had a drink and sat on the terrace of the hotel overlooking the sea. Very pretty there and regretted having no time to bathe. Returning from Mount Lavinia the bus ran into and fatally injured an old Indian man. Our bus took the man to hospital while we were transferred to another bus. Returned to the city and taken by two people to their restaurant. We had lunch there—quiet lunch, though the ambience not too savoury. After lunch a little shopping. As I was not feeling very well I left the others and returned to ship. They presented a letter of introduction to a woman doctor there and were entertained by her and her friends until midnight. I did not go ashore but tried to keep cool on the ship—the sister of the ship's purser dined at our table and then introduced me to the chief steward. We sat in his cabin and listened to War Comrades' Armistice dinner speeches. One of the young pursers spoke exceedingly well against war and keeping up war toleration by these anniversaries. Was rather worried by the late return of the others feeling I had left them too casually but the concern was unnecessary and unwarranted. And so off to sea at 1 a.m.

12.11.36-16.11.36

Slept a good part of the day. Sports competitions began again. I entered only for deck tennis and ping pong. Studying Spanish and French as much or as hard as I can. Ship life continues amusing—dances, cinema, shows etc.

17.11.36

Arrived at Aden. All went ashore and walked around the town—Macfarlane and self-photographing the rest in turn. Lowson changed Indian money donated at Colombo. We were pestered by amusing small imps for baksheesh, while walking round the shops. An army officer drove us to the post office in his car, then we walked back to the Crescent Hotel to drink beer. Aden attracts me always with its grim rocks clear cut against the sky. It's a brave place and the inhabitants please me more than the Cingalese of Colombo. They laugh more.

Left Aden—fancy dress ball at night. All four dressed up: Lowson as Chinese Flower girl, Wilson as Shakespeare's Miranda, Macfarlane as Peter Pan and myself as the Gay Caballero—more colourful than accurate. Wilson was very much admired and we all enjoyed the dance and appreciated the company's effort to entertain us.

21.11.36

Sports and diversions continuing. I won the tennis singles again and chose [photographic] film for my prizes. Weather extremely hot in the Red Sea, very glad of cool drinks. Entered the Suez Canal—were delayed while other ships had the right of way. Very interesting watching the work by the canal, camels feeding—an Italian troop ship passed but the troops didn't look very happy. Weather becoming cooler.

21.11.36—Port Said

9 p.m. Arrived at Port Said. As I have a cold I did not go ashore. At that hour there wasn't much to see and I did not want to spend money.

The other three went ashore, but stayed only a short time because they were so pestered by the Arabs and it was late and dark. Wilson bought herself a fez and was highly delighted. They had their fortunes told. I watched from the ship the lights of Simon Artz and Port Said; the pontoon bridge moved out to the ship and the troops came aboard and overran the decks and sitting-rooms. Lowson received letters from Sydney and France—the latter written by John Fisher208 who had written on spec. He promises to do all he can for us, bids us welcome and told something of the unit already there, and the shortage of equipment. He doesn't anticipate we'll have much difficulty getting to Spain. Some friends of mine on board are becoming very anxious and are trying to persuade me not to go.

Sailed from Port Said—weather completely changed. Rough sea, cold and windy, Wilson and I went to church. Service at sea always impresses me.

23.11.36

Passing close to Crete—lovely hilly or mountainous wooded coastline with small villages dotted here and there. The sea is grey and smooth again, fine rain came drizzling down, but the sun has come out. The journey nears its end and Europe shows us some of its loveliness, may it be preserved from wanton destruction.

24.11.36

Passed through the straits of Messina. Reggio and Messina were well lit up—couldn't see Etna. Stromboli at 10 p.m. was sending up the odd sparks and small flames. We danced.

25.11.36—Naples

A sad situation. I was invited the day previously to go ashore for lunch if the host was able to get away. Until it was decided, and until we reached Naples and could know what our reception was to be, and from previous experience of discussing hypothetical plans, I decided to say nothing to the others. Unfortunately I did

---

208 An Australian journalist and son of the Labor Prime Minister Andrew Fisher, John Fisher had travelled to Europe with Egon Kisch in Feb 1935. Until the end of 1937, when he returned to Australia, Fisher acted as an unofficial Australian representative on the Committee for Spanish Relief in London, while travelling widely in Republican Spain reporting on the war.

not know until after breakfast that this other plan was definitely possible. As soon as I knew I went in search of Lowson and saw her already on shore getting into the bus. She shouted to me, was I coming, and I answered no. I regretted very much that the announcement should come like that as I would have preferred her blessing.

Having been to Pompeii before I did not want to go again and in such a large party. Italy means so much to me—I knew as the others could not be expected to understand that I would not enjoy the Pompeii trip. In reality I would have preferred to go ashore alone, but going in the company of one of the ship's officers I welcomed the protection that fact gave me.

There was no sign at all of any antipathy or hostile feeling to us. I was taken for an Italian when asking any questions and the people as usual could not have been kinder. This meant a lot to me convinced me that I knew my Italians that as private citizens *we* would receive all courtesy. And Mussolini himself *arrived* in Naples that day. So much for their concern about us. Also, the fact that being women was protection in itself among Italians. Of course, had we made ourselves objectionable things might have been otherwise. It is pointlessly rude to declare in a loud voice one's disapproval of a race and its leader. I regret that active pacifists are so belligerent. I went to eat chocolate cakes at Caflisch's in Via Roma, drank a vermouth and watched the people.

We drove in a *carrozza* from San Ferroira to the consulate in Santa Lucia and I was back again in 1933. We went by train up the Nomera to San Martina and lunched at the Meranapoli sitting out on the terrace in the sun. We ate *vermicelli alle vongole, scaloppa alla marsala, mozzarella bagnola*, coffee (expresso) and drank a bottle of Capri wine. After-effect of Capri wine not too good, shan't drink it away from Capri again. Did not have time to go over San Martino—returned to Naples and bought a cake of *sapone di sita* and so back to the ship and the righteous anger of our leader. But I couldn't have enjoyed my day better and for that reason I don't regret it.

Depressed by the attitude taken and further depressed that Lowson was really suffering. She refused to discuss it with me and stated that she knew when she was beaten. *Dio Santo che miseria.*209 Received postcard from Mabel who disapproves of the mission, blast her.

26.11.36

Packing and preparing for disembarkation.

27.11.36

Arrived at Toulon—weather cold and grey—rained later. Four men came aboard and inquired for us. They were the Acting Deputy and Secretary of the Communist Party and two others members of other Popular Front organizations. None of them spoke English but we trustingly went ashore with them, rather disconcerted that no one was really certain of our arrival. One of them spoke Italian and asked me to explain to the others who he was. He then demanded to know our plans. Our luggage was deposited in various parts of the Douane. We all ran hither and thither and nobody would listen to me. Lowson searched for someone speaking English. The Orient agent obliged but for a long time it didn't get us any further. Our bags were passed and then it all had to be explained again—which contained equipment—they had to go in bond to Marseille. Our anxious enquiries about Egon Kisch elicited no information—unknown to these people.210 Finally, the luggage departed for the station, and we were taken by taxi to a communist restaurant.

---

209 'Holy God what misery.'

210 Egon Kisch, a Czech writer and member of the German Communist Party in exile, had been invited in November 1934 to address the Australian Congress Against War and Fascism in Melbourne. The Australian government, led by J A Lyons, declared Kisch a prohibited immigrant, and after administering a language test in Gaelic, prepared to deport him. An Egon Kisch Defence Committee was formed; and after several months of legal battles, the High Court ordered Kisch's release. See Egon Kisch, *Australian Landfall*, 2nd ed, (London, Macmillan, 1969); and K. Slater, 'Egon Kisch: a Biographical Study', *Labour History*, 36, (1979).

We drank coffee, rather the others did, I drank a vermouth—feeling the need of some stimulant amid such utter confusion and babble of tongues. There we told our story as best we could, Lowson and Macfarlane were welcomed as communists. I agreed to a statement written by M saying that I was not a communist, having as yet no precise politics, that I am against war, and sympathize with the Spanish government in their struggle. From there we were taken to the communist headquarters on rue Jean Jaures and met several of their comrades who were all very nice. We were photographed leaving the restaurant. They telephoned then to Marseille to an M Cristofol to find out what we should do and when we should leave for Marseille. It was decided we should stay the night at Toulon and then go to Marseille in the morning.

We were then taken for an aperitif by the Anti-War and Fascism Secretary, and back to the restaurant to lunch. We ate a very excellent lunch. We took rooms at the Mirabeau Hotel (Grand) and went to meet the Secretary of the Movement Against War and Fascism at home in his café. There we met other enthusiasts and the women's representative of *Contre la Guerre et Fascisme*. She asked us would we convey a packet of woollies to Spain for her. Again, we went walking in the rain, this time round the front by the sea to Worms & Co, Orient Agent. We left our political friends below while we were received by the agent, who wanted to know where we were going, etc. Lowson gave his assistant an article to translate which he very kindly did—he had offered earlier to translate for her, but apparently had not expected an article. We spent some time there and they were all very kind. By this time, we were slight less confused. I was able to understand or follow the conversation in French and even to speak a little.

After leaving the agents, we went around to the post office, having gathered our political friends we went forth into the rain. At the post office we stood long while Lowson was sending a cable and having much difficulty, and worry about the price. Alas I couldn't, and she wouldn't, let me help her much.

I had, as politely as I could, requested that we be allowed to return to the hotel to rest but the Women's Anti-War and

Fascism member requested us to take tea with her. When I refused politely, she searched for a post office official who knew some English and the request was duly made in English—there was nothing for it but to accept. We were then taken to a fashionable patisserie where we drank tea and ate rich cakes.

It was such *ambiente di alta classe* that we didn't dare to smoke among those women.*211* There we sat, nodding on our chairs and often quite silent until it was time to go to the reception arranged for us and for 15 French volunteers for service in Spain. It was a purely communist meeting, the people looked so fervent and excited I was a little afraid. We were greeted heartily and the communist salute was given. I felt it was almost more than I could bear. Lowson was happy, but *noi altre stavamo sbalordite*.212

Then we were officially welcomed. My speech was read out by the wife of the Anti-War and Fascism man. Lowson's translated speech, telling of how the movement was formed, was also read out and cheered lustily. Then the volunteers were cheered and one of them began to speak—he was interrupted by one of the audience who seemed intoxicated by something. Anyway, he wanted to speak, much to the consternation of the officials—they didn't dare to put him out so had to let him speak for a couple of minutes, then they clapped him ferociously and rather taken aback and chagrined, he sat down. A volunteer then made a brief speech after which the 'Internationale' and some other songs were sung and the salute given. I felt most uncomfortable and ready to run away from it all. We left shortly afterwards and went to the station to collect our night attire. While M and I were putting the luggage in the *depósito*, the other three thought themselves deserted, and returned to the hotel. Lowson and Wilson had gone out to buy fruit when I returned. We decided to eat at the restaurant again (they won't let us pay for anything). We had soup and veal cutlets and chip potatoes plus a lovely

---

211 *ambiente di alta classe:* 'high class surroundings'

212 'we others were disoriented.'

salad. And so to bed.

28.11.36

Met communist and anti-fascist members at the café, and were escorted to the station. Comments were made on my not giving the Left salute, and protests that it is the salute of the international democrats. Much talking at the station and laughing. Lowson was angry with me. I was angry too finding it all a little too much and was near chucking the whole business. Information is so difficult to get and people are ready to rush us to Spain, almost without a by your leave. M accompanied us to Marseille and took us to 82 rue Cerbère—headquarters of the Communist Party.

We were taken to a private apartment for lunch great chattering young things mostly members of the young Communist Party of whom there were over 4000 in Marseille; an amusing noisy party. Many questions asked about politics in Australia; again the chief means of conversation was Italian—two of the lads spoke a little English. After lunch we were taken to Cooks—money there received a letter from Isabel. Went in search of the English Consul but the office was closed; enjoyed walking alone anyway. Tension is still rather high. Lodged in Hôtel de la Poste—all four in one room. Taken to a big reception at Cinéma de Saint-Lazare—M Cristofol introduced us.

Lowson spoke in English and it was translated afterwards. After the meeting I was told I should have spoken in Italian as so many people there understood Italian—but it was better t'other way. Communist members and members of the Movement Against War and Fascism were present.

The Henri Barbusse Society (Movement Against War and Fascism) has 1,000,000 members, 10,000 in Marseille, of which 3,000 are women. Women are very energetic and fervent. After the meeting drank a vermouth then taken to dine—excellent dinner and all very pleasant. After, we were taken to a dance given by the Women's Organization Against War and Fascism. Songs, the 'Internationale' and 'Marseillaise' were sung; children in costume sang Soviet songs. Lowson was presented with a magnificent bouquet of flowers—we were rather tired and not really amused by the dance—though appreciating their intentions. At midnight returned to hotel and so to bed.

29.11.36

Met at 10 a.m. by various members of the Marseille fraternity—snapshot taken outside our hotel. Talked to a singer and her husband and heard tales of their difficulties in South America—how she had sung one night in favour of the families of victims of a minor revolution and she had escaped arrest by going to the house of the Spanish Consul. He slipped them off to Spain the next day. She had changed her name eight times, because of her communist sympathies. We walked about Marseille after hanging about the committee rooms. We went down to the old port, crossed over the water in a rowing boat to a restaurant in the sun and ate a good meal slowly. Returned to the hotel, rested then went to meet more people at a café by the water. Drank vermouth and answered many questions about Australia. Walked again up and down rue Cerbère. Then ate at a small restaurant. Hunger of all four amazing, ate spaghetti and pork and then delicious French cream; went back to the café where we met an Italian woman singer who studied at Bologna with Pinza and Toti del Monte and Zambilli. Talked there, then went to the Opera, *The Barber of Seville*. The Mayor presented his box to us—poor opera and a lot cut out—Basillo and Figaro were quite good. We were taken behind the scenes of the theatre by the director and at the end to meet the Mayor. Most amusing interlude. Returned to the hotel after the opera.

30.11.36

Went shopping and to Cooks for money and to the Spanish Consul who kept us waiting but was very nice and promised to let Barcelona know of our arrival. We were given a letter of safe conduct and passport visas. Wilson and I then went to the English Consulate where they were very nice to us and insisted we should call at the British Consulate in Barcelona. He promised that they would not like us, but that we must make ourselves and our whereabouts known to them.

Wilson and I then had lunch at a funny little restaurant, then shopped and wandered about—back to our hotel for an hour and then went to the committee rooms before going to the *hôtel de ville*. Hung about as usual till long after the time given for appointment. Finally, we were taken in and presented to the Mayor. I began my prepared speed in Italian—just as I was getting mixed with French and Italian, the Mayor, M Tasso, began a political discussion with our French companion. He was very nice and offered us a box at the theatre. Then we went buying medical equipment. Serum and anaesthetics, £15, then began at other pharmacies on sutures and needles. Had to leave the rest till next day.

Went to dine with the Secretary of the Women's Communist Party at her apartment—again ate well and despite language difficulty, mixture of Italian, French and Spanish, we got on very well. Then to the theatre; quite amusing as we had a box over the stage. I understood bits here and there—the juvenile lead sang several songs very well. And so to bed.

1.12.36

Went to Cooks. Lowson booked tickets to Port Bou, and settled the hotel bill. We went to Sphinx Farjest Pharmacie and bought equipment, instruments, cotton wool, gauze, rubber aprons, bandages, strapping sutures. All very exhausting—because we had no interpreter. Had an excellent cheap lunch at F's. Very windy day. Lowson and I went to the station uselessly, then to a pharmacy off rue Cerbère to spend the rest of the money. No interpreter—went back to our hotel and wrote letters. Posted a beret to Isabel and an air mail letter. Back to the pharmacy— ordered more anti-tetanus serum, anti-gangrene, haemostatic serum, anti-phlogiston, Epsom salts, iodine, lysol and other disinfectants. Mlle Marcelle Dupont collected us and took us to the committee rooms. We three waited downstairs while Lowson talked. Then went to a café for a vermouth. Ate early then Mlle Dupont collected us and took us to café where her committee were working with woollen clothes. It was the same café headquarters as of the Anarchist Party. Stayed only a few minutes, returned to the hotel, collected grips and set off for the station. Entrained. A group came to see us off, very cold night.

Mlle Dupont brought us chocolates and fruit. We were the only passengers in a second class carriage for Port Bou. Settled down to sleep at once—I did not sleep until early hours but we were warm and comfortable. Moon shining; passports stamped at Cerbère and arrived at Port Bou at 5.30 a.m. After a little confusion we were interviewed by the man in the Militia Committee who talked Italian—Lowson showed the Consul's letter and a first class ticket was presented to us. We had to pay for our excess baggage—we had our carriage to ourselves. To save expense we did not have breakfast on the train—chocolates and mandarins consumed instead.

1.12.36—Barcelona

Arrived at Barcelona 9 a.m. *Mucha confusión*—went to the *Comité de Milicias* no one to meet us—showed our papers and demanded an escort to the Hotel Colón. A polite young man packed us complete with luggage into an omnibus and we drove to the Hotel Colón, the headquarters of the Communist Party.213 More confusion—Lowson found a man to talk English and he gave us the address of the British Medical Aid Unit at 407 Muntaner. So, complete with luggage we drove there and Lowson was happy to find Mr O'Donnell.214 We descended from the omnibus and went up to their flat—dividing luggage to be taken to a hotel and that to be left at BMAU's flat. Beautiful flat— previous owners having left the country. We were very well

213 The Hotel Colón was the headquarters of the PSUC (Partido Socialista Unificado de Cataluña, the Communist Party of Catalonia. See Chapter 2, see Footnote 24.

214 Hugh O'Donnell was an English communist organiser in Barcelona for the British Medical Aid Unit. Mary Lowson later relied heavily on his assistance in purchasing supplies from funds sent from the Spanish Relief movement in Australia. O'Donnell and the British Medical Aid Unit parted company in 1937 over differences with the disbursements of money and general dissatisfaction with O'Donnell's behaviour. See Jim Fyrth, *The Signal Was Spain: The Spanish Aid Movement 1936-39*, (London, Lawrence and Wishart, 1986), pp 57, 189; and conversations with May MacFarlane [Pennefather] Annandale, Sydney, Nov 1986.

received and stayed there talking for some time and were given tea. All very hungry and tired. Taken to the Strangers' Department to get permission to stay in Barcelona and stayed there waiting till 2 p.m.

[This entry appears at the end of the diary]

Arrival in Barcelona. First impression at the frontier was of khaki balaclavas and coats. Unshaven men carrying guns and wearing dirty white and black rope-soled sandals. Black of eye, dark skinned and bearded. Everything scrutinized - we realized that we were in a country at war. Luggage in the omnibus was taken to the Hotel Colón which was full of people, red banners and photos of Lenin and Stalin on the facade of the building. Hotel Colón was no place to leave our luggage, guards about and sandbags at the windows which were all smashed and marked with bullet holes. Drove to the unit's flat, Loutit and O'Donnell were there.215 Had tea. Una, May and self were left to hang over the balcony and view Barcelona while Mary told her tale - reported me as a fascist. Then to the Strangers' Department of the Socorro Rojo—an interminable wait—told to call again. Finally inter-viewed by Felice (?) a French communist and head of the SR who questioned me about my travels—how had I been able to afford to travel—what had I seen of fascism in Italy etc. At the Ramblas Café, where one met everyone, one was warned that this or that foreigner was unreliable. The British Unit ate in a nasty little café, bad cheap food but the waiter spoke English. Atmosphere of suspicion everywhere, among the foreigners at least.

---

215 Kenneth Sinclair-Loutit was the administrator of the first medical aid unit sent in August 1936, from London to Spain by the Spanish Medical Aid Committee. See his *Very Little Luggage*, https://spartacus-educational.com/TUloutit.htm; and 'The Largest Frying Pan in the World', in Phillip Toynbee, ed., *The Distant Drum, Reflections on the Spanish Civil War*, (London, Sidgwick and Jackson, 1976), pp 105-108.

2.12.36

Much waiting here in Spain because they are all so busy. I had lunch with Mr Loutit from BMAU. He took me to a Catalan restaurant where we ate well—but much garlic flavoured food. He drank wine, pouring it into his mouth out of a special Spanish vessel—very skilful proceeding. We talked a bit then went for coffee up on a hill, his chauffeur coming with us. Lovely view of hills and harbour. Sun setting—looked at destroyers and foreign sloops outside port—saw a seaplane arriving on the water. Returned to the British Medical Aid Unit's flat to await other colleagues. Had tea and met other members of BMAU down on leave—one played the piano and tuned his violin. Danced a little with Mr Loutit, dancing in gum-boots. I was very tired. John Fisher, an Australian journalist, arrived to find our whereabouts and Lowson arrived shortly afterwards. We went to the Hotel España where the Government have billeted us. Had a glorious bath. Mr O'Donnell introduced three British engineers of the party who are working here. The others did not want to eat again but as I did John Fisher asked me to dine with him at his Hotel Nouvel. Went for coffee to the Ramblas Café and met several journalists and interpreters. Stayed talking and waiting while John Fisher made enquiries, and so to bed.

3.12.36

Were taken for breakfast, cold coffee and croissants. There are shortages of milk, sugar and no butter to be had—all the best food being sent to the front. Then met Mr O'Donnell in the Plaza Cataluña in front of the Hotel Colón, with a big square fountain, peanut and sweet sellers and lots of pigeons. We had our photographs taken—a militia man was asked to be photographed with us.216 The photo is to be sent to Australia.

We were taken to the Strangers' Department to fill in forms. I was interviewed by Comrade Felice—I talked Italian with him. I was rather confused after trying to talk French, and was asked

---

216 This was the Australian, Jack 'Blue' Barry, whom Agnes had not met before. See Footnote 220.

how long I had spent in Europe before—how I had the money to travel, what were my impressions of Italy, and my reasons for coming to Spain.

Went to a miserable café for lunch—shortage of meat—food mainly spaghetti, potato, garlic and gravy. I had coffee at the Ramblas Café and met John Fisher, who invited me to meet him again in the evening. Returned to the hotel and washed some clothes and went back to the Strangers' Department. The others were interviewed and we waited a couple of hours.

Had a vermouth at the Ramblas Café and went back to the hotel. I listened in to a Spanish lesson given by Mrs Bates to two of the engineers.217 Went to dine and met Mr O'Donnell at a better café this time.

Ate and joined John Fisher at Ramblas café and met J Barry,218 who had been reported dead in a dramatic fashion, and Kitty,219 an American journalist, and several others.

---

217 Winifred Bates, wife of English novelist Ralph Bates, worked for the Republican Information Services and was a liaison officer for the British nurses in Spain, in Imperial War Museum, Dept. of Sound Recordings, 'British Involvement in the Spanish Civil War1936-1939', Winifred E. Sandford [Bates], Acc. No 00 0816/06.

218 Jack 'Blue' Barry, a seaman and a member of the Communist Party of Australia (CPA), had trained in Sydney at the Workers' Defence Corps gymnasium in Glebe, in preparation for what he saw as the imminent 'stoush' with fascism. In November 1936, he worked his way on a coal steamer to Europe in order to join the defenders of the Spanish Republic. He was wrongfully reported as having been killed and, after some language difficulties, joined up with the British XV Brigade. Around this time, he also made contact with the Australian nurses in Barcelona before leaving for the Madrid front where he was killed defending a machine gun position in the ferocious battle of Boadilla del Monte on 16 Dec 1936. See Nettie Palmer and Len Fox, *Australians in Spain*. (Sydney: Current Book Distributors, 1948), pp 11-12.

219 Kitty Bowler, a radical American journalist was drawn to Spain in order to support the Spanish Republic. In Barcelona, she met, and later married, Tom Wintringham, a member of the Communist Party of Great Britain and a journalist in Spain for the *Daily Worker*. In Spain he was moved to join the International Brigade, eventually becoming commander of the British International

Mary Lowson, May MacFarlane, journalist John Fisher, International Brigader Jack 'Blue' Barry, Aileen Palmer, Agnes Hodgson and Una Wilson. The Plaza de Cataluña was a favourite site for photographs of newly arrived foreign volunteers in Barcelona. 1937.

4.12.36

Had breakfast near the hotel. Missed the escort at the hotel, then went to the Strangers' Department and waited a couple of hours with no result. Evidently, we had gone to the wrong place—some mix up. Had lunch at another café; a little difficult with the lack of language but very cheap. Drank coffee and walked down the Ramblas to the Christopher Columbus monument and the port and so back to our hotel for a while. Went walking, I tried to lead the party back to the ex-Square of Mirrors—but only succeeded in leading them down narrow streets—and then to the Telegraph

Battalion. However, increasingly disenchanted with the CPGB. he stood down from his position. See Paul Preston, *We Saw Spain Die: Foreign Correspondents in the Spanish Civil War* (London: Constable,2009), pp 122-134; and Hugh Purcell, 'Kitty Bowler: The English Captain's Spy' *History Today* 62 (Feb 2012).

Office near the port. Back along the Ramblas where the birds were going to roost in the overhanging trees causing embarrassment to the promenaders.

Came on the cathedral—all ruined and barricaded—bought soap, looked at shops, things were fairly cheap. Lowson and Wilson decided to have tea at Jorba—a large shop run by the workers. The roof garden has a large fountain and aquarium beside its bar and café. MacFarlane and I kept on walking—went into a sweet shop and ate chocolate cakes—then went to the Ramblas Café and read the news. Much prominence is being given to King Edward's affairs. John Fisher, Belcher,220 Kitty the American journalist and others came in. We had the various political parties explained to us.221 The CNT and UGT are the main trade unions—a union of these two is aimed at.

Anarchists want each village autonomous under its separate anarchist leader, because if there is no central government there can be no wars made by the government and no interference with the liberty of the village. Not too clear, but hope in time to understand more the aims and objects of all these groups of people. Went to eat at a small restaurant and so early to bed.

---

220 Australian-born William Belcher, a Cambridge educated engineer, went to Spain with the first British Medical Aid Unit as a cinematographer but was injured in an accident on the journey. Later, when he returned to Barcelona, he was moved to join an anarchist militia, La Batallón de Muerte (Battalion of Death) which as part of the government's move to centralize the military effort was absorbed into the Republican army. He served in Tardienta and Belchite, eventually being appointed to the Brigade Staff. In early 1938, Belcher was arrested in Barcelona. After five weeks in prison he was released through the efforts of the British Consul who oversaw his departure for Marseilles on *HMS Devonshire*. Belcher always suspected that O'Donnell was responsible for his misfortune. Fyrth, *The Signal Was Spain*, p 189; and Palmer and Fox, *Australians in Spain*, p 56.

221 The references are to the political groups active in Barcelona at the end of 1936. See Political Parties & Abbreviations on p 291.

5.12.36

Had a domestic morning. Other three went up to the British Medical Aid Unit flat to rearrange packing. As I had luggage at the hotel, I repacked there. Lunched at the most frequented restaurant—did not choose so well—rice with shell fish revolted the company, and instead of veal, received kidneys. Had coffee at the Ramblas—met Barry, the reported dead man, and others. Went down to the port and hired a rowing boat for an hour. We were taken around the harbour—Spanish American passenger vessels and Spanish cargo ships in harbour—lovely and peaceful being rowed along slowly. The sun warm, the hills behind Barcelona looked attractive, a fort on a high barren hill, fine buildings down near the harbour. We were rowed over the breakwater to see the mussels growing, lots of them on wires— some wires hoisted up to dry off. And so back to the landing stage, all very pleasant and everyone pleased with the fresh air. Lowson and Wilson went to a meal at the nasty cheap place— MacFarlane and I stayed in our hotel awhile—then went to the Ramblas Café and met the usual people. John Fisher took us to dine—and we had the best meal we've had in Spain—always eating but the food is not so good because the best is going to the front. Went back to the café and talked pleasantly and read some English newspapers and heard stories of the front.

6.12.36

Marched in the funeral procession of Hans Beimler,[222] an ex-German communist deputy who was killed fighting at the front

---

222 Hans Beimler, an ex-communist Reichstag Deputy who had escaped from Dachau, formed the first brigade of international volunteers, the Thaelmann Centuria, later the Thaelmann Battalion, located near Huesca on the Aragón front. Originally, it comprised German exiles living in Barcelona, in July 1936. He was killed in early December 1936 on the Madrid front at University City. See Giles Tremlett, *The International Brigades; Fascism, Freedom and the Spanish Civil War*. (London: Bloomsbury, 2020), pp 59-60, 127-8; and Gustav Regler, *The Owl of Minerva*, (Rupert Hart-Davis, London, 1959), p 286.

here. A man very able and evidently much loved, it was a great loss to the party. An English party was joining the procession so Lowson offered us to join in. We assembled outside the Karl Marx building, and waited there until all were ready. Lowson carried flowers, and we all joined in with the women's brigade— international women, English, German and Swiss. We followed after the officials and behind a banner declaring "Vengeance for the Death of Hans Beimler"—we gave the salute continuously as we moved slowly down the street. Passing round in front of the Hotel Colón, by means of amplifiers the corpse of Hans Beimler was addressed. *Commovente*. We passed on round the square of Catalonia and down the Ramblas—saluting and being saluted as we passed by various committee rooms—Latin American students, anarchists, young communists and others—until we reached the end of the Ramblas where we international women were called to stand on one side.

We then stood while thousands of people of every party, police and militias, children and women, passed by with their myriad banners and bands. The *Internationale* hymn was played with minute intervals, the anarchists followed playing their hymn, and the *Internationale*, till at last came the carriages bearing the magnificent wreaths. Mac not feeling well so we left a little before the others and returned to the hotel for a while before lunch.

All we four have dispensed with hats as hats are considered bourgeois here. Mac developed a bad cold and went to bed early. I went to the Ramblas Café—no one there—came back to the hotel and went to dine at Lowson's low restaurant where the waiter speaks English. Company included one English technician and an English ex-soldier—food a little better. Felt very depressed—went to the Ramblas Café, Barry joined us and several others. Wilson and I stayed on talking of our lives. John Fisher joined us and accompanied us to our hotel.

7.12.36

Got up late. Mac wanted to go somewhere in the sun—walked down the Ramblas—took a right turn along a street going up a hill. Kept on walking—with the object of walking up Montjuich— came to a dead end. Enquiries led us to retrace our steps to the metro station. Took the funicular railway to its termination. Discovered that we were level with the fort and decided it was no place for us—had a marvellous panoramic view of Barcelona and surrounding hills and sea.

Took the funicular railway back to the first stage and walked round by the automobile road to the Miramar restaurant. Sat in a garden overlooking the harbour and the city—lovely in the sun—though getting cold to sit. Three o'clock and we decided to have lunch—went into the restaurant by the overhead railway. It was rather expensive but very pleasant and as we've kept down expenses to a minimum we decided it was worth it. Thoroughly enjoyed ourselves—my Spanish advanced a little. We went down again to the city and took another street—good shops—passed a fine new school and arrived back at our hotel surprised at finding it so easily.

Went to the Ramblas Café—Barry and John Fisher were there—Barry had been looking for us to join him on his last night in Barcelona. Went all four with him to a different café, food not the best. *Butifarra* means sausage and a curious one at that. Again to the Ramblas—saw Mac home to bed and stayed jabbering until fairly late. An aroma of suspicion surrounds us.

8.12.36

Still waiting. All went to have photographs taken at Hotel Colón, or rather in front of it, as the 'Australians in Spain'. Hung about for some time then lunched on rice and fruit. Saw Barry off to Madrid—sorry to see him go as he is a thoroughly fine type of Australian and it was nice to meet him here. MacFarlane and I went walking in some gardens *zoológica*.

Had dinner with John Fisher—coffee at the Ramblas and went in search of a cinema news reel. Found it eventually, *Actualidad*, an Anarchist cinema and saw the English Grand National, a bad American comic, a short bit about Father Divine in America, then views of fighting at the front—machine guns, large guns with sound accompaniment whistling of shells—men running forward—digging trenches—pack horses moving off. Brought the realisation of war nearer. Then saw Caballero addressing the camera at Valencia and 'La Pasionaria' being greeted by the crowd.223 224 Went to another café for cocoa and so home.

9.12.36

Very little doing. Got up late, walked the length of the Ramblas, had lunch with J Fisher and MacFarlane. Returned to the hotel and slept and tried to get warm. Went to Hotel Lince for dinner with Mac. Met others at the Ramblas Café—stayed talking to friends and acquaintances till midnight.

10.12.36

Up late again, lunched with John Fisher, coffee at the Ramblas, went shopping a little, returned to the hotel, feeling a bit depressed, weather dull. Tried to write but unable to concentrate feeling indigestible. Shop windows are being covered with strips of gum paper presumably against the shattering of windows in an air raid. Cigarette shortage.

We had dinner at Hotel Lince, then to the Ramblas Café—Mr Edwards invited us to go dancing at the Shanghai Café. Fisher didn't turn up—Belcher came, also a Spaniard friend of Edwards. Good orchestra and floor—we all enjoyed dancing.

11.12.36

Got up late, lunched at a different restaurant, back to the Ramblas Café. Received word that equipment had arrived. I rushed home but was repulsed by leader. Mary is anxious about

---

223 Francisco Largo Caballero, leader of the Socialist trade union, the UGT, was Prime Minister and Minister for War from September 1936 to May 1937.

224 Dolores Ibárruri, 'La Pasionaria', a leader of the Communist Party of Spain and elected to the Cortes in February 1936, was probably the most well-known Republican figure outside Spain during the civil war. Her rallying cry in Madrid in July 1936 of 'No Pasarán' ('they will not pass') became a slogan for all Republican supporters.

something but refuses to share her anxiety. *Es una lástima.*225 Ate at the Lince after walking around the town a bit. Talked with several people at the Ramblas Café and so to bed early.

12.12.36

Thought to make effort to study Spanish and do some writing. Went walking round the city, saw many fine buildings, tried the Metro but it wasn't going our way. Found el Palau de la Música Catalana and marked it well. Went to the zoological gardens (where we saw no animals) and tried to study Spanish but got cold and walked home.

Had dinner with John Fisher and an American journalist then went to a concert and film given by the PSUC. Films shown of churches destroyed here and in Madrid, a symbol of ridding the country of corruption. Film badly projected. Then there were films of soldiers fighting at the front, women amongst them, no more women are now being recruited. Casualty tents behind the lines, rows of canvas stretchers, looked well organised. Also showed a hospital for evacuation and classification. Then saw a Russian film, *Tchaipeff Revolutionaries against the Whites*— some excellent photography. Then the concert began. A saxophonist played very well, the violinist, *muy bien*,226 and a woman dressed in black sang something from *Bohème*, another woman sang better, evidently Spanish songs. After that the brass band of the Carl Marxists played some Schubert and other things very well, though tempo a little slow the cymbals were active.

13.12.36

Went with three American journalists, one woman and John Fisher to visit the convent of Santa María de Pedralbes. A lovely Gothic building from 1326, which took 14 months to build. It has been restored in places. In one chapel valuable frescoes done in

---

225 'It's a pity'.

226 'very well'.

1345 were shown to us. The nuns were all evacuated some months ago.

The wife of Jacques, King of Catalonia, after the death of her husband lived in a palace adjoining the monastery and spent most of her time praying at the monastery. Her palace was demolished on her death, and she was buried in the church here; her effigy as the Queen is in the church and as a nun in the chapel off the cloisters. The nuns paid a dowry to enter the monastery in the early years. Only aristocrats were admitted, when a large dowry was presented. The monastery or order at that time collected certain dues from the surrounding district, but recently it has lived on income from accumulated capital. It was a very rich order called the Independent Order of Santa Clara whose patron saint was Saint Francis of Assisi. Permission to enter the monastery was very difficult to obtain and it was necessary to get the Vatican's permission. The Abbess was elected by the sisters but generally it was a blue blooded one appointed. Of recent years a novice could enter with a small dowry of 10,000 or 20,000 pesetas. For the last 800 years all nuns have been buried in a vault below the cloisters. A very strict order where the nuns never went out and had their own separate entrance to the cathedral, and the priest had his entrance.

There is a small chapel behind the cathedral where nuns held their own masses—small iron grill (double) where relatives of nuns could watch the initiation or funeral masses—or see their relatives. There was also a curtain over the grille. We saw a very ancient wooden baptismal font, originally made for Montserrat but found too small and was presented to Pedralbes, with the coat of arms of Monserrat and daughter of the King of that time on panels. Lovely cloisters, orange trees, palms, a couple of old wells, with an iron head above, empty tiled pond around one, with lovely coloured tiles in green and blue and yellow. Shown small day cells of nuns—double doors—one of wooden slats and small Madonna or saint at one end of a rectangular cell—a small window where she could sit and look out, or shut with wooden shutter.

A bell was rung when any man entered the place and all nuns disappeared. The nuns had a separate garden and quarters from the novices. Sewing room, laundry and kitchen were all denuded of their utensils. Dormitories with structures for curtains nuns 'night cells' went off a long corridor—silence notices up. They slept on mats on the floor apparently—no heating apparatus visible. Nuns entered the convent as young as 12 years. There was a collection of altar pieces and pictures, and two lovely fifteenth century pictures of Madonna and child. There were some Flemish pictures also—two lovely Spanish wine flasks and other things. Some Faenza stuff with a Della Robbia—it didn't look like it.

We were taken up the tower and had a good view of the cloisters and two floors of the convent and also a view of Barcelona. It was not destroyed because of its art value and because the nuns evacuated it and went quietly to their homes.

Went back to the Hotel Nouvel for lunch. An American woman and John Fisher argued about [The English] King Edward and became a little heated.227 Present crisis is talked about here. Went back to the Ramblas Café and went walking to the harbour with Belcher and a French Canadian just returned from Madrid, also MacFarlane, and looked at the Navy, three cruisers and a submarine. I did not care for the conversation of the French Canadian. I find many of these English workers talk lewdly and I don't see why I should be expected to like it. I've never heard such filthy conversation—our own working men are far more particular about their conversation in front of their women.

Went to a pianoforte recital in the Palau de la Música Catalana. It is a Rococo building with lots of mosaic and coloured tiles winged Pegasus as structural supports, and a huge round candelabra—rather too ornate for my taste so far. Juli Pons was the artiste and played well: Beethoven's *Amora Sonata*, Chopin, various studies, Rachmaninoff and some compositions of his own and some of Granados—finished with Chopin's funeral march as encore.

---

227 The English King, Edward VII , after less than a year on the throne, abdicated in order to marry Mrs Wallace Simpson, an American divorcée. The case evoked world-wide interest, and (mostly) sympathetic commentary in Spain.

Returned home in pouring rain—dined, talked at the Ramblas Café with Jellinek and others from the unit.228

14.12.36

Received letters from Isabel and Auntie V. Lunched at a cheap restaurant—we walked a bit. My heel is giving trouble. My belching echoes in the courtyard outside! Dined at the Lince, then to the Ramblas Café where all four of the unit were gathered. Not being sleepy I stayed on longer than the others talking to Belcher, John Fisher and two American journalists joined us. Just before midnight whistles blew. At first, we thought it was a police raid on the café or some such thing. We had been jesting slightly about the promised air raids. The men quickly realised that we had to make for shelter and there was not time for me to get back to my hotel. I went with John Fisher and the American journalists to the Hotel Nouvel. We all stayed about the lobby; there seemed to be no basement—we were taken into the kitchen but nobody liked that. An American woman whom I had met previously invited me to sleep with her—she went up to her room after a while, but I didn't feel like going to bed, besides I wanted to get back to my own hotel if possible. I wasn't allowed to telephone. After about 20 minutes or so the whistles blew and the lights came on and we were told '*se ha terminado*'229—it was all a trial to see how much of a target the city was. John Fisher and Mr Taylor, the journalist, went off to telephone and the other man accompanied me back to my hotel. The others had been to the nearest cellar and had guessed I'd gone with John Fisher and Co. We all felt a bit nervous at the beginning but would have liked to have seen what was coming

---

228 Frank Jellinek, an American journalist, wrote for the communist newspaper *Labor Monthly* and was the correspondent in Spain for the *Manchester Guardian* during the Civil War. See his *The Civil War in Spain* (London: Victor Gollancz, 1938). The Jellineks were long-term guests in Tossa de Mar with Nancy and Archie Johnstone, in *Hotel in Flight*, (London: Faber and Faber, London 1939), pp 22-23. See also Footnote 276.

229 'it's over'.

our way, if anything. There was a large fire engine and ladder stuck in a tree in the Ramblas and one aeroplane was droning in the sky observing the effect of the alarm *sin duda*.230

15.12.36

Walked with MacFarlane past the University, lunched at Hotel Nouvel with John Fisher and Mowrer,231 an American journalist—then afterwards went for a trip on the harbour with Mowrer. A battleship either British or American was just outside the entrance to the harbour—still two Spanish war boats there. Fog came up over the harbour as we returned, would not be good visibility for air attack.

Went back up the Ramblas, went searching for bootlaces with Mac, and wandered round by the Cathedral and other fine old buildings, which are now a lecture room and rooms for kids. Had a drink at Café Dorée, then at the Ramblas Café, dined again at Hotel Nouvel with John Fisher and Mowrer—nice lads. He is representing the *Chicago Daily News* and said I should go to their London Office in Bush House and give them a story if I go to London. Then saw Mowrer off to Valencia and returned with John Fisher to the Ramblas Café.

Heard of the likelihood of our being sent to Madrid. Three possible hospitals for the international column—one at Albacete,232 one between there and Madrid and one at Madrid. Some person will go to Valencia or Albacete tomorrow to enquire when passes may be given to us to leave here. We cannot know before tomorrow p.m. There is a political crisis here.233 The

---

230 'without doubt'.

231 Richard Mowrer was an American correspondent for the *Chicago Daily News*. See Sefton Delmer, *Trail Sinister,* (London: Secker and Warburg, 1961), p.393

232 The headquarters of the International Brigades was established in Albacete.

233 Andrés Nin, the POUM Minister of Justice in the Catalan Regional Government, had been forced out of the cabinet in a trial of

POUM has been accused of attacking Russia for not helping more, I gather, and trying to oppose and divide the faction here. A new cabinet is to be formed—no radical changes expected and no change of policy predicted. The reason for last night's alarm—some (I believe two) hydroplanes were seen out to sea this side of Tarragona and were believed to be fascist planes. An alarm was given but as nothing further was seen of them it served to prove the efficacy of arrangements for the protection of the people. Three attacks were made near Madrid. The first was the biggest but repulsed with heavy losses. All quiet by midday.

16.12.36

Received 217.50 pesetas from Lowson. I had my hair washed by a hairdresser for the first time in my life. Lunched lightly, feeling bored, didn't do any writing or anything. Had a beer with Edwards and a couple of Czechs alias Russians and went to dinner with MacFarlane and back to the Ramblas. Went to see a film, *British Agent* and some silly American naval tripe. John Fisher accompanied us home. Newspaper reports bombardment of Port Bou today—coincided with the arrival of the mail train— no one hurt and no material damage done.

Fighting going on at Santander at 12 below zero. Another contingent has arrived to join the International Brigade. Some English among them were singing 'Tipperary'. Wilson's friend Louis departed for the front. We should have news about our movements soon.

17.12.36

Walked down to the harbour to enjoy the warm sunshine— MacFarlane lunched alone with John Fisher, and I lunched at Hotel Lince. I was feeling generally depressed and continued to be so for a time. I dined again at the Lince Café and felt better. I talked at the Ramblas Café with J F Edwards and Belcher. Went

---

strength between the Catalan Communist Party, the PSUC, and the revolutionary Left.

with Belcher and MacFarlane to eat sticky cakes and then drank anisette at a bar nearby and felt more cheerful. MacFarlane and I went in search of 86 Calle Laforja, and Mlle Ufridge Gluckselig (?) We found the street after enquiring a couple of times and found her at home, a little Jewish woman writing to Mlle Marcelle Dupont. She gave us tea and we talked politely and arranged to meet the following day. We walked back to the city and our hotel.

18.12.36

Met Mlle Gluckselig at Plaza Cataluña. She took us to the Casa Juan at the harbour end of the Ramblas. We sat at a table with a German woman, the wife of a soldier fighting at Madrid, and a French woman who had lived in Spain for 16 years. We had a good lunch and pleasant conversation and arranged to meet Mlle Gluckselig on Sunday and go walking if we are still in Barcelona.

19.12.36

I went walking in search of cigarettes. I finished an article for the *Adelaide Advertiser* and wrote letters to Lloyd Ross and P Thorne, and studied Spanish. I dined with John Fisher and Mac at the Lince, and met various members of the English Ambulance Unit, just arrived. There are more rumours of our being transported by Ambulance Unit to Valencia or Albacete if permits can be obtained in time. John Fisher is very anxious to come with us.

There are reports in the paper of Eden's speech in the House of Commons, still no intervention though he admits it has failed to aid Spain but has prevented a European war. There was a report too of Infantile Help to Refugee Children, the School of the Pedralbes which was formerly an expensive school where children are now being housed and fed. There are 400 refugee children in Barcelona and 4000 in Cataluña, and no differences in their treatment is made because of the political opinions of their parents. The same treatment is given for all, some being taught professions in many cases.

General Franco told a North American journalist that the attack on Madrid had failed and he will attack again in the

Spring.

I met Edwards, an American journalist, and Fidèle, the Frenchman who is head of the Foreigners' Department, in the Ramblas Café. We talked a little, I went to bed early, but did not sleep well. Thinking a lot.

21.12.36

I was given the commission of attending to our packets of medical equipment, and was very busy, but did not despatch the business entirely. We are uncertain as to our time of departure. However, we walked about the city this afternoon and enjoyed ourselves—Mac and I made some minor purchases in preparation for the departure. Went to the Ramblas Café in the p.m. and met the usual people. An artist in the café drew Belcher and Wilson, and made our acquaintance. He seemed a nice man who has something to do with the Department for Propaganda, publishing a review in French, English, German and Catalan. He wanted addresses in London of libraries and chain bookstalls where he could send the Catalan publications. John Fisher and I gave him some. We were told we would leave early the following a.m.

22.12.36

We were all ready to leave with the British ambulances for Albacete, but just before our departure Lowson told me that only three passes have been granted—for herself, Wilson and MacFarlane. There was no permit for me. Devastated. O'Donnell explained that mine is being withheld for the reason that the Department of Strangers asked him the night before could one of us be spared for work here in Barcelona. As I speak several languages (O'Donnell's words) they thought it would be most suitable if I was left for such a position. I asked was this the real reason, because I should prefer to know if there was some other suspicion or idea behind this rather tardy rearrangement. He vowed that that this was not so—that I was not under suspicion. The others departed—Wilson and MacFarlane were rather depressed by the sudden changes of arrangements and both rather apprehensive. I was commissioned to see about the equipment—for which I was glad. I lunched with John Fisher at the Lince Restaurant but missed O'Donnell. The address of the others is c/o Dr Newman, Sanidad, Albacete. I went to the Department of Defence, to see Camarada Conchita (Elmrich) about further authorizations on our goods at the customs house. It was a difficult proceeding. Went to 407 Muntaner and walked back to the city and so to dinner with John F at the Ramblas Café.

23.12.36

Saw John Fisher off to Paris. Met O'Donnell and handed over the equipment papers and went to the Colón re Hotel permit. I suggested to O'Donnell again about my broadcasting—he was to make enquiries. Went to the Colón again then to Hotel Ritz, but was told to come back in the a.m. Crowds of refugees clamouring for rooms.

Met one of the nurses from Grañén—she told me about the refugees, hundreds of women and children, coming down from the mountains. The soldiers carried the children most of the way, but the women walked for 36 hours over rough roads and mountain tracks. They arrived at the hospital at Grañén with the soles of their feet raw and were treated at the hospital. Wounded men coming down mountains had to walk several miles till they could get to the mule trains—then two men to each mule—they were carried lower down to the ambulances. It was several hours usually before they got treatment and the less hardy and more seriously wounded usually succumbed en route. Many wounded in the chest arrived having suffered terribly. Dined alone sadly and went to bed early.

24.12.36

Had a very miserable day. The cold is bothering me. I went to the Hotel Ritz and was given a *vale* (voucher) for accommodation at the Hotel Pasionaria. Felt very depressed at having to change my room. O'Donnell promises to find me work as soon as Fidèle comes back from Madrid. After a solo lunch, I packed and took a taxi to the Hotel Pasionaria. I was driven all round the country but no one knew where it was not even the Hotel Ritz could give directions over the phone. I landed at a Military Training School and all the guards clustered round and laughed about it; the taxi driver thought it was a huge joke but I was again feeling very miserable. We finally located the Hotel P and was deposited there cum baggage and put in a room with two other refugees.

Hotel Pasionaria is an ex-convent and very cold. I felt if I could only stand the first few days I'd stand it well, but I just couldn't bear it. Women and children refugees were all there and the noise was terrific. Everyone of course was very kind; the woman in my room was taking me under her wing. I rang up O'Donnell and managed to speak calmly. He said I couldn't possibly stay there, for which I was grateful, fearing I would have to, and said I was to meet him at the Ramblas. He arranged for a room at the Hotel Lloret, 6.50 pesetas per night for a small dirty room—still I mustn't grumble.

Went to the Ramblas Café and found several members of the British Unit there, and joined Belcher and Somerville and a German lass and we celebrated the eve a little with a rum punch.

Earlier I had listened to Jellinek talking about Spain and various political parties. He praised the anarchists for their good heart and simple sincerity. I heard an account of a ceremonial burning of a church. The foreign journalists were formally invited to be present. It was a definite ceremony symbolising the destroying of the corruption which had crept into the church. A sincere ceremony of purification such as Christ himself might approve. The foreign journalists, or their papers, reported it was an act of vandalism—the Spaniards cannot comprehend how their foreign brothers can misinterpret such an act of faith.

Met F Gluckselig—very pleased to see her and she me— together we talked of our separate difficulties. I find her very helpful as well as sympathetic. Promised to see her again.

25.12.36

Xmas day—not feeling too well. Went to Josep Ferrero and talked Spanish and French rather badly. Went in search of a medical book and thoroughly enjoyed myself in book shops. Met an English girl and though not hungry lunched and trailed about with her. After dinner we met a Mexican ex-colonel in Pancho

Villa's army with Sam Masters, the English girl's boyfriend, a very excitable round headed Jew boy.234 Stayed talking a little. He had been wounded.

It seems fairly certain that Blue Barry has been killed—he and another Briton covered the retreat of some gunners and their gun.235 Later Government forces recaptured the position and found Barry dead, rifle in hand—the other man is still missing. They saved the gun.

While waiting at the Ritz the other day, I got talking with a fifteen-year-old girl from Madrid. Her house of five stories had been complete destroyed. Her *esposo* (husband), she said, was fighting on the Madrid front. She wore no ring, but assured me she was married and could not believe that being 30 I was not married. I felt a very strange animal.

26.12.36

Lunched at a different restaurant, 2.50 meal all included, rather an amusing place, the cook was arguing in the kitchen, very heatedly, the other waiters and employer looking round nervously and trying to quieten him. Could only catch the word *'la miseria'*. Nice old toothless woman sitting opposite me. They gave her a hard end of bread and she demanded other bread and

---

234 Sam Masters came to Barcelona in July 1936 for the Workers' Olympiad and was one of the first English volunteers in the International Brigades. He was killed at Brunete in July 1937. See Bill Alexander, *British Volunteers for Liberty: Spain 1936-39*, (London: Lawrence and Wishart, 1982), pp 36, 41-271.

235 When Agnes was asked to comment on Jack (Blue) Barry's death, after the Spanish civil war, she stated: 'He was a man of few words, greatest and happiest in action. At Boadilla, he bravely covered the retreat of a precious gun and the gunners, and one [can] imagine what happened . . . without a thought for himself he took up his position and he and a British volunteer saved the gun . . . and his dead body was found with his rifle still in his hands. Words are inadequate to pay such heroes just tribute,' in Nettie Palmer and Len Fox with the help of Jim McNeill and Ron Hurd, *Australians in Spain*, p 12.

they gave her a roll. Then she wanted more and I offered her my soft bit so she filled my wine with some lemon mineral water. We are all sisters now.

Went on the harbour with an English ambulance driver who had been resident in Minorca and forcibly evacuated from there by a British warship. He is going to the front as an electrical technician. The boat took us quite near the ships in port, naval vessels and a submarine (Spanish) only one foreign cruiser here now. Past the liner *Uruguay* and the *Juan Fernández Elmando* (?) one of which is used to house political prisoners.236 The two fascist generals who began the Catalan uprising were tried on board. Passed all the other cargo ships tied up and looking helpless. One beautiful three-masted sailing ship, newly painted grey on the slips. Went to the Hotel Colón and got a note to take to the Hospital Montjuich—'please let bearer give some blood for the wounded'. From Plaza de España walked up through the exhibition grounds—several people offered their company, which I refused until held up by militia men with guns—then I produced my note and one of them kindly escorted me to the hospital, leaving word there that I was to be escorted away again in case I got lost. The lad at the hospital when I was leaving asked a couple of militia volunteers to escort me they asked why and didn't seem anxious so I took myself off. Five cc's of blood taken for test, and shall be called upon next week. Felt much better at doing something.

Received a grand batch of letters. Mr O'Donnell arranged with a Hungarian, Doctor Stefan, that I should go and assist him at a clinic in the Cuartel Pablo Iglesias—Regimiento de Férreo—tomorrow. Bit afraid of language difficulty and rustiness.

26.12.36—Tarragona

Submarine (unknown) fired two torpedoes at a Spanish cargo ship just as she was leaving the Port of Tarragona. Calm sea and

---

236 The *Uruguay* held Republican political prisoners. See Sefton Delmer's description of his visit to the ship at the end of 1936, in *Trail Sinister*, pp 349-357.

the torpedoes were launched quite close but the ship was manoevered quickly—*a las acometidas de los piratas*.237 The two torpedoes shot up on the beach of Río Cla without explodiing. They were of Italian fabrication and measured 6.5 metres.

A group of *milicianos* (militiamen) blew up a train with dynamite. A lot of German fascists have been killed on the Aragón Front near Talavera.

No embrutezcáis a los niños dándoles armas, anulad los juguetes de guerra.238

27.12.36
Went to Cuartel Pablo Iglesias and was introduced to a couple of doctors. Had a quick look at some patients in a cubicle—VD clinic and small dressings mainly I gather. Two or three nurses, but being Sunday there was not much work. Examined the drug cupboard and other medicines.

[This entry appears at the end of the diary]
Hung about and played a species of ludo with a couple of doctors. Taken over to barracks for dinner, freezingly cold in an underground dining room and everybody shouting. Good dinner of rice and potatoes, meat and fruit and wine. Coffee in the square later. Myself very silent and confused. Couldn't discover my duties. Felt very weary and excused myself as the doctor had left at five. Asking what time I should come the next day, was told—just when I pleased.

28.12.36
Went at 9 a.m. to Cuartel Pablo Iglesias and trailed after the nurse taking temperatures. Then did the odd dressing of fingers and sores generally. Sat about a lot and helped the cook with the

---

237 'At the pirates' assault.'

238 'Don't brutalize children by giving them arms, get rid of war toys'.

potatoes and the dishes. I went to lunch in the barracks where there was absolute bedlam—all lads and all very cheerful—but what a noise. Ate soup with beans and potatoes and two small hunks of meat to follow, plus *vino* and orange. Huge dishes were put in the middle of the table and everyone helps themselves and cuts their meat with a spoon. Good spirit present. I listened in a little to an argument between a nurse and a young boy—he had pinched her photographs so she took his pen. Dr Hassaszti had to settle it, and lectured them both. The nurse wept. I went to coffee with her and a male nurse. The male nurse lectured her on her responsibility as a nurse. He told me that nurses' training here takes two years and nurses never make beds or anything menial like that. She is purely the doctor's assistant and takes temperatures, etc. A very dull business really.

The younger nurse told me she didn't like the place; it wasn't a hospital or a clinic, merely a place. She's right. I'm completely deflated and so help me I'll stick it as long as I can, but more I cannot do. They don't need me there, and if they can't make better use of me, why stay and torture myself.

Heard that the others were held up 12 miles out of Valencia with the ambulance lorry broken down. Also that women were being kept out of Albacete and Madrid.

La Noche. Concentration camps are to be formed and the Committee for them consists of the General Director of Prisons, two members of the CNT, two UGT, one Partido Comunista, one Socialista, one Left Republicana and one Unión Repúbl. They already have two big buildings in the province of Murcia to house them. They will work on the construction of a canal for a dam on the Valdeinfierno which will considerably increase the worth of the land in that zone which is now dry and unproductive.

Reasons for the camps:

1) El gasto inútil de mantenimiento del gran número de presos fascistas, se convertirá con el trabajo de éstos, en un beneficio positivo para el Estado.

2) La riqueza que ese procedimiento irá reportando a las zonas de España en donde se vayan instalando los campos de trabajo.

3) Este es el aspecto moral del proyecto; puesto que con él podrá llegarse a la rehabilitación y dignificación de no pocos presos,

*ya que se habituarán al trabajo y se convertirán en hombres
útiles, no pocos que acaso, hasta ahora, no habrán hecho otra
cosa que vegetar sin provecho ninguno para la sociedad. Esa es
la moral generosa y ése es el sentido humano del proyecto.239*

29.12.36

At Cuartel Pablo Iglesias made beds, did various small dressings
and gave injections. Dinner very noisy, I'm talking less—but felt
happier on the whole. On my return walked from Sarriá to
Muntaner, through back streets, with nice buildings some exactly
like Morocco—then up a hill past some lovely villas taken over by
the CNT-UGT and across the railway line and finally down to the
Diagonal. I had been searching for Calle Laforja but couldn't find
it, and so to my room. Dined all forlorn and met Belcher, and the
Jellineks at the Ramblas.

30.12.36

Slept later but arrived on duty on time. Fairly busy morning and
afternoon. Feeling pretty stupid. Had a beer at the Ramblas but
nobody was there; then had a meal at the Cervecería Bavaria
good salad for which I had craved. I called on Frau Gluckselig,
she was in bed with a cold; we were glad to see each other. Very
fed up still with this bug and life in general.

31.12.36

At the *cuartel* (barracks) all day—invited by Dr Hassaszti to go to
a meal there at 9 p.m. Fiesta to celebrate New Year's Eve. Feeling

---

239 1) The useless cost of supporting a great number of fascist
prisoners whose work could be converted into a positive benefit for
the state.
 2) The value that this plan will return to the parts of Spain where
the camps are to be set up.
 3) There is a moral side to the project because through it a good
number of prisoners will be rehabilitated as worthwhile people, as
they will become accustomed to work and will be transformed into
useful people, because until now they have done nothing but
vegetate without contributing anything to society.

acutely miserable all day and having great difficulty not to weep. I felt I couldn't cope with more difficulties, the language, etc. So I went to bed with a temperature and some sort of throat, painful.

1.1.37

Felt better, work slack and everyone in festive spirit. A special lunch was served to the militia, rice with chicken liver, chicken and green peas, some sort of nutty *marrón*, and sparkling wine. In a better temper generally and feeling more at peace with the world. Went to Café Dorée and listened to light music, the 'Princess Maritska' and 'Blue Danube', and so home to bed.

2.1.37

At the *cuartel* again, busy morning, patient (TB) haemorrhaged; I was busy doing dressings, when later I went to see his state found the bed empty. Marisa said he wasn't dead. I gathered he'd gone to hospital. To my surprise later in the day I found him back in the bed, he'd evidently been for X-ray! Went for coffee in the square and talked with some militia men, at least I sat while they talked. Back to work, all three nurses had our photo taken. Marisa said for me to give her the 'tú'—complicating my language. Everyone uses the 'tú' now.240 The other nurse was very cross that the beds had not been made. Marisa is too beautiful and *'molto simpatica'241* to concern herself much about beds. The other nurse then began giving me instructions on how to make beds. I managed to tell her I knew very well how to make beds.

I'm to have a free day, *mañana*. Walked and walked to enable me to eat a doughnut and found *no hay bollitos*.242 Met Edwards in the Ramblas and had a beer with him. Dined with

---

240 The familiar 'tú' form of address was widely adopted, instead of the formal 'usted', signifying a shared camaraderie among Republican soldiers and their supporters in the Spanish population.

241 'too genteel'.

242 'there are no doughnuts'.

Mrs Bates at the Lince and then went to the Ramblas and the Café Dorée with Belcher where we met some Spanish friends of his. I was told I talked Spanish very correctly and well for five weeks—inflated immediately. We went on to dance at a nice place but the floor was awful and played up with my leg. We were all brighter however.

3.1.37
Went to the Palacio de Bellas Artes for a symphony concert by the Barcelona Municipal Band. The played the '5th Symphony' well, but not superbly and Andalusian gypsy themes. Interesting. It ended by the *'Internationale'*, and Spanish and Catalan Republic hymns all being played. Dined at the Lince. O'Donnell was there and agreed to paying my bill and suggested my going to Grañén if it could be arranged.

[This entry appears at the end of the diary]
Told O'D if I wasn't sent to the front I would leave Spain in a week. He made mention of the hospital for the International Brigades. He seemed alarmed and said I must have a reason for this. I stated that my reason was that I didn't believe in the hospital idea. I did not know what their idea in keeping me back really was but that I had come to nurse and if long waiting was necessary I could wait more comfortably in England. Also I thought I would go direct myself to the Spanish Authorities and offer my aid. *Bien.* The next night word was left for me to leave for Grañén the following morning.

So be it. Gave my bed to Miss Holman243 of the London Committee of the British Medical Aid and she went in search of her things. Very pleasant walking in the morning in the Plaza

---

243 Portia Holman, the daughter of Ada and W A Holman, the ex-Premier of New South Wales, had been a medical student at Cambridge when the war broke out. She travelled to Spain several times for the London Spanish Relief Committee. See Palmer & Fox, *Australians in Spain,* pp 35-36; *Australian Dictionary of Biography,* vol. 9, (Melbourne: Melbourne University Press, 1983), pp 337-338, 340,347.

Catalonia where hundreds of young people were dancing in circles, quiet footwork then more energetic sort of jumping and crossing feet. It was most impressive to see the whole crowd dancing like that and new circles forming.244

I went to see Mlle Gluckselig. Dined with Edwards—stupidly let myself in for it, but a Frenchman and an American writer woman Anna Louise Strong245 joined us. She and Edwards are old friends. Edwards told me what a great woman she is, with what style she writes, etc. She appeared in a badly cut greenish suit and woollen cap, very bright eyes, rather crinkly, pointed small nose and a thin mouth. She and Edwards talked during the meal of airplanes sold by America to the fascists, sent via Italy; and rotten planes at that. 2000 American volunteers, ready to sail, were stopped by the American Government. I learnt that certain planes could not be converted into good fighting planes and only American pilots are of any use to fight with these planes. Many good civilian flyers proved too expensive, and they can't afford damaged planes. Anna Louise Strong had visited three fronts at Madrid or nearby and is on her way to America to do propaganda work.

She is a very enthusiastic, ardent communist member, and lives I gather mainly in Russia, and I think is married to a Russian. Edwards has been a party member since a youth and knew Jack London and Upton Sinclair. He says Upton Sinclair is now too old and tired, a back number, and has been running a party which was a racket in Edward's room. Afterwards I went to the Café Ramblas with him, where he talked to me about the fallacy of the anarchist theory put into practice. Every man doing as he pleases is no good and anarchists therefore have made room for pseudo-fascists and stool pigeons. I went to bed in a bad mood.

---

244 The Sardana is a traditional Catalan dance.

245 An American journalist who had lived in China and the Soviet Union in the 1930s. See her report of her visit to Spain in 1936 in *Communist Review*, Sydney, Jun 1937, p.24.

4.1.37

I did very little work; went to the cuartel at 9 a.m., but it is useless doing so. Both nurses are working there now so I hung about and froze most of the day. Felt very miserable and sick, home at six, studied, wrote letters. Went to dinner at Ramblas and so to bed.

5.1.37

Rebel planes have been fairly active—plastered Albacete—a few houses hit.

1.30 p.m. Frescoes of Goya at San Antonio de la Florida are intact and being protected by some special process. Málaga, Murcia, and Bilbao have been bombarded, Bilbao in the afternoon by nine bombing planes. One fascist motor plane fell, its occupants used parachutes, and a burning fascist plane fell on the neighbourhood of Arraiz. One of the pilots who died was of '*la categoría de alférez de aviación de Heselchdingen'*246 domiciled in Berlin and 27 years of age.

Almería 12.40 p.m. Four biplanes put to flight by loyalist planes with no damage. In Málaga, eight women and children wounded and a house facing the port was destroyed. The Chief of a Submarine Flotilla at Málaga died from wounds received in the bombardment.

Ration cards are to be given out here shortly. Flour has been bought in France and Russia as women have been protesting to the President about being unable to give their children bread. There is a great outcry about the women standing in queues for hours for bread, and cafés still supplying bread rolls, etc and a suggestion has been made that they should not be allowed them. Looks as though I'll get no more doughnuts and p'raps not even croissants for breakfast.

The papers comment on the Moors being brought into Spain to defend the Christian religion. The Union of Democratic

---

246 "the rank of lieutenant in the German air force'.

Catalonia is a Catholic association and the government respects liberty of conscience and cults. But true Catholics and conservatives ought to be on the side of the Government because it is the legitimate constitutional power, by the laws of Spain and because the gods ought to render unto Caesar the things which are Caesar's. There are 40,000 Italian soldiers disembarked for Madrid, giving a painful impression in London after the Italo-English pact. Six thousand arrived in Cadiz on 22 December. A German warship held up a ship with a Spanish cargo of potatoes. Rebel ships are holding up English and Russian ships outside the three mile limit and England is protesting that they mustn't do it again. In Bilbao the old transatlantic ship *Habana* is to be converted into a hospital. I heard that Lowson and Co are working at a small hospital at Casselton. Lowson telephoned O'Donnell and ordered £10 worth of toilet paper, among other things.

6.1.37

Still at the *cuartel*. There was a gathering of the Medical Aid Unit. I met Edwards and Belcher at the Ramblas after dinner and talked with the Jellineks. The Spanish Government is vigorously protesting about German interference in Spanish waters.

Various dancing cafés have been raided and young men unable to produce sufficient papers were taken off to clean the markets. Why should they dance and be frivolous when their brothers are fighting in the trenches? Much protesting about the bread queues. People waiting for hours, beginning at 3 a.m. and lasting till afternoon. Whole families line up and some of the petty bourgeoisie send their servants. Two were arrested on complaints made by a servant that on Sundays they listened to mass broadcast from Rome. They were liberated through insufficient evidence.

I was told an anecdote from the Thaelmann Battalion. During a hectic fight the artillery found that the munitions were getting low and they sent a message to the nearest *pueblo*. The words, badly written on a small piece of paper, said, 'Send us as soon as possible a truck of *granadas* (grenades)'. Shortly a truck appeared accompanied by several peasants beaming with satisfaction. To the amazement of the German comrades they began to unload from the truck the cargo of pomegranate fruit. They were *granadas*. With great pride in being able to offer a gift from the earth to the *compañeros* who had left their countries to come to their aid, the peasants said, 'You have what you asked for. We have brought you the most beautiful *granadas* that we have in the pueblo'.

8.1.37

Feeling rotten, sneezing all day, and did very little work. A dumb soldier conveyed by gesture that I was very cold and ought to skip and run round the garden. He showed his officer too why the officer was getting corns . . . bad boots. Then he opened his throat and indicated to Dr Hassaszti that he had a sore throat.

I bought a pair of boy's woollen socks. Dined with Redbeard and talked awhile with Mrs Jellinek then to the Oro del Rhin. Very sore throat.

9.1.37

Decided not to go to the *cuartel*. Stayed in bed in the a.m. Then walked and sat in the sun. Had a coffee with Gluckselig and went back to my room and washed clothes and myself. Went to the Ramblas and had a drink with the Jellineks and Volunteer Peel— of the Skull and Crossbones Brigade (FAI), and later went with Redbeard to the Oro del Rhin. J's and Peel came in later and by then I was tired and rather bored by the late hour and the excluding conversation. Things are not going well in Madrid— much fighting and bombardment but they have not made any considerable advance.

10.1.37

Went to Tibidabo with F. Gluckselig. Day rather colder, sun not so warm, enjoyed myself but feeling restless. Returned to Barcelona about 4 p.m. Dined alone and met Edwards and Co. Margot Miller247 has returned from Tarragona with a broken

---

247 The Australian, Margot Miller, had joined the first British Medical Aid Unit in London in August 1936 as a driver and clerk.

arm, bruised eyes, etc. While she was driving to Valencia, the Bulgarian driver had gone to sleep (probably carbon monoxide fumes) hit a tree and Margot got the wind screen. I returned to the hotel to find I was to depart for Grañén in the a.m.

11.1.37

Left Barcelona 8.30 a.m. O'Donnell saw us off. I travelled up to Grañén with Prof. Marrack248 and Miss Anita Bolster. The journey was very interesting. The country as far as Tarrasa was covered with young pine woods. The timber was being cut and the soil is red copper coloured. Last seasons stubble (corn?) is still standing; vines cut back, thick green crop just shooting; the land looks very dry. There were round haystacks and large white washed stone or stucco houses. The country undulates with a type of fir forest. In valleys there are small vineyards in between olive trees, vegetables in dry river beds and cultivated olive orchards. There were sudden depressions in the ground and cracks in the middle of town. Tarrasa is a large industrial town. I saw a flock of black goats going off to pasture. There are hardly 10 acres on the same level. Stony ground. More mountians and mineral looking country.

She was shot in the leg in September 1936 on the Aragón front and rescued by militiamen. See her dramatic interview in *Australian Women's Weekly*, 26 Dec 1936; *Daily Telegraph*, 25 Aug 1936, p 1; 23 Oct 1936, p 1 and Palmer & Fox, *Australians in Spain*, pp.34-

Soon after she returned to Spain she was again injuredin a truck accident on her way to Valencia.

248 Professor J R Marrack, a Professor of Biochemistry at Cambridge, was the Treasurer of the Spanish Medical Aid Committee in London and the British representative on the Paris International Medical Centre, Central Sanitaria Internacional (CSI) for the coordination of medical services and the distribution of funds raised. The Australian Spanish Relief Committee sent most of their funds raised in Australia to the CIS as well as to the British Medical Aid Committee. See Palfreeman, *Salud: British Volunteers in the Republican Medical Service during the Spanish Civil War*, pp 55-57, 35.

Olesa. High hills and gorges, a fine road and terraced earth lying fallow and stunted trees. Later, rising all the time, we came to flatter agricultural country where there is a sugar-beet industry and a large factory at Monzón; the biggest sugar-beet factory in Spain.

At Lérida when asking for the WC Anita[249] was taken behind a screen by a squaw who began feeling her all over—then she demanded money—we didn't understand what it was all about but I shouted angrily at her and dragged Anita away. In the train we talked to a doctor and chemist who worked in the hospital trains. There are three, one going from Grañén to Lérida and another from Lérida to Barcelona. They gave us drinks at one of the stations. After Lérida there was no restaurant car aboard—we had to change carriages there too. The last two hours the train crawled along in darkness, stopping for long periods at the stations. We listened to amusing conversation amongst the militia. One man was wearing a magnificent lambswool cap.

We arrived at Grañén all in the dark and asked our way and were kindly led by a lad to the hospital, slipping in muddy streets by the light of a torch. We were welcomed heartily and shown round the place.

We had a good meal and sparkling wine to celebrate and a ration of chocolate and cigarettes and so to bed pretty tired. Heard that t'others (Aust. nurses) were in a hospital with four French nurses and 1500 wounded passing through.

12.1.37—Grañén

Spent the morning being shown about and getting acquainted. Misty morning and cold. It is a large rambling house with a courtyard being filled in with stones. We sleep in a loft with mattresses on the floor. The two male members keep on t'other side partitioned by a Union Jack. The Spanish doctors and *practicantes* (medical students) sleep in another dormitory. There are two theatres and a common anaesthetics room. Two largish rooms adjoining each other with two alcoves serve as

---

249 Anita Bolster, see description below 23.1.37 and photograph with Agnes, Grañén 30.1.37.

wards and the alcoves house women patients. Another room upstairs serves VD patients. There is a large dining room and common room adjoining with a ping pong table. The kitchen and bathroom or wash house is more or less underground with three large cellars smelling of wine.

In the afternoon I turned in for night duty. Just my luck—somehow had forgotten such a thing as night duty was possible. Went on duty at nine p.m. An ambulance had arrived in the a.m. bringing several wounded and walking medical cases. At night others arrived, an arm, leg and cut face. Had a busy night with a woman with a retained placenta.

*Grañén main street with an ambulance of the
British medical aid unit. Feb 1937.*

13.1.37

Went straight to bed, slept fairly well. Head case arrived at night and began to haemorrhage soon after admission. Taken to theatre and blood vessels tied. Another wounded brought in—cut face. Again had a busy night with the woman.

[This entry appears at the end of the diary]

Bolster came on duty also a few nights later. Bolster is Irish and had been a stage and film actress, and a seller of beauty products,

and had run a Left book shop which she had sold before coming
to Spain. She had a sense of humour and is a very good worker
and never complains and is determined to learn Spanish dancing
with castanets which she practises in the kitchen.

14.1.37

Went for a walk in the a.m. There was a thick grey mist
everywhere, but pleasant walking along the road by the river. I
wore gumboots because of the mud, and came back with dew on
my hair. Women were washing in the river below the bridge and
wagon loads of sugar-beet were being drawn by four mules going
to the railway.

I passed by fields, maize stubble, and a man pruning saplings.
I sang to myself lustily. Coming back the same way I saluted the
guards and the women carrying vegetables and the men driving
the water carts: a couple of barrels slung between shafts and
drawn by two mules. An Alsatian dog in friendly fashion bit at
my hand. I passed the chemist's shop and bid him good day. And
so to bed in a room by myself which Stone uses at night.250

Had a rotten night with the woman, barely a quarter of an
hour passed but she called. A wounded man came in with a nasty
shrapnel wound in his arm with a great tear on both sides, bone
broken near the shoulder. Put it in an aeroplane splint after it
had been tied and sutured. The man was an awfully good patient
and rather a pet.

15.1.37

Did not go out but stayed talking with one of the nurses. I heard
lovely stories of the unit and of Margot Miller's little
escapade.251 She had gone out in an ambulance, she and Bird
and the driver, to dress a *miliciano* (militiaman) and to save
going the long way round, M voluntarily and foolhardily crossed

---

250 Jack Stone was a driver for the Spanish Medical Aid Unit in
Grañén.

251 Margot Miller, see footnote 46.

a stretch of no-man's-land, got hit and four Republicans rushed to pull her back, risking their lives.252 Miller was treated as a heroine and Bird was sent back to England for letting her go. B threatened to take morphia tablets (she had been issued them when she had volunteered to go to Abyssinia). Two nurses, one in fluffy night attire, rushed down, scared, to tell the BMAU medical men. They were so intrigued they stayed half an hour comforting the girls with brandy. Then they came up to B armed with a stomach pump. B had not taken anything and promised not to. Miller is rather neurotic and very miserable unless she can be doing something spectacular. She had come out as a nurse but to keep her contented they had to let her go out in ambulances despite the rush of work and a shortage of nurses in the hospital.253 The other story was of the Australian who tried to commit suicide because of someone who read her diary.254 The lass was rather unstrung living in a slightly hostile atmosphere. They nicknamed her 'Creeping Jesus', because she was always snooping round and making notes. She asked to be told what person had seen or heard about what was in her diary. No one paid any attention and she jumped out of the window on the floor below and was unhurt. Two men (one of whom had called to her to shut the window after she had jumped) rushed downstairs, stopping to get a stretcher and found her standing snuffingly. They begged her to sit on the stretcher but she

---

252 Doris Bird, one of the original nurses that came in the first group to Barcelona. She had served in a medical unit in the First World War and in Abyssinia. See Palfreeman, *Salud*, p 243; Fyrth, *The Signal Was Spain*, p 50.

253 Margot Miller was not a nurse. She came to Spain as a driver with the British Medical Aid unit. See footnote 47.

254 Aileen Palmer, a translator and medical records clerk, was part of the first British medical aid unit sent to Grañén, where she was secretary to the unit administrator, Kenneth Sinclair-Loutit, later transferring to Albacete to join the International Brigade medical service. See Keene, 'A Spanish Springtime: Aileen Palmer and the Spanish Civil War' and Martin, *Ink in her Veins: The Troubled Life of Aileen Palmer*.

preferred to walk with assistance. She was given brandy. The girl who had been told what was in the diary, appeared, and told the silly story again and then the Australian asked who had told her and was told she'd have to jump out of a much higher window for that. These young things should not be allowed out, this one was too sensitive and not sensible yet. Went to bed and slept well. Night began better, the woman quieter. Neurotic patient arrived—seeing things and fighting—and seemed to be lousy too.

The British Embassy in Madrid has been bombed.

Having much disappointments and discomfort about lavatories. Serious if amusing problems, because the floors and seat are always wet, and used by all. It definitely lacks all modern conveniences and gives rise to thoughts of returning to nature as definitely more pleasurable and hygienic. Weather dull and misty and cold. We wear riding britches and woollies, woolly socks and uniform over the top. We must look comic but there are few mirrors about. My eye giving me a little trouble but otherwise I am well and happy. So much for work and its effect on the spirits.

16.1.37

Had a good night: busy but not tense. Lovely red dawn and sunny morning. Washed my clothes on the terrace in the sun.

I went walking with Vita Prout up past the church to view the landscape over miles of cultivated plain, soil unproductive looking, though there are signs of irrigation, with small low bushes growing and never a tree, but lovely hills and mountains.255 There is a village on a hill and several villages nestling at the foot of the hills. On the other side of that range is the front with, in between them and another line of hills, a flat stretch which is no-man's land. There were larks twittering and flying about and a cold wind blowing across the plains. Returning we looked at the church door; it has an 1888 date on it, but the church or organ supposedly is 200 years old. The external

---

255 Vita Felber was an Austrian exile in Barcelona who joined the SMAC unit as an interpreter. Her love affairs drew suspicion, she later married Denis Prout, a British ambulance driver in Grañén, in Martin, *Ink in her Veins*, pp 141-142.

appearance of the church is pleasing though like a fortress; the church has been denuded and used for a granary. Below in the Plaza de Castilla a few old heavy stones hiding some cellars is all that remains of a castle. The church is very high and dominates the village.

Wakened early, ironed, went to the local café after the meal with some of the German Battery. They sang cheerfully, a terrific din in the café with everyone singing their own songs. I drank some nice liqueur, and so to the night's work.

17.1.37

Some Germans left by the morning train. We had to get them off in time, and they talked a lot, and disturbed the ward.

18.1.37

A severe headcase admitted. In theatre till 3.30 a.m. Anita came on night duty with me. Busy night.

19.1.37

Vita Prout and Jack Stone went to Barcelona. We shall miss them.

20.1.37

A shot hand case admitted.

21.1.37

Sat in the sun on the terrace and washed my hair. I received a letter from Auntie Vincent. Heard another Australian nurse has arrived in Barcelona this morning.

22.1.37

Another shot hand case in the theatre.

23.1.37

Raining, went walking—nice wind blowing—getting a little fed up with night duty.

*Grañén Nurses' Quarters British Medical Aid Unit Hospital,
February 1937.*

24.1.37

Slater had a birthday so the Spaniards gave her a party. Bolster and I were called—it was a good feed and champagne and good cheer.256 Ward very quiet.

25.1.37

Head case died, only 24 years of age, poor lad. Raining and cold, did not go out nor sleep too well. I am trying to read some political books in Spanish. Played ping pong with Dr Aguiló.257

---

256 Mary Slater, a 'Lancashire lass,' nursed in Grañén and Poleñino and later successfully managed preventing a widespread a typhoid outbreak in Lérida hospital but herself brought down by it and repatriated to England, in Jackson, *'For Us it was Heaven'*, p 44; Palfreeman, *Salud* p 251.

257 Dr Gonzalo Aguiló Mercader, Provisional Medical Captain of 27th Division, was the highly effective and much-admired chief surgeon at Grañén and Poleñino. In Poleñino Dr Aguiló met and later married the Scottish-born BMU nurse, Susan Souter. Linda Palfreeman, in her comprehensive and thoughtful research, notes

Went for a long walk over towards Huesca, or rather Huesca road. Walked across fields, jumped ditches and channels and walked on the road to military headquarters on a hill between here and the range of hills. Huge lorry loads of oranges *en route* for the front passed us—we were thrown a couple—and other foodstuffs, bags of grain. Various CNT and UGT officials passed us coming and going. Dentist fraternity has come to live with us.

27.1.37

Went for walk alone, glorious warm morning, snow thick on the higher peaks but no cold wind. Walked in breeches and sweater. Burning off stubble and fields being ploughed with single disc ploughs, two mules to each three ploughs and teams closely following the other. Another man was ploughing with two black oxen; and other men clearing ditches and channels and carting manure. Vegetables and barley are doing fairly well after the rain and soft warm days. The cart trace ended in a manure heap—a nice stable smell.

I went on the high bank overlooking a thin muddy river, which takes up only half its bed with lots of poplar and olive trees about. The remains of the maize crop is in low-lying sunken paddocks or plots. I sat on the river bank in the sun, chewed grass and thought of the lovely day. Because of the fine day the guns were a little more active. It's incredible that the war is just beyond those hills. On return to the hospital I went with Murray,258 Aguiló and Fábregas,259 to see some relatives of large whites, baconers penned up to be fattened, quite good as to

that their daughter was born in England and years after the end of the civil war, they were able to be reunited in Spain. Palfreeman, *Salud*, p 252.

258 Ann Murray was a nurse from Edinburgh. See Ian MacDougall, *Voices from the Spanish Civil war. Personal Recollections of Scottish Volunteers in Republican Spain*, (Edinburgh: Polygon, 1986), pp 69-75.

259 Ramón Fábregas, Agnes's 'particular friend', was the dentist attached to the hospital.

length, line, hair and bone but no hams, a bit pot-bellied. A sow had ten nice piglets, and has produced 31 in a year in three litters. No visible stock only pigs and hens in the yard too, all covered with manure

We have one sick patient shot in the abdomen, several pieces of shrapnel were removed from his guts and part of the liver. He has bronchitis too. A very nice lad. I received a note from Lowson telling me that she was in Barcelona for a few days—*Albaxacena* is where they are working.260 She gave no other news.

28.1.37

Danced a while with the hospital staff which was very pleasant. We had a nurses' meeting because one member refused to do a duty, her reason being that one nurse should run the ward.

29.1.37

Walked down to the river—day colder but sun shining—sat on the terrace. Not so much work.

30.1.37

Went for a lovely walk again down to the river but further, José Cepero and Morales came with us. José took a lot of photographs—rather fun. Stayed up until 1.30 p.m. Went for coffee after dinner with the dentist to the house of the pigs. Then to work. Our pet patient was having a very bad night. Heard that Lowson, Wilson and Macfarlane are being overworked. Mary Lowson is in Barcelona to complain. Their convalescent home is one on the coast about 70 kilometres from Barcelona.

2.2.37

Went for another walk with John and Jerome, both of whom talk some English. We saw some partridges flying. John and Jerome are in Grañén to purify the drinking water for Pancho Villa because P. Villa does not like wasting water, but now he refused John and Jerome gasoline for their needs so they are unable to

---

260 Lowson and the others were in Albacete.

purify the local drinking water.261 There is some dissension about this hospital remaining with the Carl Marxist column, i.e. of the PSUC.262 Either we stay here at loggerheads with the FAI,263 or become part of the CNT,264 or else, if remaining with the Carl Marxists, we move to another village one and a half kilometres from Grañén.

Grañen, Agnes exploring hospital surroundings with camera and sturdy boots, Feb 1937.

261 The leader of the Grañén Village Committee, Pancho Villa. The English staff tended to refer to him in a derogatory manner. See footnote 52, chapter 2 for Margot Miller and Kenneth Sinclair-Loutit's unflattering portraits of the Grañén committee. For a more positive Spanish description of the Grañén organization see Augustín Souchy Bauer, *Entre los campesinos de Aragón. El comunismo libertario en las comarcas liberadas*, (Barcelona, Tusquets Editor, 1937), pp 70-74.

262 The Communist Party of Catalonia.

263 The Spanish Anarchist Federation.

264 The National Anarchist Labour Federation.

5.2.37

On day duty and went with the dentist to Pompaniles Las Casas
and Lanaja at the front. I assisted while he removed teeth. There
was no fuss about fillings but he's seemingly painless and skilful.
The doctor at Pompaniles is tall with trousers low on the hip and
a magnificent soft curly beard and side whiskers—like Robert
Louis Stevenson—or reminded me of him. He seemed quietly
efficient. We inspected the frontline trench 300-400 metres from
the fascist line. It was a good trench covered over and with a
machine gun in a little dugout. Behind barb wire entanglements
the militiamen were having a lunch of rice, etc.

A trip to the front near Huesca. Note the miliciana.
5 Feb 1937.

6.2.37

Various cases in the theatre. One lad had been wounded in the abdomen and had shrapnel and three perforations in the small intestine, two in the transverse colon and two in the stomach. A laparotomy was done and the perforations sutured, and four pints of blood were given, and one of saline. Also, a bad leg injury admitted with two pieces of shrapnel in the leg. One would become septic after four days and was opened and drained. Another pneumonia patient admitted but died after four days. The hospital is full to overflowing with influenzas and tonsilitis. We are very busy. The lad with the laparotomy to remove the shrapnel in his abdomen and liver developed bronchial pneumonia. He now has recovered, his sutures have been removed and he evacuated. He was called Pascual. Several hands and thumb wounds, mostly accidents, admitted last night, some suspected of being self-inflicted. A bullet wound through the eye arrived and was cleaned up and sutured. Very busy on the ward but managed to get out for one or two walks.

12.2.37

Received letters from P Thorne, Isabel, Jean Kelso, Gordon Mosely and Macfarlane. Started writing to Mr Thorne. Have not been out much, too busy. Moved to the dormitory. The question of our removal is still in the balance. The village has become rather hostile to us, the girls from the kitchen are behaving badly, and the Spanish nurses are now not being paid. They are being too evasive.

An ex-bullfighter arrived on the ward and is most amusing. I went down to the river and watched the others bathe, but *too* cold for me. The ex-bullfighter swam naked and the others nearly so. Rather fun watching them sport in the water.

I stayed in bed with laryngitis for a couple of days but got up sooner than I should have and the cough is still hanging on and keeping me awake at night.

My dentist friend went to Barcelona, and I have had no time to learn Spanish in his absence. Exhausted and have more or less gone straight to bed after duty.

16.2.37

After much negotiations it is finally decided that the hospital must move to another village where people are of the same group as ourselves. If we remain here, the wounded of our column will be sent elsewhere, and this hospital would remain to heal the local sick.

Barcelona was bombed on Saturday from an Italian warship, with 16 killed and several wounded. Valencia also has been bombed from the sea—ten people killed and 60 wounded. Port Bou, too, bombed from the sea and some of the civilian population killed. The mark on the Valencian bombs coincides with the classic make used in Italy.

The Governor of La Coruña, formerly a professor of Madrid University, and his wife have been shot. They were recently married and his wife was five months pregnant when her husband was shot and she was taken to the hospital and lost her infant. She was taken from the hospital after the operation, put in the grave already prepared and shot—then covered with earth.

19.2.37

Five aeroplanes (bi-motors) passed overhead flying too high to distinguish their marks. We heard later from a lad returning from Lérida that they had been seen from the train dropping bombs. The paper says that quantities of war material and large numbers of soldiers are arriving at Zaragossa, that the offensive on the Aragón front has begun, and that Tardienta is in ruins. We have not heard any firing today but have been indoors mostly. There was a request broadcast by the UGT for more loyalty and unity from the anarchists. The lad who has just returned was saying that in Lérida he had a meal of four plates, soup, rice, fish and meat and dessert. This is against the wartime regulation of two plates.

There is an excellent atmosphere about and a tense feeling of things about to happen. People are talking more seriously. The people here being mostly Catalans, the bombardment of Barcelona has affected them all. A woman was brought in today for a stomach washout as she had drunk permanganate of potash because Barcelona had been bombed. She was not seriously affected, more hysterical than anything.

British rearmament plans and loans are causing consternation to Germany, and Austria may cause a break in Italo-German friendship. The restriction by England and France on volunteers coming to Spain operates from tomorrow. Germany and Italy, on paper, have agreed; Portugal has her own plan which may scupper the whole thing it seems to me. Madrid sadly bombed again.

Grañén, Agnes 'on a dirty job'. Feb 1937.

20.2.37

[This entry is from a diary fragment in A.H.'s papers held by Ralph Tonkin]

Tonight, our lights have failed, and my pen likewise, but I'll carry on, and by candlelight. Tonight, I was over at a house across the street where most of us go for coffee the doctors took their gramophone and played it. Some of the records are of flamenco songs. It's not quite gypsy and it is very similar to what we heard in the summer of 1932 in many ways. I hope someday to be able to do it. Some of the men here sing flamenco duets quite well. They sing with their heads together looking very solemn and a little as though it is hurting them; and we all shout '*olé*' when they have managed to be particularly flutey. Our chief doctor is quite good, and very naïve and sweet, giggling a little with mixed pleasure and irony when he has finished.

Last night when we were at the Comité de Investigación, my dentist friend arrived for the evening.265 He went on leave to Barcelona and was then sent to Barbastro; he hopes to be coming back to Grañén in a few days. I shall be very sorry if he stays at Barbastro because I regard him as my particular crony and I was learning Spanish much more quickly with his assistance. He is engaged to an American and wants to learn English. We had a cheerful gathering in our kitchen afterwards opening the package his grandmother sent him (he doesn't look as though he should have a grandmother) of dried fish, and very high sausage, squashed butter, chocolate, oranges, and Barcelona nuts. Then we danced to the new records he had brought up. Just as we were going to bed the dentist's chauffeur came down to the kitchen livid with fury, he had put his leg through his bedroom floor and the ceiling of the common room. We had to take off his puttee and inspect his knee, no damage done, and then we all trooped up laughing, I'm afraid, to see the damage done to the floor. People are always going through floors here.

---

265 Fábregas, see footnote 59.

21.2.37

Chas Hunt returned from Barcelona with stores for the hospital and the medical ones to go to Poleñino.266 He tells me that my trunk is missing, and that Lowson is still in Barcelona. She has an X-ray plant from Australia and is waiting for a transformer and asked whether we would like it here. I spoke to Aguiló and of course he was delighted as it saves them buying one. He requested that the machine be held in Barcelona until our hospital is moved to Poleñino. I received no letters and am feeling a bit mouldy.

I copied a leaflet dropped by fascists over the nearby republican line, saying that they (the fascists) had captured Málaga with guns, cannons, machine guns, warships, etc., and that the men who had deceived the poor people had fled, robbing the banks and leaving the poor fools who believed in them to follow. The leaflet asked how long people will believe in the Red Deception and urged people to open their eyes and read the papers that we (the fascists) send you and from them see the truth of the catastrophe. Profit by these moments, it said, to present yourselves in our lines abandoning those who command you if they won't come too, and so obtain the clemency in which all penitents who presented themselves can believe. (sic) Printed in Saragossa.

A quiet day otherwise, sitting in the sun.

22.2.37

Grey day but clear visibility. Fairly continuous heavy bombing in the a.m. over Tardienta.

23.2.37

A head wound was brought in, but not very serious. He was in a room in Robres asleep when a shell burst. He received a couple of superficial wounds on either side of the head. Another head

---

266 Chas Hunt was an English driver for the British Spanish Medical Aid Committee.

wound arrived and an acute appendix and another with a poisoned hand.

25.2.37

Dr Bethune, a Canadian working with blood transfusion people in Málaga, has reported in Paris on fascist atrocities.267 There are 150,000 people on the road to Almería, among them 15,000 children, without food or anything, walking 200 kilometres.268 They were bombed and machine gunned from the air and then Almería, full of refugees, was bombed. The Non-intervention Committee has still not settled about which country patrols which part of the coastline. England means to put 10 000 sailors round the coast. Oviedo was taken by Republicans.

For that reason, it is a really good thing we are leaving. Goodness knows when we will make the move to Poleñino— there's a brand new ambulance waiting there, and the Australian X-ray plant is waiting in Barcelona to be sent there. The ambulance I think is going to be a mobile hospital. This new place is actually further away from the front than we are here.

One of our nurses is returning to England on Monday, so we are all changing over. There had been a lot of trouble here with the staff (English), before I came, chiefly because of the political and non-political business. It's caused by the politicals, who begin by rushing in, protesting that everyone is equal and the Spaniards mustn't do the dirty work, and then if there is any likelihood of their having to do the dirty work themselves, they cry out again. Everything is more or less running smoothly now among the nurses, except for one who is a nit-wit and a talker,

----

267 Norman Bethune and the Catalan doctor, F. Durán-Jordà, devised mobile blood banks that could be transported to the front. Ted Allan and Sydney Gordon, *The Scalpel, The Sword: The Story of Dr Norman Bethune*, (New York: Monthly Review Press, 1973).

268 In the early days of the civil war, the port city of Málaga was controlled by the CNT-FAI. In January 1937 it came under sustained attack by Franco's army and by the end of the first week of February had fallen decisively under Nationalist control forcing the major surge of republican citizens, under intensive shelling, to flee along the Mediterranean coast to Almería.

who is happiest cleaning bed-pans. Nobody wants to work with her; she wants to go in the theatre, yet is scared, and actually I don't think capable. Our chief does not want her, there. But we have decided that she does her turn of theatre at this change over, chiefly to keep her quiet.

*Spanish Relief Committee to Aid Victims of Fascism.
Ambulance No 5, from Sydney Australia.*

The Scots lass who really runs the place as far as real contact with the Spaniards is concerned is going on night duty.269 I'll be running the ward and shall have to get down to responsibility. I think my reputation is fairly well established, still I am not too satisfied with my work; following other people's methods, I never take the same interest. We have two VADs here and we have to be very tactful; though they are good scouts, they can do amazing things, if one is too tolerant. A little self-confidence and they cheerfully burn patients, and give them brandy when it is the last thing they should have.

---

269 Ann Murray, see footnote 58.

I am thinking of going to England at the beginning of April. I shall be due leave in April; and I might just as well spend it in England as in Barcelona.

4.3.37

We have been very busy with *enfermos*. Old Escarabajo is back with erysipilas.270 Juan de la Parc and Barba with the legs were evacuated; no old patients in now, and no *heridos* (wounded). One ghastly leg wound in the theatre yesterday was evacuated that night.

Preparations for our move to Poleñino are going ahead. Everyone else has been to see the new place but me. The weather has been extremely cold and snow fell one day, and there is snow on the hills all round. The village empties and fills with militiamen. I have not had much time to read the papers lately. I sent letters by Woodifield to Isabel and P Thorne and Bertie, also a few pages of my manuscript diary notes.

Went for a ride with Fábregas to near Poleñino. We rode as far as a sheep-fold where the shepherd was putting his sheep away for the night. It was a lovely day, hills clear and blue, and we could see villages here and there. It was a Sunday and had the peace of Sunday, which is still taken as a day of rest from toil by the farmers. It was sunset when we turned back and dark when we rode back along the road cut deep by cartwheels.

We are still very busy with *enfermos*—another brace of pneumonias. Rather pets all these lads and certainly good patients.

9.3.37

I am feeling very depressed about the international situation and world affairs generally. Read in the paper the English *Dempster* liner had been sunk, with everyone lost, and turned out it was a Spanish American ship. We need more information.

10.3.37

Wrote to Geoffrey a very depressing letter. Fear I am getting a

---

270 A bacterial infection of the skin.

little moody. We started packing our things for Poleñino. There have been heavy guns firing most of the day between Tardienta and the Hermitage. I walked along the railway line with Fábregas, the country is looking very lovely with lucerne patches and trees in blossom and spring in the air. There has been fairly continuous firing. I climbed up a ladder into an unfinished house on the second floor where the militiamen are camped. I looked through binoculars at smoke, but couldn't see where the shells were falling, but it was thought it was our guns.

13.3.37

Left Grañén for Poleñino. We were all up early packing all and sundry into the ambulances. We went to have breakfast at the butcher's house, fried eggs, wine and *anís*. The butcher's wife is really lovely to look at. After fairly fond farewells, as we were crossing the square, a woman rushed out with a cord screaming that our dog Tom was her dog. Many angry expostulations. Anita and I ran with Tom and took him up to the bedroom and I kept watch prepared to be undressed and waiting if the guard attempted to come in. Much chatter between the guard and the woman and a crowd of children gathered around. We had to leave Tom and finally the woman dragged him away. The whole atmosphere was exceedingly hostile to us—Pancho stopped me on the stairs taking pillows and said 'nothing was to leave Grañén'. Ramón and Paulino were to be held for investigation but they fled secretly in a car. Aguiló left his hat at the butchers, but we dared not go back for it.

There is lots to do at Poleñino. Mary and Murray had our room arranged very nicely, six beds in a room 12 x 20, but nice and clean. The men are all sleeping in a room half as big again. There is a lovely large ward with a tiled and marble floor which holds 17 beds, and a small room leading off it with two beds is to be used as a nurses' room.

18.3.37

After one night relieving on night duty, I went for a short walk round the village. All very pretty with lots of straw stacks in all shapes—some nice conical ones.

Men are working on the road to Robres. The river winds round below high banks and rocks, poplar trees in blossom, and the hills very clear.

There was a fiesta in the village, and the local band played in front of the hospital. The population danced and all the village belles turned out; one, in pink and frillies to the ankles, wore gloves.

Yesterday the Cavalry from Grañén paid us a visit.

I received a letter from Lady Mary and Phil Thorne, also a cutting from the *Sydney Morning Herald* of my article on Barcelona of 23 February.

Heard over the wireless from Seville that on the Aragón front, at Huesca, the fascists had caused us heavy casualties and captured war material, etc. Lies. There has been never a casualty and probably only about two shots fired.

19.3.37

Louis, the German battery man, was here today and tells of more captured Italians. His battery is moving higher up into the mountains. There is a possibility of the Carlos Marx Division going to Madrid and some of the Madrid Division coming here to cope with the anarchist political people and their indecision. If so, it means that we will go with them.

We went for a long walk today among the cracked and creviced ground, here and there, on little flat bits, green crops are sprouting. Walked until I got a view of another valley that looked more prosperous—or more fertile. This village is much prettier and cleaner than Grañén. I was very glad to be alone and must go walking more; sat and read then walked back along the dry river bed, resisting the temptation to paddle in the pools. The Pyrenees looked magnificent beyond the coloured spring loveliness, a lovely curve of snow was on the highest peak. It took away my bad feelings.

Letters arrived from Doug, Geoffrey, F Forest, Ralph, Jean, Jean R, Mrs G, Auntie V and Tizzie. What a mail. Wrote to Isabel.

23.3.37

Went to Sariñena with the dentists, Ramón and Moussons, and enjoyed myself. The drive was lovely, round by the *sierretas*, lowish hills of curious formation, one rather like a cathedral, another a water tower.

Sariñena is a bigger pueblo than here with a small square and church, shops and narrow busier streets. I saw over the hospital which is quite large though the operating theatre is not so good as ours. The Superintendent complained to Moussons that the surgical cases evacuated from Vicien were practically all septic whereas those from here and Grañén did well.

"Outdoors after night duty", Agnes with Anita Bolster,
José Cepero and Dr Morales, Jan 1937

I bought oranges and *anís*, a thrill to get in a shop again. We drove home in the bright moonlight. Three men hailed us, and the driver pulled up and other lads had their hands on their pistols but we were only asked were we going to Barbastro. Went to bed early but didn't get much time to write or do anything.

24.3.37

Hernia op. and two pneumonias, rather sick, and keeping busy.

25.3.37

Aguiló received a letter from Bolster saying that the X-ray was to be given to the International Brigade, and that Lowson didn't consider it necessary here. Having had it promised and our waiting for it, it gave a very bad impression of Australian integrity. Lowson is making a bad smell generally all round with her high-handedness and lack of conscience regarding nursing. I wrote to Lowson re the X-ray and forwarded a receipt for five pounds.

A youth arrived with a shot hand. Our aviation has successfully bombed Huesca and Saragossa. The aeroplanes passed over here at 2.30 a.m. but I was asleep.

31.3.37

Bad hernia operation in a.m.—operation excellent. I spent the afternoon cleaning instruments and finding my way about a theatre again. At six o'clock the ambulance arrived with the results of a fascist shell in Tardienta—wicked maiming. One dead on arrival, another with pulp below the knee and the other leg probably to be amputated. Later I undid the dressing and exposed what remained of a leg. Later it was amputated above the knee. Another lad had an arm blown off and two fingers amputated from his other hand. Another shot in the buttock and a fragment lodged in his heel died later despite being given blood transfusions and saline.

Went to bed at 2.30 a.m. shocked to the core. Had I been able

to write then I could have written strongly about the grimness of
these wounds and the suffering. They were all terribly brave.

2.4.37
Put leg in plaster of lad whose other leg was blown off.

Sariñena front: Agnes with Dr Aguiló and associates.

3.4.37
Received word to have everything in readiness for an attack. We
were to advance and the two ambulances were sent to Torralba.
We prepared everything in the theatre—all dressing supplies,
sutures, etc. Ramón was busy making splints. Another

ambulance went off at 2 a.m. but at 8 a.m. the attack was postponed. There was a general feeling of disappointment.

6.4.37

Word again given of the attack on the morrow. Again, everything beautifully prepared, postponed my departure on leave. Two ambulances went off to Torralba at 6 p.m., another at 10 p.m. Angel left alone poor lad. We all went to bed early, Rosita convinced that this time it would happen. T'was my turn to doubt and feel I'd postponed departing to no purpose. All patients evacuated by 1 a.m.

7.4.37

No wounded arrived by 8 a.m. I got up early and washed the theatre floor and after that we waited till the ambulances came back about 3 p.m. with one solitary wounded with several bits of shrapnel, but flesh wounds, poor lad. We all went walking in the sun after that. The wind a little cold.

The X-ray arrived from Barcelona. Aguiló is very pleased. Other equipment too has arrived from England: quantities of bandages which are not needed. Other things too were unnecessary, awful old clothes and filthy instruments practically all of which we've got, air cushions of the wrong type, back rests OK etc. and my hat, poor thing.

8.4.37

I left for Barcelona on leave, a very long and extremely tiring journey. Arrived in Barcelona at 8.30 p.m. and went to the Hotel Lloret. I dined at the Lince, and went on to the Ramblas, but met only the Spanish artist who greeted me pleasantly and we chatted. Left at 10 p.m. and went home to bed.

9.4.37

Dashed about today getting passport stamps. When I went to the British Consulate, I found that O'Donnell had never registered us there and so I could not be given a special stamp, to enable me to return, without difficulty. Went to Café Bressen for lunch expecting to see Vita and Louis but drew a blank. A nasty lunch, and I feeling rotten. Received a wire not to go to England. Met Louis and Prout in the Ramblas Café and went on to the Konsomal Café with party affairs and had a filthy meal and so to bed.

10.4.37

Shopped, went to the British Consulate and registered and changed money. Lunched with Louis in the Plaza de la Universidad. Saw Vita after and had tea, back to hotel and the Café Ramblas for a beer. Reorganized packing. Feeling filthy with an awful headache.

11.4.37

Left for a break at Tossa de Mar. It was a lovely drive by the sea and I so pleased to see it. Took the train to Blanes, a bus to Lloret and another bus to Tossa. Found the Johnstones on the beach.271 Hermann escorted me and Chas H and we went up to the hotel and me straight to bed after lunch. A German couple, an American journalist, Alec Wainman,272 two Charlies,273 and

---

271 A British couple, Nancy and Archie Johnstone, at Tossa de Mar ran a hotel for expatriates that later in the war was converted into a refugee children's colony. See Nancy Johnstone, *Hotel in Flight* (London: Faber & Faber, 1939; London: Clapton Press, 2022) for the description of the British Medical Aid Unit nurses on leave in Tossa de Mar, pp 46-49 "Edna" as Una Wilson; and 104-106, 'Faith' as pseudonym for Agnes; and Miguel Berger, 'From Blue Paradise to the French Camps: Nancy Johnstone's Narratives of the Catalan Costa Brava at War', *Catalan Review*, 25 (Jan 2011): pp 119-129.

272 Alec Wainman, an English Quaker who came to Spain as a driver for the British Medical Aid Unit. Having studied Russian at university and been employed by the British government in Moscow he was drafted by the PSUC to aid as a Russian interpreter in Spain. A gifted photographer he amassed an enormous photographic record of the civil war, including photographs from his visit to Tossa de Mar. See his *Live Souls: Citizens and Volunteers in Civil War Spain* (Vancouver; Ronsdale Press, 2015), pp 107-109.

myself and Nicholas were the guests.

18.4.37

Left Barcelona for Poleñino, a very long journey. Travelled with some railway men whom I'd met on my way down. One man with a dog. After Lérida some militiamen got in. One nice man from Valencia talked to me a lot. He is at Almuniente and Tardienta and told me that the Carlos Marx division got into the fascist trenches and the fascist planes machine gunned them. Hermitage has been taken twice and lost and we still haven't got it. Our aviation didn't play its part and two of our commanders were shot in Sariñena. I waited at the station for an ambulance then walked to the hospital Two letters had arrived in my absence, one from Geoffrey and t'other from Tizzy, nice ones.

19.4.37

On duty on the ward, full of laparotomies, all pretty sick. One with two perforations in the intestines holding his own. The hospital had been hectic for three days, two days before, everyone working day and night, we handled 250 wounded.

20.4.37

Another busy day. A German's leg amputated during the night, and a number from the Battalion of Death (anarchists) with minor wounds from Tardienta in the a.m. The German had been seven days without food, and his leg was alive with maggots as he had been lying among the fascist wounded. We have had about a dozen fascist wounded prisoners here, treated exactly as other patients, to their astonishment. Also officials who interviewed them questioned them politely.

Later in the day a fair number of wounded were brought in from the Carlos Marx battalion. A lung case and one with 11 perforations in the abdomen were admitted to the ward. A very busy day. The Political Commissar, on the eighth day after his perforated stomach, began vomiting and haemorrhaging. A very

---

273 The 'two Charlies', Hunt and Hurling were ambulance drivers from Huesca, Fyrth, *Signal*, p 50.

bad patient, possibly his own fault, as he drank water from the ice bag. He has been given blood transfusions and all manner of things but he will probably die. It is a hard job getting used to the ward in these conditions. Two hernia operations were done today as well.

21.4.36

Went with Aguiló, Sutor and Fábregas in the a.m. to the front at Sariñena. There has been an explosion in a house, the cause unknown. The two homes were completely destroyed, and the windows of the hospital were broken and patients, laparotomies and all, were run out of their beds. Dr Aguiló operated with obsolete instruments and no asepsis practised here.274 The other surgeon with bloody gloves borrowed some of Aguiló's instruments, bloody from his own case. He just picked them up and took them off, and everything was thrown on the floor among the blood and sawdust. The girl assisting in the theatre was quite annoyed when Aguiló stopped her sweeping and raising dust. She brought a drum of gauze which was dusty on top so she blew the dust 'pouff' all over the sterile table and Sutor. A woman badly injured and shocked, with a leg for amputation, was lying on a glass table, a rag covering the pubis, or clad in a tourniquet only, while the doctors discussed the case. Another case was under anaesthetic before the surgeons had scrubbed up. Aguiló did a marvellous eye enucleation with outsized scissors.

23.4.37

Doing relief work on night duty. The Political Commissar is either bad or mad, or a bit of both, as he gave me a whacking blow on the face and tried to kick me, etc. Nearly his last moment but I restrained myself. Cries of shame on him came from other

---

274 The command headquarters of the Anarchist battalions was located at Sariñena. For a more sympathetic description of the same hospital see Franz Borkenau, *The Spanish Cockpit: An Eyewitness Account of the Political and Social Conflicts of the Spanish Civil War*, (London: Pluto Press, 1937), p 104.

patients. A fair number of minor wounds arrived too. The Political Commissar was evacuated this p.m. The weather is getting very hot.

24.4.37

Listened in to the radio for a while to a fascist station telling lies about their capture of 350 bombers of ours; more than we possess. Also that all foreign volunteers captured will be expatriated because they have been deceived into coming here.

X-ray apparatus is useful, two pieces of shrapnel in a lad's arm were discovered by screening and removed.

11.30 p.m. Aeroplanes passed over the hospital. Sariñena telephoned for an ambulance urgently to be sent, don't know the reason why. The Administrator returned. Off night duty. Heard several guns during the night, and half expected that we should receive wounded this a.m., but none came. Went down to the river and lay on the bank in the sun and bathed. Slept a while in the afternoon. The ward is much quieter now, and the outer wards have been evacuated. R and I were going to the café, and about four of us had coffee and listened on the radio to the fascists giving lists of their successes and captures.

25.4.37

Relieving in the theatre. Nothing doing. Went down to the river to bathe before lunch. I went to the café with R and the stretcher bearers and drank beer and we had a good lunch.

1.5.37

The Divisional Band, after visiting the café here and returning to their digs in the crevices by the station, took the first curve at 70 miles an hour and one *camión* overturned. Twenty of them were hurt, one with a fractured skull died, the others mainly concussed, abrasions, broken ribs and arm. It was absolute bedlam attending to their wounds, all were put in the lower salon. We had a busy morning. I went riding in the afternoon, all alone, on a broken winded stumbling horse, but a nice beastie for all that. I rode up a river bed thinking it would be softer on the beast's hoofs but it skidded and the pebbles were numerous. Rode up to a wheat patch amid the barren rocks and gathered a handful.

4.5.37

There has been fighting in Barcelona and the remainder of the Police Guard has been wiped out with a great number of casualties.275 The hospitals are full and the radio is calling for all doctors to attend.

[This entry appears at the end of the diary]

In May the news of fighting in Barcelona depressed us all. The Catalans were anxious about their families and we were worried about one of our nurses who was on leave in Barcelona at the time. None of us knew definitively what the cause of all the fighting was about when it had begun. It was tragic that it should happen when anarchists and socialists were both fighting a common enemy. The result of it was reorganization and more unified control of our forces. During the Barcelona trouble some of the anarchist divisions had been withdrawn from our front just when a big offensive had been planned. Two English lads, volunteers in the Battalion of Death occasionally walked the odd 20 kilometres to visit us. They wore very smart blue-green uniforms with skull and crossbones badges. Each time they came to see us their beards were longer and more unkempt. They did not intend to shave until the war was over. We celebrated their visit at our local café one occasion. There was beer, and laden with books and any English food we could find some of us walked along a little of the road with them. On the last occasion we treated the café to some English songs—the crowd gathered

---

275 The street fighting in Barcelona in the first week of May 1937 was part of a concerted effort by the central government and the Spanish Communist Party to exclude from power the anarchists and the POUM, who opposed government centralization and the growing strength of the Communist Party.

round us while we went from one song to another.

8.5.37
Belcher and Peel arrived and told me that the Ascaso, the Durruti and another anarchist division have withdrawn to Barcelona to subdue the trouble there.276 Lacking those divisions our proposed attack has been postponed. The attack had been arranged on this front to necessitate the fascists' withdrawal of troops from Bilbao. Had a swim before lunch, played deck tennis after lunch, and went to the café at night; the party was merry and bright, and all sang. We English gave voice to English ditties with a surrounding audience, one of the military band played the concertina. Afterwards we went for a short walk down the road all together and set the dogs howling. Too dark for Peel and Belcher to find their way home so they slept at the hospital.

9.5.37
Received three wounded this afternoon, one severe lung wound, one in the neck, and t'other in the leg. A hand wound cleaned and sutured in the a.m.

10.5.37
An accident case arrived from Grañén and had an amputation of his left forearm. Busy day. Later a chest case was in theatre, with the muscle sutured his condition improved. Still later, leg case X-rayed and *metralla* (shrapnel) pieces seen and removed in theatre.

11.5.37
Another accident case, a militiaman handling explosives blew off the first joint of three fingers.

---

276 See footnote 20.

12.5.37

An appendectomy in theatre, the appendix rotten. Went walking afterwards and collected feed for the rabbits.

14.5.37

Hermia operation. I had a very short ride on a good grey horse and galloped around the village. There is news of possible changes in hospital staff which is very disturbing.

15.5.37

Still no definite news of a move. A crowd of us went to the café where they were singing flamenco.

Hospital surroundings with ambulance in Poleñino street.

23.5.37

Awake in the early a.m. At 4 a.m. two fascist planes passed low to the left of the hospital and bombed Alcubierre and the Sierras returning again about three quarters of an hour later flying higher. Reorganization of everything going on.

24.5.37

Four *practicantes* arrived—awful bums and sissies. Everyone disliked them on sight and resented their intrusion.

25.5.37

Practicantes at work—one told me I could give a lad Pantofon.

31.5.37

Letter received from Tizzy, praise be. Barcelona bombed yesterday, 100 killed which has caused great indignation. Ramón tells me the war will finish with a pact and that is the general impression. One feels the acceptance of the inevitable depressing, as is all the reorganization.

1.6.37

The *Deutschland* at anchor in the port of Ibiza has been bombed by Republican planes. The *Deutschland* was there for international control and fired at the Republican planes. Eighty killed and about 100 wounded on the *Deutschland*, and also some Italian officers were killed. There is much German indignation, and two German cruisers and three destroyers bombed Almería in retaliation.277 All this has caused much chatter among the Powers, and Germany and Italy are threatening to retire from the Non-Intervention Committee of Control. Their ships have been withdrawn, causing consternation

---

277 The *Deutschland* was bombed on 26 May 1937 by two Republican planes, killing 37 and wounding 75 of the crew. In retaliation, on 31 May a cruiser and four German destroyers shelled Almería, destroying large sections of the two and killing 19 civilians. See Thomas, *The Spanish Civil War*, pp 685-6.

to the other powers. England disapproves of acts of retaliation, and Germany is abusive about England's disapproval. The Spanish press have censured the lukewarm support in the English and French democratic press which refer to the bombardment of Barcelona as the action of Franco's air planes, instead of openly calling them Italian ones which they are.

4.6.37

General Mola died as a result of a plane crash.278 With three others he was on a reconnoitring flight and crashed over his own territory.

5.6.37

There are great changes on the Aragón front. 279 Only military trains are running now and our post is coming in by truck. War material and troops keep coming. Two thousand Ascaso troops (FAI) have been sent to the Madrid front, and 2,000 from the Madrid front are being sent here, and the others are moving up. General Pozas is inspecting this district,280 to Torralba and

---

278 General Emilio Mola, the commander of the Nationalists' northern divisions, had been the principal organizer of the Spanish generals' rebellion in July 1936.

279 After May Days in Barcelona, the Catalan army was reorganised and brought under the control of the central Republican administration. A new Republican offensive against Huesca was begun in late May 1937. Led by General Pozas Perea, its objective was to draw the Nationalists away from their offensive in north-western Spain. The Huesca campaign was a failure, with heavy Republican casualties. Bilbao fell to the Nationalists in the third week of Jun 1937.

280 General Sebastián Pozas Perea was a career army officer who had commanded the Civil Guard during the Popular Front and became Minister of the Interior in July 1936. By May 1937 he had joined the Communist Party and had been placed at the head of the Army of the East on the Aragón front where he put down attempts by anarchist and POUM militias to return to Barcelona in the May Days street fighting. Pozas led the Huesca offensive in May 1937, the Belchite offensive in October 1937, and dispersed the anarchist

Tardienta. Tardienta is being bombed daily so the General Command of the front has moved to Torralba, leaving only about 40 people in Tardienta. Food has become a great difficulty for us. The hospital has now to buy its food and pay local staff from the monies received from the Brigade, which is ten pesetas daily for each patient. 281 The Brigade owes us 25,000 pesetas, but as yet we have no money.

We have meatless days mostly, an egg for breakfast and water (we have tea still). The local committee is still not forthcoming. Paolino gathers snails and searches for mushrooms to cook. We are all feeling abdominal discomfort in the epigastric region, appeased a little by food. There is no jam, but dry hard bread, beans still, and we have some honey. With luck we might get some fruit soon.

7.6.37

Word received that the Estado Mayor (General Command) is moving here from Almuniente. There is also some talk of an attack being made in a couple of weeks.

A little paragraph in the daily newspaper said, 'I believe in the fear, almost insuperable of England and France before the bravado and provocation of the Italian and German dictators'. There was also reference to Mola's two boasts before the Madrid campaign: 'In a few days I shall take coffee in the Gate of the Sun Café in Madrid'; and the other that 'if Bilbao doesn't surrender I shall convert Vizcaya into a cemetery'.

Germany wants the Non-Intervention Committee to agree among other things that, 'in the case of aggression the ships' commanders can take rapid reprisal methods against those who violate international rights without waiting for counsel of four powers'.

Council of Aragón in August 1937.

281 This arrangement was part of the general reorganisation of the Republican army whereby militias and units attached to particular regions or parties were disbanded to bring the entire military effort under a central command.

8.6.37

A *Sanidad* man was admitted with a perianal abscess. He made no fuss about modesty and was put in position before the anaesthetic. Went walking to the station in the p.m. with Murray, Susan and Patience, to enquire if any fruit had arrived.282 We met the Blood Transfusion Outfit and begged a lift. We waited for the train, and oranges and tomatoes arrived. Also there was a package from England sitting in the waiting room which we hoped would be chocolate and cigarettes. We had a terrifying journey back to the hospital in the Blood Transfusion coach, rolling from side to side and going round curves, simply terrifying. The pups with us were terrified too, much to the amusement of the doctor. I had thoughts of the band's performance round the curve at 70 mph. It was though a pleasant little excitement after the general feeling of boredom here. There was great disappointment on opening the English package as there were no cigarettes, and no package for me. How childish one feels. Ramón came down for a moment. Letter from Tizzy to cheer me.

9.6.37

A hot morning. We bathed in the river which is very muddy and running fast. I am feeling bored and homesick. The hills looking lovely, fresh breeze, just the atmosphere to make one long for peace and idle content. I don't really want to leave Spain but am sick of nursing and hospitals. Sat out in the afternoon sun looking down at waving silver trees like birches and the green gardens on the other bank. The village sheep trailed past, poor-looking rams leading with bells round their necks, backwards and forwards and round about, no quiet grazing for them. Why

---

282 The English nurse, Patience Darton who had travelled to Spain in February 1937 in order to to nurse the seriously ill commander of the British International Brigade, Tom Wintringham in Albacete, was transferred to Poleñino at the end of April 1937, in Angela Jackson, *'For us it was Heaven'; The Passion, Grief, and Fortitude of Patience Darton.* (London: Sussex Academic Press, Cañada Blanch Centre for Contemporary Spanish Studies, 2012).

they don't go down on the bit of river flat I can't understand, where there is good lucerne and clover there enough for them to graze quietly for a while. The shepherd follows slowly. Now they are nearing the river bank. No they don't go down.

A gypsy family has camped in one of the huts on the outside of the village. The woman in a red sweater with a red kerchief round her head is busy cooking some sort of stew over an open fire and a half-naked very brown infant stands by, and a mongrel long-haired lean dog barks at all intruders. The gypsy man is fat and swarthy, with a shirt hanging out, and walks around the village always going somewhere mysteriously. All the village women sit in the street at the doors of their houses, knitting and sewing or feeding their infants. There is very little difference between this village and a Moroccan one as far as outside appearance goes. There are low doors and mules disappear through the entrance hall and one almost expects them to mount the stairs to the *primer piso* (first floor). The restless sheep and their tinkling bells go by, goats with them. The sheep have fairly recently been shorn.

Hospital vehicles in the hospital courtyard. Note ambulances with the capacity to carry multiple wounded from the front on tiered stretchers.

11.6.37

News has come of preparations for the attack. Our big ambulance departed for Barbastro with Ventura and the other nice fat chauffeur. I felt sad at so much change in the staff.

We spent the day getting things prepared scrubbing and cleaning instruments. The German, Waldie, came begging provisions and cough mixtures and importantly whispering 'there's to be an attack, have you got everything ready, you'll soon have plenty of work to do.' The wretched little French doctor of chemistry told me I ought to clean instruments only with alcohol. The doctor Taberna arrived and all present patients have been evacuated. We are all feeling restless and a bit depressed. Catalan coastal villages have been bombed.

12.6.37

After the routine work went down to the river, bathed and sun-baked. A lovely warm day. The gypsy encampment has been enlarged, an old man was making baskets and the kids searching each other for lice. Two men passed us carrying fishing baskets.

The guns have been busy all day and three planes passed low over the hospital, two bi-planes and one *chato*. We have heard the noise of planes intermittently during the day. There are rumours at night that we have surrounded Huesca, leaving it cut off and we are advancing towards Saragossa. The Fascist offensive against Bilbao intensified after a couple of days of quiet. The visibility has been bad against rebel planes. All quiet round Madrid. I was talking to Patience about the Catalan village bombings. She tells me that the British Embassy at Valencia has had adequate proof that Germans were bombing these small villages and it was announced that they were bombed from the *Canarias*. But the *Canarias* was in several other places at the same time. The British Embassy cook was killed. Now the English staff sleep down the coast and see the Embassy only as an office.

13.6.37

Huesca is said to be surrounded, completely cut off, and the end is only a question of days. Waldie arrived, agreeing with this story. Saragossa has been bombarded. There are other rumours of seven fascist planes brought down and the newspaper is complaining bitterly of extensive espionage in Aragón. Aragón they say will be the deciding factor in the war.

No guns or planes today since it's Sunday. We received seven wounded, five early in the a.m. Leg sutured and all evacuated by midday with two others. One amputation of a leg done in Alcubierre, t'other both legs with shrapnel splinters. Two hospital trains wait at the station. The news tonight is that all hospitals except Grañén and Poleñino are full.

Ramón came down from Torralba with *enfermos*. Tardienta is still being bombed and Santa Quiberia will probably be attacked tomorrow or the day after. Then we'll get the wounded.

I went walking with Luz to the cemetery to look for a mythical spring. The cemetery has been enlarged since our coming to Poleñino. Bilbao is still hanging on.

14.6.37

The rumour is that Huesca is burning after an air battle over Huesca by 40 planes, Gloriosas and Asenias. A lass here who escaped from Saragossa says it's fairly easy to escape as the guards are awfully silly. In Saragossa nobody is allowed to walk about in pairs, not even small children, all houses have to be left open night and day, and no one is allowed to talk at all about the war. Men are stopped 'hands up' in the street, and if after three times of asking they don't say 'Arriba España' and give the fascist salute they are shot.

A couple of planes passed over today but no guns. One chest and spine wounded arrived, very ill, poor lamb, and paralyzed, but insists on doing everything for himself. He died later during the night.

16.6.37

Went for a walk with Patience in the lovely windy evening. Ramón came with *enfermos* who are now all evacuated. The Blood Transfusion Ambulance arrived in time for the meal. We made fairly merry after supper waltzing to the radio.

The news from Bilbao is not good. Dr Sostres denied rumours of Huesca being surrounded and burnt. Our planes have bombarded Saragossa. The International Brigade only has been fighting. They are very well organized with their own doctors etc. Barbastro we hear is full of wounded waiting to be evacuated to Lérida or Barcelona. The big hospital train is waiting at Poleñino. Jerry returned from Barcelona and brought my photographs, most of them a washout. Feeling rather bored, but received a letter from Anita.

We decided to lunch by the river and just got nicely settled when Fábregas arrived for Suzanne. Grañén had telephoned for Aguiló and a team to attend to wounded there. They have been away all day. We stayed on by the river, bathing and sunbaking.283 Today is my last day in theatre.

Nine bombing bi-planes passed over on their return to Sariñena, and were inspected by a Russian chaser plane. On its melancholy journey through Poleñino it crashed near Grañén, or rather made a forced landing but none were hurt.

The theatre at Grañén is now full of flies with nothing ready; blood transfusions were given cold and after-treatment is not given promptly. One fractured humerus with the elbow halfway up the arm died on the table from loss of blood and shock. Aguiló and Co were not welcomed so they didn't send for us. They treated 160 wounded and arrived back at 3 a.m.

17.6.37

A touring party left for Grañén after all hands cleaned instruments and gloves. Murray and I went instead of Suzanne and Aguiló drove. At a narrow stretch of road, with a car coming towards us, and a reaper and cart on ahead, we slid off the road but fortunately didn't capsize. Two mules were hitched on to the truck and off we went again. We arrived at Grañén to find *practicantes* sitting at the door and no more wounded. Aguiló inspected a man with a wounded bladder and a head case who

---

283 Patience Darton noted that the local anarchist mayor and local people disapproved of nurses swimming in the river, in Jackson, *For Us it Was Heaven*, p 48.

was propped up, and the bladder lad without a pillow.

The hospital is full of *chicas* running about. It is now a beautiful hospital with 70 beds, a bathroom, a douche upstairs, large wards and a couple of small ones. The operating theatre has been painted and there are hand basins outside and an autoclave, but otherwise not much has changed. We went over the hospital train; about five coaches for wounded, one with two operating tables, office supplies, x-ray apparatus, and a dressing room with several patients lying there under a tree. There is a huge engine to pull the train and the dining car was all set ready for the meal with wine and fresh bread on the tables.

18.6.37

A typhoid patient died during night, he shouldn't have died but was probably perforated on arrival. Very pale and shocked poor lad. Not sleeping well. Ramón was here in the a.m. Robres was bombarded yesterday; no casualties but houses were destroyed and the ambulances missed the bombs. Today Gloriosas was busy again, more rumours of Huesca surrounded and it should be ours tomorrow? Bilbao is still holding out but it is difficult to know the real position, only that it is still in Republican hands. The blood *camión* came by for a moment. Ramón again came in during the afternoon to gather maize to put camouflage on top of the ambulance. I went cutting it with him and afterwards we drank some champagne he had brought. Today I learnt a new expression, *'fotre un cop de pal al cap'*.284 Feeling flat, after supper I went walking over the bridge, met the *chicas*, and it began to rain. I bathed late in the afternoon with Marcelino. I sold some film to Suzanne, 20 cigarettes for the film and a packet of Celtics for use of the camera.

19.6.37

Ramón brought some champagne. Morales came and asked about dental instruments which are very short and can't be got in Barcelona. The aeroplanes have been very busy but our front or

---

284 A Catalan expression, 'to get a bang on the head with a stick'.

division is still not in the fight. When they attack Santa Quiberia it touches us. This lack of work is demoralising. Received a letter from A.G. Phillips.

20.6.37

My turn for night duty, but Francisca slept in the alcove and as there were only three *enfermos* in the lower ward I went to bed. During the night five *enfermos* were admitted but I was not called and a little bad feeling was roused.

21.6.37

A meeting of nurses today to protest against various irregularities in the distribution of work and to clear up a slight misunderstanding between Spaniards and ourselves. All amicably settled. And so to night duty in earnest, five patients in upper ward sleeping fairly soundly.

Earlier in the night Fábregas and Taberna, bright boys, searched or glanced through my diary for frivolous references or I know not what. The keeping of a diary seems to afford Fábregas much mirth so we have decided to give him mention honourable or otherwise as food for its curiosity. Bilbao is reported to be in the hands of the enemy and Sariñena was bombed this a.m. causing damage to the aerodrome; fortunately the planes were absent, (hearsay). Depressed by war news and night duty though it was a lovely moonlight night with Henry and Gladys, the rabbits, sitting peacefully in the middle of the terrace. When do rabbits sleep! The guns have been a little busy during the morning. Went walking with P in the evening along the road, sky cloudy and Sierra (Alcubierre) a dirty blue. The lower Pyrenees are a very pale misty blue with the odd patch of snow showing.

22.6.37

Bilbao has been evacuated, the papers report, and there has been a withdrawal of Republican troops and armaments.

23.6.37

The hospital is full, mainly oddments and no evacuation patients sleeping in the men's dormitory.

24.6.37

I went walking while five fascist planes bombed Alcubierre. I saw them clearly and the smoke and the noise of the bombs sounded very close. I walked on to the other side where smoke was still rising and saw one plane come back and swoop down behind the hill, probably machine-gunning shock troops whose tents are over there. I just got back to the hospital when the ambulance arrived, but failed miserably to do anything, stood about foolishly and so went to bed. Heard another ambulance arrive and got up, trying to tell myself the things I must do quickly. Seemed it was false alarm but found they'd taken the patients into the dining room. Managed to pull myself together. An old paralytic came in the ambulance too—too good an opportunity to be missed. Apparently there was a military parade in Alcubierre and the fascists must have known. Four houses were completely destroyed and people buried under them. Our wounded were not so grave. One head case died after the operation, pretty hopeless from the beginning; several concussions but so far no abdominals, mostly bits of shrapnel.

25.6.37

Had a hectically busy night. Other ambulances arrived after I had gone to bed, with people rescued from the fallen houses, mostly concussions, but needing observation. One man was absolutely pulseless and was given all the stimulants, salines and blood transfusions. Doubt as to whether there would be further evacuations. There are patients sleeping on the terrace, in the men's dormitory, the dining room and down by the stairs. After much insistence, the *auto-chir* came plus our large ambulance from Sariñena.285 What a thrill to see it, I nearly wept with relief. From one bombardment we had 100 odd wounded. All day long ambulances arrived; at first with the wounded and later

---

285 *Auto-chirs* were large enclosed lorries containing a full scale mobile surgical theatre.

with those who had been injured or buried under the houses when these people were finally excavated. The ward floors and beds were full of bits of stone and dust from their clothes. One old woman of 90 blind and deaf was brought down to be evacuated. Her only son had been killed. Why, she wailed, should she be left old and infirm and tired of life and her son killed. Our casualties had never been so heavy since the attack in April. Finished evacuating patients at 3 a.m. then began clearing up in between looking after the transfusion patient, a perfect lamb, who never murmured. The whole hospital seemed full of dust from patients who had been buried. One of the sixteen-year-olds who was wounded slightly in the leg previously, is back with a wound, (superficial) in the chest and has lost a lot of blood. The blood transfused man died, probably his ureters crushed.

26.6.37

Spent most of the day in bed. We had a case in theatre at night, a strangulated hernia. The old boy said his condition was aggravated by carrying dead and injured from the fallen houses in Alcubierre. Nice old pet. Taberna went back to Sariñena, a nice lad.

27.6.37

The hospital is full again but no evacuation as they are mostly *enfermos*. Mary expected back from England and there is great excitement.286 Two *practicantes* went to meet her. Aguiló shaved and put on a clean shirt. Fábregas talked about his little dog, who would bring him cigarettes and we tried guessing what she'd bring in the parcels mentioned. But no train arrived from Barcelona. Not daring to expect anything I wasn't so disappointed, but a feeling of flatness prevailed everywhere.

Night. Still no evacuation, this is getting chronic and with it my temper is getting very bad. A poor old girl in the alcove is pratically blind. Her son was killed in the bombardment of Alcubierre and she is being evacuated and will go where she has

---

286 Mary Slater, Palfreeman, *Salud*, p 251.

no friends. The old girl asks continuously for food.

I have decided to leave here in a month.

28.6.37

Morales is away. Specticasy (?) in bed but we lifted him out and carried him downstairs. I got up for lunch and went with A. F. and Martin to Sariñena. A rather pleasant outing. Mary didn't come though we searched the train at Sariñena and later at Poleñino but she wasn't on it. The truck stalled both at Sariñena and Poleñino and we all had to push. Ramón and José came in for a while. More difficulty about evacuation, which finally began at midnight. We are all exceedingly tired.

*Poleñino "chicas", Julia, Luisa, Pilar, María, Ramona and
Marina helping in the hospital, June 1937.*

29.6.37

Mary arrived back from England, but no parcels for me. Had a party in the alcove, but I was very depressed and felt like crying. Dreamt of Bela today, dancing in some tremendous place to the 'Dollar Princess' waltz, so nice to see him. Weather windy and cold.

2.7.37

Murray went on English leave. We had a fairly quiet night and the weather is warm so we went to the river to bathe and sunbathe. We heard planes but couldn't see them, but heard six bombs exploding but at a distance probably in the Sierras. No casualties arrived anyway. We had a youth in with a possibly self-inflicted wound in the foot, and possibly going gangrenous. On night duty alone and had an almost uncontrollable desire to throw things. The desire for leave is growing daily.

7.7.37

There was an article in the paper telling of libraries and classes held in the trenches for lads learning to read. Seventy per cent of the population is unable to read or write. In Madrid before the Revolution there was school accommodation for 60,000 and there were 160,000 children of school age.

Alcubierre is to be evacuated and Robres will hold the General Command. The Almuniente staff are coming here. The church will house soldiers and our bar also. They are building temporary offices on spare ground and the place is beginning to hum with workmen and militiamen. I went inside the church where the heads of all the figures have been smashed and the church completely denuded.

The floor is very old, inclined to a Gothic nave with nice old designs on the tiles of the chapel. The agricultural machines have been turned out of the chapel—one was an H.V. Mackay Sunshine harvester.287 Back in the theatre I did throw a pair of scissors across the floor. Perforated gastric ulcer in a.m. in

---

287 An Australian machinery company.

theatre.

8.7.37

Very bored and depressed. No letters. There is mention in the
paper of fighting in Aragón south of the Ebro. A Swiss and a
Czech in the ward who say that Belcher and Peel are in
Barcelona. The anarchist Battalion of Death has been disbanded.

9.7.37

Just after breakfast an ambulance arrived from Vicien. There
were four severely wounded arms. The first one an amputation of
the right arm, another with a very compound fracture and an
arm badly gashed and legs and body burnt. Later in theatre we
did a nephrectomy with a ruptured kidney. All very bloody. One
lad was yelling in what sounded like Chinese and was upset at us
all because we couldn't understand, but he swore in Spanish. All
the result of a bombardment.

11.7.37

We had a hand injury in the a.m. and a head case in the p.m. In
the afternoon about 50 cavalry arrived and tied their horses
below. Antonia knew some of them and said they had been
quartered in her village. They are ex-POUM people, and are
supposed to have deserted their officers as fascists and are
joining some other Republican group. They are a fairly tough-
looking lot, one heavily spectacled man seemed to be in charge.
Some wore scarves spotted and coloured round their heads, or
big straw hats and militia capes, with blankets and bags strapped
to their saddles and guns, bottles and even a pullet.

Some of the horses were beautifully groomed; one chestnut
particularly with a saddle newly polished. A few wore spurs and
most of them wore the usual rope sandals. They exchanged a fair
amount of back chat from the terrace. Practically all of them led a
spare horse, either with or without saddles and pack.

The village maidens appeared in their Sunday best very elegant
and pretty most of them. They came in twos, threes and fives
giggling girlishly, surprised to see the horsemen of course and

frightened to pass the horses. They walked past amid the impertinent and appreciative remarks and glances of the men. Finding no beer and just resting awhile they rode off again though some had time to start a meal in the houses and came running out when the other half had gone, their mouths too full to speak.

Spanish military cavalry from a dismantled POUM unit arrives in Poleñino plaza, 11 Jul 1937.

In the evening after supper, and after I had received a letter from Tizzy and was jubilant, I went walking a little with Fábregas and Pila. Behind the hospital there was dancing in the street. The soldiers sprinkled water on the ground to lay the dust, but we danced with dust and pebbles in the shoes.

Afterwards I danced a circular waltz with one or two people in the room beside the wireless. It was good fun. Pila, Jerry, Patingón, Pérez, F, Margaret and myself, etc, plus of course the village. Very hot again.

12.7.37

I received a card from Lowson telling me of her possible return to Australia, and expressing surprise at my probable visit to England.288 Two hernias in theatre in the a.m.

13.7.37

Again two hernias in theatre in the a.m. Patience sick. Belcher and an Irishman, Patrick, walked over from Sesa. They were full of tales of their Battalion of Death about to be joined to another division. They were intended as a shock battalion of indeterminate, but mainly anarchist politics, but failed to get the arms and equipment promised. They have been in the trenches for weeks with one rifle between five men, and had the fascists attacked they had nothing but stones.

Each man who gets a rifle guards it with his life. One of four airmen who had been bombing Huesca relates that there is a huge red cross on the hospital roof, with four anti-aircraft guns on the red cross. In their battalion there was a lack of organization generally, roll was never taken so no one had any knowledge of the dead or wounded in the last attack. Men periodically go off on leave (after an attack) without permission and stay away a month and return to claim their pay. Patrick, an ex-Irish soldier of HM army, had been sentenced before the Irish Republic to 15 years imprisonment for rebelling, I gathered,

---

288 Mary Lowson returned to Australia in August 1937 to carry out fund-raising for the Australian Spanish Relief Committee.

among other things. He was sent to a prison ship out of Belfast which was hell on earth, minimum of food, one blanket, no boots, thin clothes, food lowered down in a bucket etc., many of them died of TB. After 18 months he was released by the Republicans and treated to champagne. Patrick is an ardent anarchist but a fine fellow. The battalion sat in the front line trenches waiting to attack, and after about three days without ammunition and the attack not coming off, most of the battalion walked back to the village. B and P and an American youth stayed and the others were all put in jail. There were bullrushes in front of their trench and B and P wanted to cut them down since the Fascists could use them as a screen to walk right up to their trench. So finally the commander ordered them to be removed in daylight and during firing. The commander, showing a lad how to use a pistol, fired four shots into the lad's foot. The battalion has six commanders, five of whom are in Barcelona. Their pay has been reduced from 15 pesetas to ten *per diem* by General Pozas. The 15 they got before was as a shock battalion but Pozas doesn't consider them worth it.

14.7.37
All patients evacuated. Went to the *auto-chir* with the last two, one for burns. Everything ready for an attack with Susan and Patience ill in bed. Afterwards everyone a little excited.

15.7.37
Spent the day doing extra preparations, two *auto-chirs* arrived, and a large ambulance. Grañén telephoned for assistance but Dr Aguiló is not allowed to move from here. After supper we made a little merry with cognac and company. Cook's *compañera* arrived. I went to bed in Mary's room and at 2 a.m. was called by Harrison as the wounded had arrived. All the men were up, feeling thoroughly heavy with sleep and when ordered to bed again, went gladly.

16.7.37
Two lower wards are full, and there are about ten in the big ward.

Three dead, nothing very grave in the wards, mostly arms and feet, and one chest. All the wounded were evacuated by 11 a.m. and *auto-chirs* and the ambulance went back. The rumour is that the attack in the Sierra of Robres is over and that it was not meant to be a big attack but merely to relieve the boredom of the troops. Pancho Villa of Tardienta among the wounded, his fifth wound. A big bluff creature, he said that there had not been heavy casualties and neither side had gained much.

Poleñino is changing out of recognition with *Estado Mayor* arrived. Cars, trucks and motor bikes, making a noisy hell of the place. The Catalan cook talking hard to his plurry bird Blanca, '*que ets maca*'.289 Gladys had five rabbits, and Cook has a hedgehog in a box with a young rat tied by the leg, also sundry sparrowlings and the baby owls.

We went to see the school children's exposition. Quite amusing, the map of Australia was not too good though some of the copies of pictures were well done. The girls' samplers were good, as usual.

17.7.37
Two wounded arrived, an arm and a bullet through the buttocks which had ruptured the bladder. Both repaired in theatre. I received a letter from John Fisher, but feeling fairly bad tempered. Went walking with F and M and felt rather more cheerful, we all fell or were pushed into the canal.

18.7.37
The band came tonight but it was too hot to dance. The place is lousy with Estado Mayor people. Britain is talking of giving Franco belligerent rights on the withdrawal of foreign volunteers. Bah. They won't withdraw them.

19.7.37
Grañén has been bombed. Only two hurt. Leaflets were dropped

---

289 'How pretty you are.'

inviting the population and soldiers to desert to the fascists, giving the fascist *Arriba España* salute and taking their arms with them. Great alarm there and the civil population ran to cover. I didn't hear or see the planes. Two new nurses have arrived from England. One is Hobart-trained but they brought no parcels. There was a general meeting in front of the church followed by dancing to a military band. Too hot and dusty but the village was gay. I sat by the bridge and talked with the new lasses on a lovely moonlight night and no guns.

21.7.37

Suzanne is very ill—blood transfusion from staff and village.290 Eight transfusions all told. Specialling S. I had to postpone my departure.

24.7.37

Went walking with Fábregas and Martin, and we all very thirsty, decided to try the church for beer. Asked in my best Spanish and was told to go to the *Intendencia* people supplying on the patio. '*Hola guapa, que quiere?*'291 they said, but they had no beer, but promised to come to the hospital and tell me when the next lot arrived. Afterwards I went visiting in a private house with Fábregas. We drank wine and cognac and I talked better. We swallowed green plums and viewed the photographs of the youngest fat daughter who is missing in Saragossa.

25.7.37

*Molto stanco e stufato della vita; ma come si fa questa stronza a farmi arrabbiatissima. Per lo più l'altra mi da più fastidia.*292

---

290 Susan Souter, Scottish nurse, later married Dr Aguiló. Their daughter with her mother was born in England and the family were reunited in Spain years after the end the civil war. Palfreeman, Salud, p 252.

291 'Hi gorgeous, what do you want?'

292 'Very tired and fed up with life, how is it that this turd of a woman makes me so angry. And the other one annoys me even more.'

Very hot. *Estado Mayor* arranged a football match in aid of the hospital. I didn't see it. Patience kicked off amid cheers and afterwards there was dancing in one of the *plazas del pueblo*. We have a town crier now. Formerly the son of the postman went round with his little horn, now a soldier does it with better voice but more self-consciousness.

At the dance I did not enjoy myself over much, getting mostly dud partners and being tired anyway. A journalist has been spending the afternoon in the hospital—just too bad we only have *enfermos* to show him.

After supper in one of the *plazas del pueblo* we had a cinema show. Pancho Villa and couple of the telephone men were exercising their English with Dorothy. When a man dragged up a hay cart we rushed it. One of the villagers produced chairs so we had a box to view the moonlit performance. An exciting day.

26.7.37

Bought a bottle of gin. Went with Martin to the *Intendencia* to get a *vale* for beer. No beer as yet. I was taken in to see the chef, and ex-cook's assistant I believe, and was treated very courteously. Twenty-five pesetas gone in one fell swoop, but I owe the hospital personnel for cigarettes. Martin mixed us Gin Fizzes. Ramón came down from Torralba and told us that the day that Grañén was bombed tanks were due to arrive there and the place where they were expected to be was bombed. Espionage work no doubt. Susan is better.

One of the medical students told us of his experiences at the beginning of the revolution. He had been given leave from doing his military service to sit his examinations. Before beginning military service proper they did three months instruction, camps, etc, but it was customary to avoid most of this if they were able to bribe the sergeants, etc, and this he had done.

On 17 July he received orders to go to the *cuartel*. Having no knowledge of politics he did not guess at any reason for this order but had to go to the *cuartel*, where he and his comrades were kept confined to barracks, still not being told any reason.

On the 19th he and a friend were put on sentry duty at the entrance. Having evaded their military instruction neither he nor his friend had any knowledge of how to load their guns let alone fire them, and when they heard noise of firing they trembled with fright. The officer called the guards within and delivered the 60 soldiers a speech exhorting them to defend their country and their flag, which flag he didn't mention. When the mob began banging at the gate, they were lined up behind it. When the gate was broken open with a telegraph pole there appeared men in all sorts of garb, handkerchiefs round their heads, knives in mouths their only weapons. The soldiers were ordered to fire but they only fired once, the student got a blow on the neck and remembered no more. When he recovered consciousness he sat up and rubbed his neck and there were the whole 60 of them in a line, almost as they had fallen one on top of t'other like a ballet. Some had received knife wounds but mostly blows. They were then lined up against the quadrangle wall to be shot, but an old sergeant protested that the soldiers were not to blame. They were released and told they had been pardoned.

On leaving the *cuartel* in every street and every square they were fired at, 'pim, pim, pim', machine guns in the squares, on the roofs and from the houses. When they were not running they lay flat in the gutters or crouched in doorways. Taking off their soldiers' tunics they ran clad only in their trousers. Two of his fellow students were killed. It took him the whole day to get back to the hospital.

Two days later they came to the hospital and took him off to the *cuartel* again telling him that as he had done some military training he must go to Zaragossa and fight. He was forced into a *camión* with men and women singing and drinking merrily. He sat behind a benzine tank and after one of their many stoppages for more drink and food he hopped out and found his way back to the hospital.

Another two days and again he was ordered to the *cuartel*. Refusing to go to Zaragossa with two companions he was imprisoned and given bread and water, but little of that. But after a day he escaped through the window and went back again to the hospital. Asked why he always went to the hospital, he told me that his people were away in the country. He had no money and at the hospital he got his food and living.

So another two or three days and back to the *cuartel*, this time he demanded to see the chief, explaining to him that he was a medical student, knew nothing of fighting and could serve in the *Sanidad* (medical service) or looking after the wounded in hospital. 'So you're a medical student and can look after the sick? Well, you can stay here and look after our 20 sick mules'. For three days he cleaned the stables and brushed the mules, using a paint brush he applied a veterinary medicament to some. He had to ride one mule too, never having ridden before and riding minus saddle. This *cuartel* was controlled by the CNT and then the FAI, CNT and UGT united to form a government and the *cuartel* came under government control.

Our hero took the opportunity to return again to his hospital. He had picked up an official stamp at the *cuartel* and, half in joke on one occasion being asked for papers or permit, he had said bring me paper and applied the stamp and to his surprise was treated like royalty. So then for about a fortnight he had a glorious time, treating his friends, male and female, to sumptuous meals at the best restaurants, ordering benzine for them, and stamping a receipt for it. Four of them went to the best hotel in Sitges and stayed for ten days. Paying at the end with the official stamp, they were farewelled like royalty. Those were days when there were many uncontrollables about.

Then his friend invited him to work on the Aragón front. Here he has been for ten months acting as a *practicante*, all but finished his medical course, while those who were luckier and who stayed in Barcelona are not being forced to serve, but having been able to finish their course, serve as doctors.

I went to see the nice villagers last night in company with F. The old boy told his daughter to stop fanning herself with that thing as he couldn't see the *Inglesa*.293 We drank wine and *anís* with them.

28.7.37

S not so well. The man wounded in the bladder has died. There is

---

293 'the English woman'.

a rumour that the recently settled *Estado Mayor* (headquarters) plus a division is going to Barcelona to stop the anarchists who are opposing the end of the war. One of the *Estado Mayor* people has been in the ward and has two horses. I was allowed to ride one today, a lovely beast. I went over towards the east at a beautiful canter. I went for a swim in the a.m. and was too late to get my coupon for beer. There was a magnificent thunderstorm with the entire sky lit by streak and sheet lighting. Lovely to watch, then glorious loud crackles of thunder. Very little rain. I had a nasty night with leg cramping. The blood transfusion *camión* arrived. Patience prepared to depart in my place.

29.7.37
Patience went off in the blood *camión*. A case of shot fingers in theatre. We had beer to drink. Ramón came and said the division was moving first to another pueblo to reorganize and then going to Madrid.

30.7.37
Ramón came, brought me a bottle of *anís*. They are departing tonight. Rumours now that we too will follow the division. Sent letters to Johnnie, Fred, Isabel, John Fisher and Phil Thorne.

2.8.37
We are to move or being moved to Fraga tomorrow and will only take surgical cases there. The other wounded can go direct to Monzón. Had farewell binge in a private house, singing and carousing. It was pleasant at first, but M got rather painful, imitating pansies, and spoilt an otherwise pleasant choral singing.

5.8.37
Packing in process, but I am a bit sick and stayed in bed. Half of the staff left for Fraga yesterday. A fine birthday! Still feeling rotten and not working.

8.8.37

Have come to Fraga. We left fairly early in the a.m. Stopped at the station to take a look-see for fruit. My burst of energy has passed. Lovely hot hazy morning complete with sun glasses, temp and fever. I felt in the real tourist mind. We passed through the various pueblos, the glasses accentuating the greens and the houses, I felt t'was either in Ceylon or Africa, only there were not enough people. Plenty of bare-legged children, loaded donkeys and strange vehicles. By-passing Sariñena we stopped by a well to fill water bottles. I had Fossic to nurse all the way. We passed through Sena and below Caspe running along by a river. Somewhere en route we met air force mechanics and trucks. We saw lots of fig trees and luscious-looking fruit trees, patches of lucerne and vegetables. We passed the *intendencia* settling themselves in under shady trees and green gardens in cool-looking bungalows. Along the road and across the river by a long iron bridge, back by the side of the river, below tiers of untidy mud-coloured houses, winding up a steep road to the main square, where we had one house requisitioned from a tailor, and the floor of an ex-hairdressing establishment. The latter has been headquarters for some days and holds all our packages, beds and bundles. In one room they sleep, in t'other they eat, going to both when they could find space, time and food.

There is an indescribable muddle, and very little drinking water. I stayed in bed most of the morning and after lunch, an effort to get some coffee was abandoned because of lack of air, heat, a concert around a piano and inability to get served. I withdrew to the new house and installed myself in a large room with a pull chain lavatory and a wash basin attached to a balcony. There I stayed sweating while t'others worked a bit and until I heard a band. Feeling a bit better I went out and had an innocuous drink. Walked up the street with M and sat on a seat and was raided by four small girls, priceless pettlings, dressed in their Sunday best, looking very sweet and clean. They patted my cheek and I believe we kissed. The onslaught was so sudden. I think, because of my overalls, they mistook me for a militiawoman and a heroine. We exchanged names and played the odd tickling games until soldiers marched up the street.

Great enthusiasm. Very infected by it myself. Soup and tomato for supper. Went to bed immediately but slept rottenly and couldn't lie still.

9.8.37

Feeling much better and brighter. Got up for breakfast, some very thin coffee. About 10 a.m. the military review began. Four battalions of our division were reviewed by General Pozas. Cheers and clapping. Such enthusiasm. Such fine lads. One was affected, but brought near to tears thinking of such a senseless waste of life. Shock troopers, signallers, artillery engineers, motorcyclists, mules, pack, stretcher bearers, and ambulances. In addition about 14 tanks passed.

Did the odd spot of cleaning, felt fine, but sticky with heat. Went for a swim in the river, a little open air treatment for my complaint. Whatever it is it reacted badly and so to bed.

10.8.37

Stayed in bed all day. S and M arrived with the men and our livestock. The livestock, rabbits, chooks and kids, have been put in the room above. Mary L and D started work with the ill at the hospital. Things were not easy for them as there was a certain amount of antagonism from the resident staff. It was arranged, in theory at least, that we must have a hospital of our own. Everyone cheered up. Felt better for the day in bed. Letters from Tizzy and Jean. Wrote to Tizzy.

11.8.37

Still feeling rotten. Decided to get up for lunch. Blood *camión* at hospital so decided to go on leave and go to Barcelona in the *camión*. It was a lovely journey. We stopped on the roadside and drank *anís* (my bottle which they'd brought at last) and ate melon. Sostres, Vidal and Pérez were in great form singing and laughing. Made a detour by Montserrat but it was getting dark. Arrived at the flat about 9.15 p.m. pretty tired. Joe Coombes, Eric Muggeridge and a French journalist were at the flat. Sybil came in later and Patience and David, chauffeur for the *Ayuda a los*

Niños Españoles. Slept very badly.

12.8.37

Passport office closed. Lowson out. Gluckselig moved and left no address. Drank an aperitif with Sostres and to bed early.

13.8.37

Got passport fixed. Went out to lunch with Phelps, decided to leave on Monday morning, did some shopping late in the afternoon.294 Went to Jardín Apolo where Spanish dancing and turns were put on, lovely costumes and dancing. Went on to Café Oriente but didn't like the place at all and am feeling lousy

14.8.37

Saw Phelps off and Jeger.295 Morgan and Co left by car. Went to the Oriente and Shanghai for supper. Met a Swiss ambulance driver, danced a bit at the Shanghai Café. Very hot in Barcelona.

15.8.37

Left Barcelona for Port Bou. Train crowded with militiamen going on leave to Gerona. Very happy and funny crowd of kids, one bigmouthed lad kept all t'others laughing by his antics and remarks to civilian young men. Train crawled into Port Bou where the one lane bridge has a large hole in it and little ones from shrapnel. At Port Bou the customs guard found my diary at once, but started selecting my best photographs for himself till another officer passed by and muttered something. He hastily gave them all back and didn't even look at my diary. Searched by a woman who felt me all over, looked in my purse and raised my beret as an afterthought. Guards or militiamen going with the train to Cerbère were very attentive, one invited me to marry him

---

294 Penny Phelps, an English nurse in Aragón with Agnes, later became the highly decorated honorary medical officer to the Garibaldi Brigade, Palfreeman, *Salud,* pp 248-9.

295 George Jeger was the secretary of the British Medical Aid Unit.

but the other not so polite. I had to tell t'other I didn't like men. Passport Official and Cerbère thought I was Spanish and was all for sending me back to Barcelona for a French visa till I protested I was British. Crowded train of trippers from Port Vendres to Perpignan, all speaking a form of Catalan. Took the hotel bus to Hôtel de la France and a nice big room, had a bath without soap. but was too tired and went back to bed. Ate at the hotel and went out for a walk and perhaps a concert

16.8.37

Went to Credit Lyonnaise and collected 1300 francs, bought the ticket and found I had the day to spend there. Shopped a bit enjoying being in France but felt rotten and went back to the hotel and slept. Had dinner at a café near the station, meals are all more expensive in France. Left Perpignan at 8.20 p.m. for Paris, talked with a Frenchman and later with a Catalan couple. At Toulouse some International Brigade people got in and did not sleep. Arrived in Paris 9 a.m. Took a taxi to Gare du Nord and caught a train to Boulogne—crowded with dull English people. Sick of tipping French porters.

One old English woman buying her ticket bothered the French. She knew all about trains, is used to them, born in one. Another old girl, feeling her stomach upset, feared the crossing. The crossing was quite fair, but cold, and I was glad to get to Folkstone. Utterly exhausted and looking awful when I arrived in London. Auntie V. and Muriel met me at Victoria and took me to Camden Street in M's car—a great thrill. Drank sherry and went latish to dinner at Maurice's and so to bed.

17.8.37

Wrote letters, went to the bank and to 24 Oxford Street where there was a letter from Phil Thorne.296 Met Jeger accepted £12, talked over affairs with him about foodstuffs promised for Poleñino. I was shown bills and correspondence. Went to dinner

---

296 The headquarters of British Medical Association were located at 24 Oxford Street, London.

at Mars with Auntie V. and Muriel and so to bed still feeling pretty rotten.

18.8.37
Went in search of Mr Mason, called at the Orange Tree Café, went later to Australia House. Went to the theatre and sat in a box for 'French without Tears' which was most amusing.

19.8.37
Letter from Lady Mary hoping to see me on my return from Scotland. Went down to Gerard's on the Chalford with Auntie V. Very quiet.

20.8.37
Got up late. Ate, sat in the garden, went to see a cricket match, drank a cocktail at the lovely Chalford Hotel and walked back.

Poleñino Nurses with Dr Gonzalo Aguiló:
L-R, Rosita Davson, Margaret Powell, Mary Slater,
Annie Murray, Susan Sutor and Agnes Hodgson

21.8.37

Returned to London. Letter from Aunty B saying they were going away in September, so I decided to go up to Scotland on the morrow. Saw Woodifield, jabbered a lot, went pub-crawling with her and some friends.297 Not feeling well enough for that and they drove me home.

23.8.37

Came up to Scotland and had a good journey on the Royal Scot.

20.9.37

Left London by night crossing, stayed on the boat till 8.30 a.m. then by train to Paris. Called on Richard Mowrer of the *Chicago Daily News* and had lunch with him and later an aperitif. I found we had missed the third-class section but got a second class carriage to ourselves. Slept hardly at all.

21.9.37

Arrived early in a.m. at Toulouse and straight to the plane after a hurried breakfast. There was a great fuss and bustle and the plane was very pleasant and thrilling. The clouds in great banks were so white and exciting with the dawn lighting them. The wings of the machine obstructed my view but I could see roads and fields and then endless mountains. Went to sleep to my amazement until over Barcelona. Very nice to be in Spain again, though I am still utterly dumb. Arrived at the flat after a perilous car journey on a bad road with the driver gesticulating and missing things by a hair's breadth. The flat is full of un-congenials. I shopped a bit.

22.9.37

Left Barcelona with Manolo, Vidal and Pérez and Susan on the transfusion *camión*. Such pets. Stopped for a beer en route at Lérida, then Fraga, where nobody could tell us where Aguiló was.

---

297 Jean Woodifield, an English nurse was part of first British Medical Aid Unit in Spain, Palfreeman, *Salud*, p 244.

Held up before the bridge, and on it, at Bujaraloz and stayed the night there, in an anarchist hospital, very dirty—mainly *enfermos*.

23.9.37

Left about 11 a.m. after changing a wheel. Manolo running here and there for *vales* and very pleased at getting a new wheel there. On to Sariñena where we saw Taberna, then left for Lanaja and Poleñino. Saw Alejandro and *'Pies Tranquilos'*.298 The hospital was full of beds and soldiers quartered there. We were told that Aguiló had gone to Boltaña with the staff. Went to Grañén and had lunch there, then on to Vicien. Saw Huesca, and passed through Sietamo, all in ruins but people still there. On to Barbastro where there is a big hospital and there got more petrol and oil and on to Boltaña. It was a lovely trip up the mountains, in the moonlight night but couldn't see what must be splendid country. Arrived at Boltaña but discovered that Aguiló was not at the hospital. The hospital people were not very civil except one doctor friend of Taberna's. They were very unpleasant to our blood transfusion people and said we couldn't sleep there, without our having even mentioned such thing. Enrico arrived with wounded and we fell on his neck. Manolo and company went off to the village café. The hospital ice chest was out of order, so they left blood at the café. Very sad at parting from them particularly as there is not much chance of seeing them again like before in Poleñino.

24.9.37

Left Boltaña about 1.20 a.m. on a very twisting narrow road, going near the edge and having to stop to let anything past. We were challenged by guards and ordered to put out our light. We arrived at a wayside house at Molina about 3.30 p.m. Went to

---

298 *Pies Tranquilos*, literally 'Quiet Feet', the gravedigger at the Poleñino hospital, took the responsibilities of his job seriously, his wife and child had been killed early in the war and had hardly been sober since' from Margaret Powell's diary, in Ruth Muller, *Margaret Powell: An Extraordinary Life*, pp 25-26.

sleep in a tent, in bloody blankets and with dirty dressings, etc. all over the floor. I had a disturbed night. Aeroplanes flew over about 7 a.m., probably ours. Feeling damn depressed and unsettled and pretty sore that I'd come. Rested most of the morning and wounded arrived continuously in the afternoon. In theatre till 12 midnight, all wounded evacuated as soon as possible, rarely staying the night. Our conditions are primitive and equipment rather short.

25.9.37

Slept with Mary in an airless small room in the only house. We eat al fresco. Ramón Santerban (?) is bringing down the wounded from the front. Reinforcements kept going up this a.m. We have been and are attacking, with the fascists counter-attacking. Yesterday they said we had advanced 12 kilometres. Optimism reigns up here. Our operating theatre is set up in a former slaughter-house, a suitable place.299

26.9.37

[This entry is from a diary fragment in A. H.'s papers held by Ralph Tonki.]
We are here as a mobile ambulance unit for the 27th Division. The divisional chief of the *Sanidad* chose the place, an isolated farmhouse-cum-mill on the Boltaña-Jaca road some four to twelve kilometres from the firing lines. There we have arranged our *Casa de Urgencia*. It is far from ideal and could not by any flight of imagination be called anything but an emergency casualty station. The *Sanidad* supplied us with a small *auto-chir* (theatre ambulance); but is more practical to use the farm slaughter-house as an operating theatre.

Four days before our arrival the Spanish staff and two nurses came up to Molino in ambulances loaded with theatre equipment, medical supplies, bed, blankets, etc. Tents are

---

299 Margaret Powell, writing in April 1938 in the *British Journal of Nursing*, about the mobile hospital dealing with the relentless stream of wounded in high Aragón in late September 1937, reprinted in, Muller, *Margaret Powell: An Extraordinary Life*, pp 77-80.

pitched in a cleared ex-pumpkin patch opposite the house, branches of trees are draped over and around the tents for camouflage. The slaughterhouse has been cleared and set for action; the only attraction of it as a theatre is the concrete floor because one can throw buckets of water over it which drain through a hole into the stream outside. The handbasins and sterilising outfit from the *auto-chir* are installed in one corner with the water tank for it outside; it is the job of the *auto-chir* chauffeurs to keep the tank filled. The rest of the furniture consists of an operating table, wooden table for instruments, an anaesthetist's stool and large packing case on top of which are put the sterile drums, sutures, sharp instruments, etc. A few nails were driven into the wall on which to hang gowns and aprons. Most of the sterilising is done by the roadside.

In the storehouse there is just room for seven beds. When it rains the earthen floor becomes sticky and a couple of the beds stand in puddles of water. Two of the *practicantes* found some bricks and put them in the worst patches. We have beds, blankets and some pillows, but no sheets and apart from the shocking wounds, blood on the beds, mud on the floor and flies wherever there is blood, makes work more grim.

Six men sleep in one tent, which also serves as an office and common room, while the other tent is used by two nurses when not required for the overflow of wounded. Some of the doctors and staff sleep in a cave across the shallow river, but when the river rises they have to wade over to bed.

When our equipment arrived, the troops were already attacking, they had captured several villages, among the wounded were a number of fascists—those received treatment and were evacuated with our wounded. Some of our wounded produced cigarettes, a large supply of which had been found in one of the captured villages. We were given fascist honey, other soldiers produced 100 mark notes and Italian medals, and one man had a pair of Russian boots taken from a white Russian serving with the rebels.

Aguiló only operates on the most urgently wounded; abdominal and head wounds, amputations and a couple of gas gangrene cases. Those less urgently in need of surgical aid are evacuated to Boltaña. We try and keep the abdominal cases as long as possible, about two days at most, sometimes they are evacuated two to three hours after their operation. The ambulances take three hours to reach Boltaña and the road is a nightmare to the drivers, twisting and turning; they have to stop to let other cars pass, and descending to Boltaña there are more than 30 hairpin bends; to go round some of these they must drive to the edge, then reverse, one slight mistake and the ambulance would fall hundreds of feet. There are no chains to put on the wheels during the heavy rain and when the ambulances are late coming back we worry until they return safely. They are well-sprung vehicles so that it is the length and tediousness of the journey rather than the unevenness of the road that the wounded suffer.

As the troops advance, the engineers repair and make roads bit by bit to enable the ambulances and trucks to follow the soldiers, but mules are still used where there is no road. The wounded are being brought down to us promptly, though occasionally it is as long as 36 hours before they are found and reach us. This service is much better organised than in the early days of the war when often days passed before the wounded were found. I had not realised that about 70 per cent of the stretcher-bearers lose their lives bringing in the wounded.

At first the sick militiamen suffered, having to sit and wait if there were badly wounded to be evacuated, but a large house seven kilometres lower down has been requisitioned, and there at least those not too ill can remain in comparative comfort until cured or the urgent evacuations have taken place.

The divisions were attacking a strongly-fortified position when the weather broke. The wounded arrived day and night, mostly hurt in the head and limbs. All are soaked to the skin, and we have been kept busy only cutting their clothes off and trying to warm and stimulate them. We have very few dry clothes to give them usually they are evacuated wrapped in blankets. It has rained heavily for four days and held up the attack; food transport was delayed too, and the sick and wounded have arrived not having eaten for three days. We had little more than coffee and milk to give them and not always milk.

27.9.37

A stream of wounded. A head case died. One laparotomy, and a couple of hands and a foot, otherwise all evacuated.

28.9.37

Busy night for all except me. I had a busy day, not feeling at all like work and very sorry for myself. Getting used to this primitive place and feeling its discomforts. Mary and I share a tiny airless room in a large farm house where also live some of the *Parcomobil* and *Intendencia* people. There is neither peace nor privacy. The owners also live in the house. There seem to be lots of daughters all busy washing and sewing and feeding the men. There is also another *al fresco* kitchen behind the store houses where some of the men eat. Mule teams come down in the afternoon to load food and provisions for the army. The same mules serve to bring wounded down to the ambulances. Engineers open up the roads bit by bit for the ambulances and trucks to go up as we advance but it is perilous work and perilous driving. The country is mountainous but not very pretty just here, hills rather bare. Haven't seen a paper, though they come regularly. Haven't had a proper wash for a couple of days. The weather is hot and oppressive. There was a badly wounded lung case in the theatre in the a.m. Feeling rather like retiring.

29.9.37

Kept busy giving water to laparotomies, very difficult to refuse them. Makes one miserable and bad tempered when they keep on asking, poor devils. Some fascists arrived with armaments but too busy to find out much about them. Ramón came down for some time. Took a head case in the theatre, poor devil. Feeling better and working a little better.

1.10.37

Eighteen kilometres from Saragossa. Government troops are 15 kilometres from Jaca. Ten of our planes passed over and I thought of peaceful flying in England. We had a laparotomy and an arm case in theatre. Other lighter cases have been sent on.

2.10.37

Our troops are attacking the enemy position on a concrete parapet. The enemy artillery is very good, with small cannons worked by electricity. We are attacking in heavy rain and our casualties are heavy, coming in all morning. Others tonight were mostly head and limbs. All are soaked to the skin, half the work was cutting off their clothes. None of them had eaten for three days. One lad had a ten mark note taken from a fascist, also an Italian medallion. Some say our troops have taken the position and attacked. Raining hard most of the day. Everywhere is mud and puddles. A gas gangrenous patient in tonight, evacuated after opening and draining leg. Barcelona bombarded yesterday; 40 odd killed and 80 wounded. A bomb landed on a school. The bombardment took place at 4 p.m. and lasted an hour.

3.10.37

Raining heavily most of the day, because of that and being Sunday, no wounded and probably no fighting. Towards evening we received a few *enfermos* and a couple of slight wounds. We have all been issued with rain capes, amusing things. Found my first bug in the bed. Went walking with Fábregas to see a small village. Very hot walking, puffed up the hill like an old woman. Very dull having nothing to do in the rain, nowhere to sit. The people and house-dwellers played cards, a couple chess, *del resto*, we wandered around aimlessly. I cleaned the ward instruments in the mud, my main work for the day, beyond making the bed and cleaning the room and washing my feet. Everyone feeling tummyish these days.

4.10.37

Practically no work, still raining and very muddy. One self-shot hand in the theatre, sent back to the front. Leg and foot evacuated and a number of sick with pneumonia and 'flu. Truck loads of recruits and conscripts going up—*buena suerte* (good luck) to them. Slept in the afternoon and walked up and down the road at night, sighing to myself, as the mules passed me by, coming down for their loads. Everyone rather bored by the weather and nothing to do.

5.10.37

Still only the wounded and a few *enfermos*. Numbers of troops went up to the front during the night and a number of men from here left this morning. Feeling very dirty and depressed and arranged with Laura of the house to wash my clothes, and washed myself. After that I felt better. Went walking to the village of Jessera over the hills. Awfully pretty little pueblo, white houses and a little church surrounded by houses and a wall

We went to buy a piglet. One of the Intendencia people of the 124th Brigade presented us with a couple of bottles of beer and the people of the house offered us some very excellent bread and ham. We carried the pig home each taking turns. Lovely evening light on the hills, night cold and starry. The light question is becoming acute as the candle supply is running low.

7.10.37

Fairly busy day with laparotomies who were very sick and a couple of head cases. I had a crisis with the rest of the nurses tonight. It began as usual over a trivial incident. I was told that Susan was sleeping with me, and being rather tired of never being consulted, which is ordinary manners, I mentioned I would prefer to sleep alone this night. This brought down much invective as to my selfishness and that I was always going sick, etc. etc., and that they'd made many allowances for me since they had to live with me. At that I definitely decided they should make no further sacrifices and neither should I. Packed and told Aguiló to arrange for my departure.

8.10.37

Left Molino in an ambulance, farewelled by Fábregas and Francisco and the other men. The English nurses were conspicuous by their absence though we parted politely enough. Chauffeurs of the ambulance were very sweet. The day was lovely and the scenery nearing Boltaña glorious, with snow on the Pyrenees and the sleepy valleys far below. The road was very narrow and twisting. Descending to Boltaña went round over 30 hairpin bends, several of which we approached to the edge and then had to reverse, so easy to slip. Three to four hours and we arrived at Boltaña and crossed to the hospital over a swaying suspension bridge. Some of the wounded hopped along, one youth who had drunk nearly a litre of cognac in the ambulance before he was stopped, sat up on his stretcher and was very happy. We had lunch at the hospital. One chauffeur had to make love or mutter endearments to the *chica* to get her to serve us, the other boy just sat and grinned sweetly.

Left there and drove up to the *pueblo* of Boltaña just in time to catch the *correo* (the postman) on another four hour journey to Barbastro. We called at all the small *pueblos* en route collecting mail, or the postmen met us and handed in their bags. Arrived at Barbastro about 7 p.m. and began my enquiries. Left my luggage with the saddler, a youth standing by offered to accompany me to the *hospital de sangre* where I'd been on my last visit to Barbastro. There I asked numerous people and finally an X-ray man, radiologist, if they expected the blood transfusion *camión*. '*No hija mía, vienen cuando quieren.*'300

My escort went with me to the *Estado Mayor*—his parting words were that I could have his bed if all else failed. A nice little Nancy boy in the office made out my passport while another youth took me to the *cuartel general* to get a *vale* for a bed.

'*No hay camas*',301 they had just assigned the last seven beds to 12 artists who had been brought to Barbastro to sing and dance '*la jota*'302 for the entertainment of General Pozas on the morrow. He is to review the troops, etc. This escort seemed to take it as a personal insult that the *cuartel* had no bed for me,

---

300 'No my dear, they come when they feel like it.'

301 'There are no beds.'

302 An Aragonese folk dance.

muttering curses on them. Back at the *Estado Mayor* another boy in the office, Antonio Chesa, said he thought his landlady might find me a bed if it would suit me. The light had failed but the landlady inspected me by the aid of a match, then offered me the matrimonial alcove next to Antonio's. '*Muy bien.*' That settled, we went off to eat. Antonio on request led me through a café to a lavatory, switched on the light and showed me the lock on the door. Such nice people all these. After a vermouth we went to dine, food very difficult to obtain anywhere. Antonio got permission for me to eat there, and we waited in a queue for an hour or so for the second sitting, entertained by the remarks of our fellow queuers. We ate well, salad, soup greens and stew of horse which I tasted all night. We had wine also. Then we went to one café for *manzanilla* (camomile) because there is no coffee in Barbastro at present. A cup of *anís*, then to another café, to drink peppermint (*crème de menthe*). After that I'd had enough to drink though Antonio doing the honours was inclined to think I might like to go to another café. It was early for him but I voted to go home and so to bed in our various alcoves. Antonio shut me into mine and I was to call out when ready and he would switch out the sitting room light which served us both.

9.10.37

The landlady called me before 6 a.m. Antonio accompanied me to the *correo* (post office) and we discovered the truck didn't leave till 8 a.m. No trains are running except hospital and troop ones. We walked about in the cold bright morning. The saddler's daughter came down at 7 a.m. to go for milk and let us into the shop to collect my luggage. After that we waited at the post office. Two small girls led a donkey along and unloaded endless packets, bread and vegetables and luggage and a couple of chickens. We all helped rearrange the empty baskets, the soldiers and other civilians dribbled along. Then the van itself. Antonio asked the driver to let me sit in front. The driver was very chatty, enjoying being the important man in that job. Very upset that he'd had no sleep as he'd returned from Lérida at 5 a.m. having taken 36 fascist prisoners and their escort the night before.

About 8.30 a.m. we left, Antonio waving me off before he went for a shave and the big day with General Pozas. This part of the journey made me want to stay in Spain. Another woman, a post office official, and myself were squeezed into the front by the driver and the chickens were on the floor by the engine. The chauffeur was very voluble and enthusiastic about equal rights for women. Antonio called him a '*canta mañanas*'303 and when not talking he sang all out of tune. But a kindly nut and waved his hands in the air. We stopped at Monzón and Binefar and again called at various places for mail. One of the chickens died half way to Lérida but the woman shrugged and said it saved them killing it; the other clung to life. Arrived at Lérida 10.30 a.m. Started off for the station with my luggage but passing the *Estado Mayor* I called there to ask about transport. The official *coche* had already left but I could go the next day. Left my suitcase with the guard and hiked my rucksack in search of an inn or a *pensión*. Drew a blank at the first, and the second were not certain. Air raid sirens sounded as I went searching and everyone made for refuges. I kept walking until I found my *fonda* then stayed there until the all clear signal given and I could attend to business. Went to a café, had coffee without sugar and a vermouth and set off to *Sanidad* and the hospital, still with a faint hope that somewhere I might find the blood transfusion *camión* if only I was diligent or persistent. Small boys noticing me, muttered and ran in front to have another look. One woman said what was my father doing to let me wear *pantalones*,304 the little girls were kinder and called out that I was '*guapa*'.305 Drawing a complete blank at the hospital I walked back to the centre of the town by back streets, this time it was small girls who ran round me in circles, and soldiers disputed '*si que es una mujer*'.306 But the narrow streets descending the hill were nicer.

---

303 'a story teller'

304 'trousers'

305 'pretty'

306 'if that is a woman'

Not wanting to go down too soon I came to a blind alley where there were fairly modern houses. A woman and a man called out did I want the main street, then the man directed me going ahead down the steps, he told me '*mujeres de la vida*'307 lived in that street. He thought I was a stranger so had followed to show me the way—at the foot of the steps he said '*que vaya bien*' 308 and went off.

I found that the *fonda* could put me up in a small inside room. Washed in a jug, there being no plug to the basin, but the bed linen was clean. I was then directed to another *fonda* where I could eat. While waiting for a place I talked to a *Sanidad* man, a doctor of the 21st Brigade which builds fortifications. We sat at a table together and discussed various acquaintances. I questioned him about his work and made polite conversation. Then he told me how boring Lérida was. He couldn't sleep alone, I couldn't sleep with anyone. What he valued most was '*la amistad de acostarse con una mujer simpática*',309 for him that contented him as a rule. I was not quite certain what I was understanding but was taking no chances and bade him farewell firmly after lunch. By then he had realized I didn't want to share my siesta or '*jugar*'310 in friendship. Called at the *Estado Mayor* but they were shut, and back to the *fonda*, undressed and prepared for siesta. But the siren blew, I took no notice until the windows rattled hard. I got dressed not wishing to be caught undressed and hurried a little as more bombs fell and went out on to the terrace with knees knocking a bit. At first I could not see planes, only where bombs had been dropped over by our aviation camp and then when I'd seen the planes, more bombs over behind the house. They were aiming at a petrol dump the *chica* said. The all clear signal was given after the anti-aircraft gun puffed a bit. Went to the *Estado Mayor*, saw the cross-eyed telephonist, a

---

307 'prostitutes'

308 'safe journey'

309 'a friendship formed in bed with an accommodating woman'

310 'to play'

Poleñino acquaintance. He advised me to try the benzine office for a lift to Barcelona. Sirens again and a few more bombs but pretended to take no notice but walked by the river, crossed the bridge and walked and walked being directed still further at each enquiry. Finally at the petrol station, one lad talking English and another French, suggested that if I bring my baggage and liked to wait there I might get a lift. I decided to take the official car in the a.m. Back to *Estado Mayor* and was given my pass pleasantly. Went to a café for vermouth. A *mujer de la vida* sat down beside me, enticing a *miliciano* to join her and a Frenchman to join me. Soon after I left and wearily went for supper (more small sardines) and bed. The proprietor of the *fonda* told me I could not be called before 7 a.m., that the girl did not get up before then. Finally he produced a small alarm clock—British at that—and I set it. He too led me to the lavatory but unrequested. After three hours I wakened and caught a few bugs, and decided to leave the light on but it seemed to worry the proprietor who kept popping his head in my door asking if I was sick. Finally I slept again and wakened at 7.15 by the clock, luckily it was fast. Flung on my clothes and raced down to the *Estado Mayor*. Nobody knew about my suitcase, but at the back they called the guard who'd been on duty and he had it beside his mattress on the floor.

The official '*coche de correo*'311 was a big bus with only about half a dozen travellers. The driver had to refuse people without passes, at the petrol station people tried to get in at all four doors, women with bundles, soldiers and civilians, some had been waiting by the roadside since 3 a.m. in the hope of a passing *coche*. But they had no passes, poor things. So we left Lérida driving along a flat road often shaded completely by big plane trees, vines and olive trees on either side, and maize and vegetables.

At Tárrega we stopped in front of the café where the blood transfusion *camión* stopped for refreshment. I went to a café beside it, then on again. Going up by the Montserrat road we ran

---

311 postman's van

into thick mist and all the lovely view as one climbs was completely hidden. Running downhill again we ran out of the fog but the sky remained grey. The summit of Montserrat showed above the clouds, yellow-brown patches showed on the steep clusters of grey rocks. The chapel of Monserrat and its treasures remain intact. The village of Monserrat looked peaceful enough and the trees by the road were autumn tinted. We reached Barcelona running to the port and the bus dropped me beside Christopher Columbus's Column. I was a dirty-looking object and put on my trench coat to make myself less conspicuous. Had the bus passed near the unit's flat I'd have gone there but the business of carrying one's luggage decided me to go to an hotel and a decent one. With the peseta so low one can afford them anyway. Arrived at the Nouvel Hotel; I washed and changed into civilised feminine garb.

Went to the flat and announced my presence. After lunch and a siesta went back there to tea. An American nurse Esther and Paddy, a Canadian chauffeur, arrived at the flat and I went to dinner with them and Sybil, Eric and a couple of Spanish secret police. Damned expensive meal and a dull one—everyone inclined to be quarrelsome after it too. Went back to the hotel walking down Paseo de Gracia and so to bed.

11.10.37

Shops shut most of the day. Washed clothes, slept nobody telephoned me. Went to a cinema and was offered a job with the 35th division and thought to accept. Lunched, slept, tea'd, vermouthed, dined and went to Café Oro del Rhin—alone. Could not sleep being indigestible and tummy upset again, blast it.

Raining. Went to Jardín Apolo with Esther Rubenstein from San Francisco, Batty (?) a Canadian and a little Jewish doctor and Sybil. Dancing very poor but had an amusing time riding in a ramshackle car with the horn detached.

12.10.37

Met Leah Manning and Churchill and they suggested my going to a new hospital near Madrid.312 313 I was almost decided for it then heard from Esther about various intrigues that go on there, etc. so decided to stick to my plan of going to England. Leah Manning said if I decided later to come back to let her know. And so to bed early. Air raid alarms and anti-aircraft gun firing.

13.10.37

Went to the Hospital de Montjuich in the a.m. and saw Dr Sostres working in the laboratory there. In the p.m. went up to the flat, the alarm was given again and eight or nine anti-aircraft busy, six killed, 50 wounded. Barcelona bombed. Had a meal at the flat and some brandy to drink. Stayed the night there.

15.10.37

Went to see about a passport and had difficulty with money. Bombardment 7.30-9 p.m. Guns firing, more than 100 bombs dropped, not sure where—shrapnel from anti-aircraft bombs fell in the streets. Went out to dine afterwards and to the cinema. *A Night at the Opera* with the Marx Brothers and so to bed, very weary.

16.10.37

Got a new coat and skirt and wore it with much success. Sat in the Café Ramblas waiting for t'others and people at my table offered me cigarettes and chatted. Then the British Medical Aid people arrived and just as we were leaving a nice artist told me I was looking really beautiful. Nice little man. Met José, the administrator, and went back to the flat and collected some money from Philip, and was escorted by him, also affected by my new coat and skirt, to Air France. He assisted me about booking.

---

312 Leah Manning: an ex-Labour MP and Secretary of the British Spanish Medical Aid Committee.

313 Peter Spencer, Viscount Churchill, was a founder of the British Medical Aid Committee and led the first British Medical Unit to Spain. See Peter Spencer, *All My Sins Remembered*, London: Heinemann, 1964, pp 158-173.

Dined alone and went solo to Oro del Rhin, *no hay música allí ahora.*314

17.10.37

Went down to Barceloneta in the a.m. Walked round the streets and saw the ruined college where 40 children were killed and 70 wounded. Lots of other buildings with floors destroyed. All the intimate furnishings of the rooms were exposed, broken glass on all the pavements, iron shutters even at a distance from where the bombs had fallen were buckled and useless. People gathering the remains of their furniture, piling it on barrows, horse carts, on anything. Trams don't go into Barceloneta, now stopping at Palau. A hen coop on top of a five storey house was practically suspended and half the house demolished and empty. The hens were sitting up there preening themselves in the sun, but will probably die of starvation. I went down to the beach, sitting in the sun, the sea calm and a marvellous blue, a man fishing standing on a ladder with a long fishing pole and a few young men swimming and sporting by the baths. Gasometers, chimney and iron foundries in the view extending down the coast. An auxiliary schooner chuffed past and another steamer was apparently at anchor. Women were buying wine at a little bar and everyone not moving.

I went up to the flat and there was an air raid. Afterwards met Eric and David Crook and went to a dance hall. Eric was awed by its respectability—rather a dull crowd, between dances couples walked in a circle round the arena. Men looked girls over and if they had danced more than once they called 'hist!' to the girls. It closed at 12.30 and we had a cocktail at a bar off the Ramblas. Eric solemnly asked the cashier to marry him. Talked with David Crook till 9.30.

18.10.37

Busy day at the French Consulate and the Generalitat. Met Sybil and Eric for dinner at Casa del Puerto near Colón. Just finished dinner when the lights went out and hurriedly gulped my beer,

---

314 'there is no music there now.'

but felt a bit afraid tonight. Went out into the street to watch, standing under cover against a wall at the end of the Ramblas. There was a nasty moment when a bit of shrapnel from an anti-aircraft shell came whizzing down. Eric and I flattened ourselves against the wall. I was afraid. Anti-aircraft guns were booming away and there were great flashes and searchlights. I wished it would stop, though I was not afraid all the time. The planes sounded very low and the moon clouded over. During a lull we walked up the Ramblas and sat down by a café when a bomb fell with tremendous noise and a flash lighting up the sky, seemingly on the other side of the houses. There was a bit of panic for a moment, some people ran and chairs were knocked over. I got to the door of the restaurant and a soldier said, '*un poco de calma*.'315 Sybil said, 'Don't go inside.' Recovered myself but there was more anti-aircraft. So difficult to tell bombs and anti-aircraft shells. It lasted from about 8.30 p.m. till 10.45 p.m. A miserable and horrible business. I had a drink at the Ramblas Café and so to bed. My last night in Spain.

19.10.37

After spending my last pesetas I met Sybil, Eric and Batty at the Euzkadi Café. Paddy, an International Brigader, was seen walking up the Paseo de Gracia. Batty went down to find out what he was doing. Apparently he is sick of it all and was trying to desert. He said he'd brought down an ambulance, the others had left goods for him to take back, but the ambulance had never come further than Lérida. Then a couple of the others had got drunk and smashed up the ambulance. Then he'd been sent to take troops to Lérida, his being the only vehicle available. All fabrications. Very worried, poor lad, because the authorities have discovered his blunders and he fears he will be shot. He was hungry also.

Sybil, Eric and Batty saw me off. We had an amusing journey down to the airport, nearly ramming a truck, ordering children off a pavement so that we could mount it and pass a vehicle. The

---

315 'a little bit of calm.'

woman at the airport very thoroughly searched me, feeling me all over, but I forgave her at the buffet afterwards where we all chatted and took coffee. Had to wait about an hour for the Valencia plane to arrive. Marseille plane smaller. It was lovely flying over the sea and I could see some traces of the damage done to Barceloneta., but nothing else from the bombardments. Catalonia looked fairly prosperous in its cultivation. Approaching Marseille there were great wastes, looked like salt deposits, and I could see land going down into the sea. A curious effect, not being able to tell where the land ended and the sea began, except on the other side where the waves crept up in a white line of foam.

Arrived at Marseille at 5 p.m. Talked with W. Forrest,316 a Scottish journalist on his way to Minorca, and had dinner with him. He told me that last November Del Vayo approached him to invite British MPs to visit Madrid, to be there when it fell, because Franco had dropped leaflets saying that if the city did not surrender all the wounded would be killed.317 As there were about 35,000 wounded there it was thought the presence of British MPs in Madrid when Franco entered it would prevent a massacre. Forrest came to London and was told by his paper, the *Daily Express*, to take a rest. He arranged for the MPs to go out and while on holiday in Scotland read in his paper a violent attack on the visit of the MPs, for which he was responsible. So he resigned. The British MPs' visit, for its initial purpose, was not necessary fortunately, but it did a terrific amount of good in arranging for evacuation of refugees and food supplies. Also Forrest visited no-man's-land of one of the Madrid front which was in a wood. He wasn't really keen but the officers wanted to show him an atrocity there. A scout went ahead in case some of the fascists had the same idea of a Sunday walk. Two men and a

---

316 William Forrest was the correspondent in Spain for the *Daily Express*. For Beaverbrook's version of this incident, see Sefton Delmer, *Trail Sinister*, pp 289-293, 396.

317 Julio Álvarez del Vayo, a socialist, was the Republican Minister for Foreign Affairs between 1936 and 1938 and was the Spanish government's representative at the League of Nations.

woman had been roped together and bayoneted and only recently the government troops have advanced near enough to get their bodies.

The Government will be moving soon to Barcelona and so the journalists will also move there. The idea is to consolidate Catalonia's resistance with the rest of Spain. There was a mass meeting of women in Barcelona to discuss mobilization of women to take over men's jobs in the cities and country, to enable them to study technical details so that more men can be freed to fight. Went early to bed.

20.10.37

Left Marseille at 8.35 a.m. Did not see Forrest again, as I left the hotel early. Plane attendants were very attentive, pointing out various places as we went along. We descended at Lyon with time for a coffee and cigarette. A Dutchman invited me to coffee and chatted. He was travelling with a German so when they heard I'd come from Barcelona they asked me various questions. I told them that all was going well with the Government and that at least they were prepared to fight another two to three years, if not longer. At Le Bourget we all went up to Paris together. I was introduced to their Parisian agent who took us in his car and suggested a moderate hotel for me. They were all amazed, I think, that as luggage for the night I took only my trench coat with a sponge bag. After that they accepted that I had a friend to see in Paris and dropped me at rue de la Paix.

Found Mowrer was in Spain again for a short time. Went to the Exposition, Finnish glass and wood and material very interesting. Visited Danish, Austrian and Hungarian pavilions and had marvellous coffee with cream at the Austrian tea room, but expensive. Spent a long time in the Russian pavilion, all new buildings rather fine, but the educational efforts for kids looked much the same as elsewhere, maternity homes and pre-natal homes were good and interesting, youth looked cheerful and happy, but the youth anywhere does. Disappointed in the children's books, other examples I'd seen elsewhere were more interesting. On the whole I didn't gather much more information about Russia from it.

The Spanish Pavilion was mainly peasant costumes of different countries and pictures of war and propaganda and in a café below, flamenco records being played. Read a front page of *Popolo d'Italia* and how they put over their propaganda. Went back to the hotel by the tube and walking, feeling that I am beginning to know my way around Paris a little.

Went to a cheap restaurant for dinner, and thought a little regretfully of the dinner and show offered by the big business men. Thought I'd go to the opera and entered the house but a bit awed by it and well-dressed people. It was L'Aiglon, but I didn't know it, and thought the price beyond me. Had a coffee, wrote to Tizzy and went to see Gary Cooper and Jean Arthur in '*Buffalo Bill*', a silly fighting picture. Went to bed and slept well.

21.10.37

Went again to the Exposition and went through the ceramic ware of the Sèvres pavilion, lovely sunken baths. Had a great desire to buy me some expensive scent so bought some cheap stuff at the Exposition bluffed by an offer of a free tube. Wandered about then found my way to rue Lafayette and gulped half a pâté sandwich and a beer and caught the bus to Le Bourget airport. I like this air travelling, so much less fatiguing, and the pleasant manner of officials. Very sleepy in the plane, a bit blasé too. Misty over the land and sea—so much of the time we seemed over the sea. We left Le Bourget at 1.15 and arrived at Croydon at 3 p.m.

England looked so green and lovely, with a coloured patchwork quilt effect and autumn coloured clumps of trees. And so ended my long journey.

Abbreviations

ALP   Australian Labor Party

ACTU   Australian Council of Trade Unions

CEDA   Confederación Española de Derechas Autónomas (Confederation of Catholic Parties on the Right)

CNT   Confederación Nacional de Trabajo (Anarcho-Syndicalist Labour Federation)

Estat Catalá   Catalan State Party, formed in Barcelona in 1922 to advocate Catalán separatism.

FAI   Federación Anarquista Ibérica (Spanish Anarchist Federation)

JCI   Juventud Comunista Ibérica (JCI): the Spanish Communist Youth – a radical youth group within the POUM.

JSU   Juventudes Socialistas Unificadas (JSU): the United Socialist Youth was formed in 1934 among communist youth groups and by 1936 had become the armed wing of the Spanish Communist Party.

PCE   Partido Comunista Español

POUM   Partido Obrero de Unificación Marxista (Workers' Party of Marxist Unification) formed in 1935 by dissident Marxist-Leninists. It advocated revolutionary socialism and was opposed to Stalinism.

PSOE   Partido Socialista Obrero Español (Spanish Socialist Party)

PSUC   Partido Socialist Unificado de Cataluña (Communist Party of Catalonia)

UGT   Unión General de Trabajadores (Socialist Trade Union Federation), formed in 1882.

UME   Unión Militar Española (a right-wing army officers' organization).

UMRA   Unión Militar Republicana Antifascista (an officers' organization opposed to the UME and supporting the Popular Front).

List of Illustrations

Page 7: Studio portrait of four Australian nurses taken in Sydney before their departure. Back row: Agnes Hodgson, May MacFarlane. Centre: Una Wilson, Front: Mary Lowson. Oct 1936. (Phil Thorne Papers, Noel Butlin Archives, Australian National University PT NBAANU).

Page 17: Badge of the Australian Spanish Nursing Unit. October 1936. Photographer JK. Spanish Nurses, N171 57. Noel Butlin Labour Archives, Australian National University.

Page 18: Leaving Sydney SS Oronsay, 24 Oct 1936. Agnes Hodgson, Mary Lowson, May MacFarlane and Una Wilson. (Agnes Hodgson photo album "AHPA").

Page 20: Members of the Victorian Spanish Relief Committee welcome the four nurses in Melbourne. Back row: Len Fox, Helen Baillie, Dorothy Gibson, Joyce Metcalf and Nettie Palmer. Front row: Australian nurses. 25 Oct 1936. (AHPA).

Page 25: Una Wilson and Agnes Hodgson enjoy ship board life, Nov 1936. (AHPA).

Page 28: Saint Lazare rally to welcome the Australians in Europe, 28 Nov 1936. (JK private collection).

Page 31: Australians in Barcelona, Plaza de Cataluña in front of the Hotel Colón. Mary Lowson, May MacFarlane, journalist John Fisher, International Brigader Jack 'Blue' Barry, Aileen Palmer, Agnes Hodgson and Una Wilson. 8 Dec 1936. (PT NBAANU).

Page 39: Hospital Staff at the British Medical Unit, Grañén, late Dec 1936. (PT NBAANU).

Page 43: Grañén, clearing the 'mud and muck' from the surroundings of the British Medical Aid Unit hospital. (AHPA, NBAANU).

Page 45: Dr Gonzalo Aguiló Mercader, Poleñino, June 1937. (AHPA).

Page 50: Pancho Villa. Banastas-Carrascal; "Miliciano in the field leaning on a shotgun with cartridge belts, hat and sash". Image front page, *Umbral* no 3, 24 July 1937. Kati Horna, photographer, Archivo Fotográfico de Kati Horna, Foto 27, Copyright Ministerio de Cultura y Deporte. Centro Documental de la Memoria Histórica de Salamanca.

Page 53: Agnes captured by an unknown street photographer, Sydney, mid 1938. (JK collection).

Page 60: Margaret Michaelis, photographer, Margaret Michaelis-Sachs Collection, 'no title', [Oct 1936] IRN 48755, National Gallery of Australia.

Page 71: Margaret Michaelis, photographer, 'No title' [October 1936] IRN 48750. (Margaret Michaelis-Sachs Collection, National Gallery of Australia).

Page 120: Fund-raising stamps from Australian Spanish Relief Committee. (PT NBAANU).

Page 123: Ray Jordana driving an ambulance for the CNT in Aragón. (PT NBAANU).

Page 127: May Day Parade Sydney SRC Aid Spain float, 1937. (PT NBAANU).

Page 128: May Day Procession Sydney, 01 May 1938. Photographer Sam Hood, Home and Away No. 18170. (State Library of NSW).

Page 135: Agnes in the Poleñino operating theatre, 31 Mar 1937. (AHPA).

Page 157: 'Australians in Spain', Plaza de Cataluña, 08 Dec 1936. (AHPA).

Page 186: Grañén main street with an ambulance of the British medical aid unit, Feb 1937. (AHPA).

Page 191: Grañén, Nurses' Quarters, British Medical Aid Hospital, Feb 1937. (AHPA).

Page 194: Grañén, Agnes explores the surroundings with camera and sturdy boots. Feb 1937. (AHPA).

Page 196 Agnes on a trip to the front near Huesca, note the miliciana, 5 Feb 1937. (AHPA).

Page 199: Grañén, Agnes 'On a dirty job', Feb 1937. (AHPA).

Page 202: 'Spanish Relief Committee to Aid Victims of Fascism. Ambulance No 5, from Sydney Australia'. (PT NBAANU).

Page 206: Outdoors after night duty, Agnes with Anita Bolster, José Cepero and Dr Morales, Jan 1937. (AHPA).

Page 209: Sariñeno front: Agnes with Dr Aguiló and associates, Apr 1937. (AHPA).

Page 216: Hospital surroundings with ambulance in Poleñino street. (AHPA).

Page 221: Hospital vehicles in the hospital courtyard. (AHPA).

Page 229: Poleñino "chicas", Ramona, Julia, Luisa, Pilar María and Marina. Jul 1937. (AHPA).

Page 232: Spanish military cavalry from a dismantled POUM unit arrives in Poleñino plaza, 11 Jul 1937. (AHPA).

Page 245: Poleñino nurses with Dr Gonzalo Aguiló: L-R: Rosita Davson, Margaret Powell, Mary Slater, Ann Murray, Susan Sutor and Agnes Hodgson. (AHPA).

Acknowledgements

In this project I have benefited enormously from the expertise and generosity of others. Among the archivists, curators and librarians I thank Ann O'Hehir and Eliza Williams at the National Gallery of Australia; Almudena Rubio Pérez, curator and scholar of the CNT-FAI photographic archive at International Institute of Social History, Amsterdam; Catherine Ziegler at the Noel Butlin Labour Archives, Australian National University; and Aleksandra Markovic at the Fisher Library, Sydney University. Fellow researchers on the Spanish civil war and associated topics have been generous with time and sharing knowledge. They include Ann Curthoys, Helen Ennis, Angela Jackson, Ann Muller, Linda Palfreeman, Teresa Ferré Panisello, Victor Pardo Lancina, Michaela Pattison, Elizabeth Rechniewski, Nuria Saura and Carlos Serrano. The University of Sydney, School of Humanities has been supportive and at home I treasure the backing of the Keene clan. Simon Deefholts of Clapton Press originally raised the idea of a new edition of Agnes's diary and in its execution has been an exemplary editor and publisher.

Judith Keene, School of Humanities, The University of Sydney.

Bibliography

Agnes Hodgson's Writing

Agnes Hodgson, 'Australian Nurse in Spain', *Sydney Morning Herald (SMH), Women's Supplement (WS)*, 23 Feb 1937; 'Life in Barcelona', *SMH, WS*, 2 August 1937; 'I Was a Nurse in Spain', *SMH, WS*, 22 Mar 1938; 'I believe in Spanish Republican Government', *Daily Telegraph*, 14 Oct 1938.

Nurses in Spain: Republican and Franquista

Anton-Solanis, Isabel, Ann Wakefield and Christine Hallett, 'International Nurses to the Rescue: The Role and Contribution of the Nurses of the International Brigades during the Spanish Civil War', *Japan Journal of Nursing Science*, 16 (2019): 103-114.

Cochrane, Archie, One Man's Medicine. *An Autobiography of Professor Archie Cochrane.* (Cardiff University Press, 2009).

Fyrth, Jim, *The Signal Was Spain. The Spanish Aid Movement in Britain 1936-39*, (London: Lawrence and Wishart, 1986).

Hanley, Jane, 'The Tourist Gaze in the Spanish Civil War: Agnes Hodgson Between Surgery and Spectacle', *College Literature*, 43, 1 (Winter 2016): 196-219.

Holloway, Kerrie, 'Empathy in Narratives of British Humanitarian Workers Assisting Spanish Republican Refugees at the Time of the Retirada: Esme Odgers, Audrey Russell, Richard Rees and Lillian Urmston', *Journal of Spanish Cultural Studies*, 21, 4 (2020): 503-517.

Jackson, Angela, *British Women and the Spanish Civil War*, (London: Routledge/Cañada Blanch Studies of Contemporary Spain, 2002; London: The Clapton Press, 2020).

Jackson, Angela, *For Us It Was Heaven: The Passion, Grief and Fortitude of Patience Darton*, (Sussex: Academic Press, with Cañada Blanch Centre for Contemporary Spanish Studies, 2012).

Keene, Judith, 'A Spanish Springtime: Aileen Palmer and the Spanish Civil War', *Labour History*, 52 (1987): 755-87.

Larraz Andía, Pablo, 'Heridos, enfermedades, hospitales y enfermeras: La otra cara de la guerra', *Memoria y Civilización*, 15 (2012): 197-210.

López Vallecillo, María, 'Relevancia de la mujer en el bando nacional de la Guerra Civil española: las enfermeras', *Memoria y Civilización*, 19 (2016): 419-439.

López, María, Rubén Mirón-González, María-José Castro and José-María Jiménez 'Training of Volunteer Nurses during the Spanish Civil War (1936-1939): A Historical Study', *Plos ONE*, 16 (31 December 2021).

Martín Moruno, Dolores and Javier Ordaz Rodríguez, 'The Nursing Vocation as Political Participation for Women during the Spanish Civil War', *Journal of War and Culture Studies*, 2, 3 (2009): 305-319.

Muller, Ruth, *Margaret Powell: An Extraordinary Life*, (Crickhowell: Crickhowell District Archive Centre, 2002).

Nelson, Siobhan, Paola Galbany-Estragués and Gloria Gallego-Caminero, 'The Nurses No-One Remembers: Looking for Spanish Nurses in Accounts of the Spanish Civil War (1936-1939)', *Nursing History Review*, 28 (2020): 63-92

Organización de los cuidados de enfermería en la Guerra Civil española (1936-1939): un abordaje histórico. *Cultura de los Cuidados*, 53, (2019): 77- 86.

Palfreeman, Linda, *Salud!: Volunteers in the Republican Medical Services During the Spanish Civil war, 1936-1939*, (Brighton: Sussex Academic Press, 2012).

Sinclair-Loutit, Kenneth, 'The Largest Frying Pan in the World', in Philip Toynbee (ed.), *The Distant Drum: Reflections on the Spanish Civil War*, (London: Sidgwick & Jackson, 1976).

Photographers in Aragón during the Spanish Civil War

Agustín-Lacruz, Carmen & Luis Blanco-Domingo, 'La memoria en encuadres. Fotógrafas extranjeras en Aragón durante la Guerra Civil española', *Documentación de las Ciencias de la Información*, 44, 1 (2021): 61-72.

Ennis, Helen, *Margaret Michaelis: Love, Loss and Photography*, (Canberra: National Gallery of Australia, 2005).

Rubio Pérez, Almudena, 'Las cajas de Amsterdam': Margaret Michaelis y los anarquistas de la CNT-FAI en la Guerra Civil', *Historia Social*, 104 (2022): 71-91.

Rubio Pérez, Almudena, 'Las cajas de Amsterdam': Kati Horna y los anarquistas de la CNT-FAI en la Guerra Civil', *Historia Social*, 96 (2020): 21-39.

Wainman, Alec and Serge Alternês, *Live Souls: Citizens and Volunteers of Civil War Spain*, (Vancouver: Ronsdale Press, 2015).

Spanish Civil War in Australia

Andrews, E M, *Isolation and Appeasement in Australia. Reactions to the European Crises 1935-1939*, (Canberra: National University Press, 1970).

Campion, Edmund, *Rockchoppers: Growing up Catholic in Australia*, (Ringwood: Penguin, 1982).

Damousi, Joy, 'Humanitarianism and Child Refugee Sponsorship: The Spanish Civil War and the Global Campaign of Esme Odgers', *Journal of Women's History*, 32 (Spring, 2020): 111-134.

Easson, Michael, 'Lloyd Ross, 1901-1987', *Australian Dictionary of Biography*, 18 (2012).

Fox, Len, *Broad Left, Narrow Left*, (published by the author, Chippendale, 1982).

Inglis, Amirah, *Australians in the Spanish Civil War*, (Sydney: Allen & Unwin, 1987).

Inglis, Ken, 'Catholic Historiography in Australia', *Historical Studies*, 8 (1958).

Keene, Judith, 'An Antipodean Bridegroom of Death: An Australian with Franco's Forces in the Spanish Civil War', *Journal of the Royal Australian Historical Society*, 70 (Apr 1985).

Keene, Judith, 'The Word Makes the Man: A Catalan Anarchist Autodidact in the Australian Bush', *Australian Journal of Politics and History*, 47, 3 (2001): 311-329.

Keene, Judith, 'A la recerca de la vida a Acràcia: un anarquista català a Austràlia', *El Contemporani*, 33-34 (gener-desembre, 2007): 85-99.

Keene, Judith, 'Amirah Inglis; Activist, Historian and Friend' in Peter Browne & Seumas Spark (eds.), *I Wonder: The Life and Work of Ken Inglis*, (Melbourne: Monash University Publishing, 2020): 240-59.

Keene, Judith, "Catalan anarchists in Australia in search of *Acracia*', *Memories of Migration* edited by Ignacio García and Augustín Macarthur, Spanish Heritage Foundation, Ministerio de Trabajo y Asuntos Sociales de España, 1998, p111-124.

Kneipp, Pauline, 'Australian Catholics and the Abyssinian War', *Journal of Religious History*, X, (Dec 1979).

Martin, Sylvia, *Ink in Her Veins: The Troubled Life of Aileen Palmer*, (Perth: UWA Publishing, 2010).

Menghetti, Diane, *The Red North: the Popular Front in North Queensland*, (Townsville: James Cook University of North Queensland, 1981).

The Red Matildas [documentary] directed by Trevor Graham, Laurie McInnes and Sharon Connolly et al., with May Pennefather [MacFarlane] Audrey Blake and Joan Goodwin, Ronin Films, Melbourne, (1985): 50 minutes.

Palmer, Nettie, *From the Battlefields of Spain: Vivid Pen Pictures from Australian Nurses*, Published by the Spanish Relief Committee Sydney: Forward Press (40-hour week), (1937).

Palmer, Nettie, and Len Fox with the help of Jim McNeill and Ron Hurd, *Australians in Spain*, (Sydney: Current Book Distributors, May 1948).

Palmer, Nettie, *Fourteen Years*, (Melbourne: Meanjin Press, 1948).

Ross, Lloyd (ed.), *Catholics Speak Out*, (Melbourne, 1938).

White, Richard, 'The Soldier as Tourist: The Australian

Experience of the Great War', *War & Society*, 5, 1 (1987): 63-77.

Spanish Civil War

Alpert, Michael, 'Humanitarianism and Politics in the British Response to the Spanish Civil War', *European History Quarterly*, 14 (1984): 423-40.

Arrarás, Joaquín, *Historia de la Segunda República Española*, Vol. 4, (Madrid: Libros de Historia, 1964).

Berger, Miguel, 'Catalans at War: Representations of Catalonia During the Spanish Civil War', *Catalan Review*, 25, (Jan 2011): 119-129.

Bolloten, Burnett, *The Spanish Civil War: Revolution and Counter Revolution*, (Chapel Hill: North Carolina Press, 1979).

Buchanan, Tom, 'British Perceptions of Spain, 1931-1939', *Twentieth Century British History*, 4 (1993): 1-24.

Casanova, Julián, *Anarquismo y revolución en la sociedad rural Aragonesa, 1936-1938*, (Madrid: Siglo Veintiuno de España Editores, 1985).

Churchill, Peter, *All My Sins Remembered*, (London: Heinemann, 1964).

Crome, Len, 'Document: Walter (1937-1947): A Soldier in Spain', *History Workshop Journal*, 9 (Spring 1980), p 120.

Friend Harding, Susan, *Remaking Ibieca, Rural Life in Aragón under Franco*, (Chapel Hill: University of North Carolina Press, 1984).

Johnstone, Nancy, *Hotel in Flight*, (London: Faber and Faber, 1939; London: The Clapton Press, 2022).

Kaminski, Erich-Hans, *Los de Barcelona* (Barcelona: Parsifal Ediciones, 1976), (1937).

Keene, Judith, *Fighting For Franco, International Volunteers in Nationalist Spain during the Spanish Civil War, 1936-39*, (London: Continuum, 2001).

Kern, Robert W, 'Anarchist Principles and Spanish Reality: Emma Goldman as a Participant in the Civil War, 1936-39', *Journal of Contemporary History*, 11 (1976): 237-259.

Loach, Kenneth, film *Land and Freedom*, (1995).

Low, Mary and Juan Breá, *Red Spanish Notebook*, (London: Secker and Warburg, 1973) (1937): 198.

Malefakis, Edward, *Agrarian Reform and Peasant Revolution in Spain: Origins of the Civil War*, (New Haven: Yale University Press, 1970).

Mangan, Kate, *Never More Alive: Inside the Spanish Republic*, with a Preface by Paul Preston, (London: Clapton Press, 2020).

Mintz, Frank, *L'autogestion dans l'Espagne révolutionnaire*, (Paris: Bélibaste, 1970).

Mintz, Jerome R, *The Anarchists of Casa Viejas*, (Chicago: University of Chicago Press, 1982).

Orwell, George, 'Homage to Catalonia', in *George Orwell in Spain*, Peter Davison and Christopher Hitchens (eds.), (London: Penguin Random House, 2001).

Preston, Paul (ed.), *Revolution and War in Spain, 1931- 1939*, (London: Methuen, 1984).

Preston, Paul, *We Saw Spain Die: Foreign Correspondents in the Spanish Civil War*, (London: Constable, 2009).

Purcell, Hugh, 'Kitty Bowler: The English Captain's Spy', *History Today*, 62 (Feb 2012).

Santamaría, B A, *Against the Tide*, (Melbourne: Melbourne University Press, 1981): 33-38

Romero Salvadó, Francisco J, *The Spanish Civil War: Origins, Course and Outcomes*, (London: Macmillan, 2005). Seidmann, Michael, 'Work and Revolution: Worker's Control in Barcelona in the Spanish Civil War', *Journal of Contemporary History*, 17 (1982), X.

Shubert, Adrian, 'The Epic Failure: The Asturian Revolution of October 1943', in Preston P (ed.), *The Revolution and War in Spain*.

Souchy Bauer, Augustín, *Entre los campesinos de Aragón. El comunismo libertario en las comarcas liberadas*, (Barcelona: Tusquets Editor, 1937) (1977).

Southworth, Herbert, *Guernica! Guernica! A Study of Journalism, Diplomacy, Propaganda and History*, (Berkeley: California University Press, 1977).

Thomas, Hugh, 'Agrarian Collectives in the Spanish Civil War', in his *The Republic and the Civil War in Spain*, (London: Macmillan, 1971).

Tremlett, Giles, *The International Brigades: Fascism, Freedom and the Spanish Civil War*, (London: Bloomsbury, 2020).

Usandizaga, Aránzazu, *Escritoras al Frente: Intelectuales Extranjeras an la Guerra civil*, (San Sebastián: Nerea, 2007).

Select Index

MEMORIES OF SPAIN SERIES
AVAILABLE FROM THE CLAPTON PRESS

Never More Alive: Inside the Spanish Republic – Kate Mangan

The Good Comrade: Memoirs of an International Brigader – Jan Kurzke

In Place of Splendour – Constancia de la Mora

Firing a Shot for Freedom – Frida Stewart & Angela Jackson

The Fighter Fell in Love: A Spanish Civil War Memoir – James R Jump

Struggle for the Spanish Soul – Arturo & Ilsa Barea

Hotel in Spain – Nancy Johnstone

Hotel in Flight – Nancy Johnstone

Sombreros are Becoming – Nancy Johnstone

Behind the Spanish Barricades – John Langdon Davies

Single to Spain & Escape from Disaster – Keith Scott Watson

Spanish Portrait – Elizabeth Lake

British Women in the Spanish Civil War – Angela Jackson

Boadilla – Esmond Romilly

My House in Málaga – Sir Peter Chalmers Mitchell

The Tilting Planet – David Marshall

Hampshire Heroes: Volunteers in the Spanish Civil War – Alan Lloyd

Remembering Spain: Essays, Memoirs and Poems on the International Brigades and the Spanish Civil War, edited by Joshua Newmark/IBMT

www.theclaptonpress.com